Latina Girls

Latina Girls

Voices of Adolescent Strength in the United States

EDITED BY

Jill Denner and Bianca L. Guzmán

New York University Press

NEW YORK AND LONDON

NEW YORK UNIVERSITY PRESS
New York and London
www.nyupress.org

Library of Congress Cataloging-in-Publication Data
Latina girls : voices of adolescent strength in the United States /
edited by Jill Denner and Bianca Guzmán.
p.   cm.
Includes bibliographical references and index.
ISBN-13: 978-0-8147-1976-3 (cloth : alk. paper)
ISBN-10: 0-8147-1976-7 (cloth : alk. paper)
ISBN-13: 978-0-8147-1977-0 (pbk. : alk. paper)
ISBN-10: 0-8147-1977-5 (pbk. : alk. paper)
1. Hispanic American teenage girls—Social conditions. 2. Hispanic
American teenage girls—Psychology. 3. Hispanic Americans—Ethnic
identity. 4. Sex role—United States.   I. Denner, Jill. II. Guzmán, Bianca.
E184.S75L345 2006
305.235089'68073—dc22   2005037591

New York University Press books are printed on acid-free paper,
and their binding materials are chosen for strength and durability.

Manufactured in the United States of America
10 9 8 7 6 5 4 3 2 1

JD: for my parents, Sonny, Madeleine, and Charlotte.
BLG: for my mother, Juan, Ana Lucia and Isabella.

Contents

Introduction
Latina Girls Transforming Cultures, Contexts, and Selves

Jill Denner and Bianca L. Guzmán

> I have to stick up for myself, because if I don't they're going to . . . you know how girls have been treated unfairly a lot, so when I think about me being a girl I want people to start respecting my sex.
> —Fourteen-year-old Mexican American girl
> in northern California

What do we know about Latina girls? Based on national reports (e.g., Coalition of Hispanic Health and Human Services Organizations [COSSMHO], 1999), the common perception of a Latina adolescent is a girl who makes poor choices and who will likely drop out of school, become a teenage mother, or be the girlfriend of a gang member. Despite this popular perception, most Latina girls do not fit the negative images typically portrayed in the media. Regardless, most research on Latina girls focuses on teenage pregnancy, depression, violent and pathological behavior, and suicide. Since research and news articles overwhelmingly focus on negative behaviors, little is known about the majority of girls who are problem-free or "fully engaged" in their environment and well-being (Pittman et al., 2003). As a result, there is little to guide teachers, adult allies, or parents on how to support Latina girls to help them succeed and to make positive contributions to their communities.

This volume is a "wake-up call" to practitioners and researchers that most Latina girls do make positive life choices, and many transform the homes, schools, and communities where they experience discrimination, limited opportunities, and institutionalized racism into safer, more equitable spaces.

Who Are Latina Girls?

To be consistent with current terminology, we define girls as Latina if they have at least one parent whose country of origin is in South or Central America, Mexico, Puerto Rico, Cuba, or the Dominican Republic. We use the term "Latina" because it includes women whose origin is Mexican, Central and South American, and the Spanish-speaking Caribbean. We also use the term to recognize and acknowledge the struggle for self-identity that Latinas who reside primarily in the Western region of the United States have undergone. However, some authors in this volume have chosen to refer to Latina girls as Hispanics.

Placing Latinas under one heading may appear problematic because they have distinct migration and cultural histories, as well as different levels of education and income. Research has only begun to tease apart the implications of these differences and how they impact the self-identity and self-development of Latina girls (Epstein, Botvin, and Diaz, 2002; Erkut and Tracy, 2002). While we do not address the topic of labeling specifically in any of the chapters, the intent of this book is to contribute to the field of positive Latina self-identity.

The need for this book is clear. Latinos are the fastest-growing racial ethnic minority in the United States. Latina girls now constitute the largest minority group of girls in the country, making up 15.2 percent of the total number of American girls (COSSMHO, 1999). Currently, Latinos make up a large proportion of the population under age eighteen in many of the largest school districts across the United States: 65 percent in Los Angeles, 50 percent in Dade County Florida, 53 percent in Albuquerque, New Mexico, 49 percent in Denver, 47 percent in Tucson, 35 percent in Chicago, and 24 percent in Boston (National Center for Education Statistics, 2001a). While these populations are growing rapidly, there is a lack of empirical data available to guide services, education, and advocacy campaigns for these young girls.

Latina girls living in the United States have unique challenges and strengths as a function of living in what Gloria Anzaldúa (1987) calls the borderlands. That is, these young women have the unique opportunity to

incorporate their cultural traditions with mainstream U.S. dominant culture. This can include coordinating cultural traditions with school and peer cultures (Cooper et al., 1998; Denner and Dunbar, 2004) and sustaining their family unit by being in charge of the family's communication with the English-speaking world (Orellana, 2003; Weisskirch and Alva, 2002). At the same time, they often must respond to low expectations by others in order to pursue their goals and stay connected to their culture (Denner et al., 2005).

Latina girls also have the opportunity to examine their cultural values and beliefs against the dominant mainstream U.S. culture and to create themselves as transcultural individuals. The term "transculturation" is defined as a multidimensional construct involving social interrelationships, language, media use, participation in rituals, and group identification (Ortiz-Torres, Serrano-Garcia, and Torres-Burgos 2000). Transculturation is different from the term "biculturalism" in that people who are bicultural share or fuse two cultures. Transcultural Latinas identify with one culture and also incorporate behaviors from another culture. The transcultural process is complex and is characterized by simultaneous behaviors, perceptions, and cognitions that could have different, even contradictory, manifestations as these young girls interact with the dominant U.S. mainstream culture. This process of transculturation presents both challenges and opportunities for Latina girls.

Research on Latinas

The last ten years have seen an explosion in research on female development but few positive studies of Latina girls. Books like *Those Loud Black Girls* (Fordham, 1993) and *Raising Their Voices* (Brown, 1998) show how African American and European American girls question, subvert, and accept social and structural constraints. A few books have focused on Latina girls' high-profile risk behaviors such as gang involvement (e.g., Dietrich, 1998; Sikes, 1998). Some recent books on Latino children (e.g., Suarez-Orozco and Suarez-Orozco, 2002; Stanton-Salazar, 2001) study strengths in the lives of U.S. Latinos but do not focus specifically on gender. The only existing volume of research to focus on girls' strengths that includes some chapters on Latinas is *Urban Girls* (Leadbeater and Way, 1996). One recent book titled *Women without Class: Girls, Race, and Identity* (Bettie, 2003) shows how Latina and white adolescents negotiate gender, class, and culture through an ethnographic study of students at one high school.

A large body of research on Latina adults in the United States challenges simplistic notions that a person's culture or ethnic background causes certain behaviors or identities. These studies use a structural and social psychological perspective to critically examine gender and power over time. For example, several books include research on how Latina women build from cultural strengths to overcome obstacles (e.g., Espín, 1999; Latina Feminist Group, 2001; Romero, Hondagneu-Sotelo, and Ortiz, 1997). A recent book by Hurtado (2003), *Voicing Chicana Feminisms: Young Women Speak Out on Sexuality and Identity,* shows how the values of familism and *respeto* do not impart a unidirectional influence on how people live and develop their identities. Instead, through a critical analysis of multiple systems of oppression, Hurtado describes how Chicana feminist thought is situated at the borderlands, where a critical consciousness allows women to move across borders. She also reminds us that border crossing sometimes results in a cost to one's sense of self. The current volume adds the experiences of Latina girls to this growing library of books that critically analyze gender, context, and migration across borders.

Research has not kept up with the rising numbers of Latino youth, and the few published articles are scattered across many discipline-based journals and books, making it difficult to get an overview of the field. When there are debates that attempt to integrate findings and advance theory, they typically focus on how Latinas differ from women in other ethnic groups, and whether acculturation increases risk (e.g., removes protective cultural values) or decreases risk (as a result of increased family income). Most of this research uses a comparative model which assumes that Latinas have an inherent deficit when compared with European American girls and tells us little about the girls' lives.

We include here a few findings from comparative studies in order to challenge the myth that by the time Latina girls are eighteen they will be in trouble, simply because of their heritage or culture. For example, only 32 percent of Latina adolescents have had sexual intercourse by age eighteen, compared with 35 percent of European American and 65 percent of African American girls (Blum et al., 2000), and rates of eating disorders among Latinas are similar to those of other ethnic groups (Granillo, Jones-Rodriguez, and Carvajal, 2005). School dropout remains an area of concern, with 23 percent of Latinas not completing high school, compared with 7 percent of European American and 11 percent of African American

girls (National Center for Education Statistics, 2001b). But even here, research fails to account for the diversity within racial and ethnic groups. And we know little about the vast majority—77 percent—of U.S. Latinas who *do* complete high school.

We have chosen to avoid using a comparison model in this book because it is inevitably a cultural deficit model that results in one group being positioned as superior (usually the majority group) and one group being positioned as deficient (usually the minority group). Instead, we look at variation and commonalities within the group we call Latinas. Following suggestions by Cooper et al. (1998), this book tells a detailed story about Latina girls' lives rather than how they differ from other ethnic groups. We believe this information is more useful for developing programs and policies to support these girls' positive development, and for generating research and theory that give voice to stories that have not been heard.

The Theoretical Context

The information in the current volume is crucial for helping programs and schools build resiliency and empowerment and for informing research and theory. A popular mantra attributed to Karen Pittman is "problem free is not fully prepared." We are not naive enough to suppose that the girls in this book are "problem free." Many come from households and communities where limited resources, fear of crime, and physically demanding work create daily stress and health problems. However, the girls in these chapters are more prepared than many to confront life's challenges because they are actively engaged in transforming systems of oppression and creating their own language of well-being. As suggested by many (Galambos and Leadbeater, 2000; Gibbs, 1998), there is a dire need for research to examine the normal developmental processes of ethnic minority adolescents and the ways they succeed rather than how they fail. To this end, the chapters in this book illuminate not only the challenges these young women face but also how they handle those challenges.

Several theoretical perspectives help us position the research in this book within a larger conversation about culture and adolescent development. Ecological systems theories (Bronfenbrenner, 1989) describe development as a process that occurs as people interact with their immediate (e.g., family) and more distal (e.g., school) contexts. Theories of social capital have been used to understand the role of schooling and academic achievement among Latino students. Research shows how families, peers, and institutional brokers provide both instrumental and emotional support to help youth avoid risks and achieve their goals (Denner et al., 2005; Denner et al., 2001; Stanton-Salazar, 2001). Theories of identity challenge the utility of demographic categories for describing their life experiences. Phinney (1996) argues that it is critical to examine the "subjective sense of ethnic group membership (i.e., ethnic identity)" to understand what importance, if any, group membership has for individuals. Finally, theories of multiple worlds describe how youth move between their homes, schools, and communities (Cooper et al., 1998; Phelan, Davidson, and Yu, 1997). In all these theories, competence is not a static part of an individual's personality; it is an aspect of the person's smooth movement between the roles, practices, and expectations in each world. These theoretical frameworks provide much of the backdrop for research on the institutions, relationships, and personal characteristics that shape Latina girls' lives.

Overview of the Book

This book brings together new research on Latina girls across disciplines to highlight the intersection of gender, race, ethnicity, and social class to provide a more complete, nuanced, and accurate account of these girls' lives and lived experiences than has been available up to this point. Each chapter in the volume critically examines the people and environments in which these young women live, the schools they attend, the programs in which they participate, and the homes in which they live. The authors invite the reader to witness the girls' lives by highlighting the ways they negotiate decision making across risks (e.g., poverty and pressures to have sex), opportunities (e.g., community programs and extended family), and expectations (e.g., gender role expectations from family, peers, religion, and community).

This volume also updates research on gender role norms in today's Latino families. Until now, most studies have referenced relatively dated studies (e.g., Vazquez-Nuttall, Romero-Garcia, and de Leon, 1987) to support a static view of traditional gender roles and the prevalence of machismo in Latino culture. The chapters here show the complex ways that gender roles get played out in contemporary Latino families, and how Latina adolescents are negotiating them.

This book includes research on Latinas from across the United States, focusing primarily on regions in California, New York, Connecticut, Chicago, and Texas. It presents descriptions of the lives of Latina girls from diverse backgrounds with regard to country of origin, generation/immigration status, rural and urban setting, and social class. The authors use a range of methodological and theoretical approaches from psychology, anthropology, sociology, geography, public health, ethnic studies, and women's studies. Across chapters, there are different and complementary data sources, including surveys, interviews, observations, and focus groups. At the same time, all maintain a focus on the dynamics through which Latinas explore identities and confront the challenges in their lives.

No one book can represent the full range of Latina girls' experiences in the United States. Due to space constraints and lack of available research, we have not addressed certain topics in depth. These include the role of religion in girls' lives, bilingualism, the *quinceañera* (fifteenth birthday celebration), Latinas in the Southwest (Arizona) and Florida (Miami), and the lives of girls in centers of new immigration such as Georgia and North Carolina. Neither do we include chapters on lesbian and bisexual Latina girls, or on those who are working to transform systems of oppression that go beyond their immediate communities. In addition, there are no studies of Latinas who have one non-Latino parent, and few chapters focus on Latina girls who are not of Mexican descent. We hope this book will encourage those who are conducting research with these populations to add those voices to the conversation.

The goal of this volume is to challenge the stereotype of the troubled Latina girl in a family with traditional gender roles. This book was created in an effort to build a research base to inform both theory and practice. As stated by Fine and coauthors (2000, p. 125), we aim to "contribute to a reshaping of the 'common sense' about" Latina girls. To this end, we bring together research on the majority of young Latinas who tend to choose positive and healthy behaviors and report happiness in their lives, many of whom are working to improve their lives and the lives of others. Each chapter provides examples of how girls regularly transform their relationships and institutions in order to flourish and succeed as they face interpersonal and institutional challenges. The chapters challenge much of what appears in the media about these young women being in "crisis" and instead focus on the issues and experiences that characterize the majority of Latina girls. Our focus is primarily on adolescent girls, aged twelve to eighteen, and on studies that provide us with the most up-to-date information on Latina girls living in the United States.

This is the first book to pull together research on the positive aspects of Latina girls' lives, and we consider it an important first step. Together, the chapters in this book address the following broad questions:

- What are the specific challenges Latina girls in the United States face in the early twenty-first century?
- What are the ways that girls are actively responding to these challenges?
- What strategies do they use to negotiate healthy decisions and create opportunities?
- How are girls' experiences affected by culturally based gender expectations from Latino culture and the broader mainstream U.S. culture?

The Organization of the Book

The book is organized around four developmental processes that are essential for Latina girls to thrive during adolescence. These include negotiating family relationships, overcoming institutional barriers, accessing institutional support, and developing initiative. Arranging the book in this format allows us to highlight and investigate the complex, creative strategies that Latinas use to negotiate in and around expectations from their family, peers, and the wider community.

Part 1: Negotiating Family Relationships

Research on families typically describes how parents influence their children. The chapters in this section push beyond this dynamic to look at relational processes and how children transform and get support from family members, peers, and teachers. The four chapters in this part by Guzmán et al., Ayala, Gallegos-Castillo, and Romo et al. describe how girls actively participate in the socialization process by challenging gender role expectations and negotiating new cultural norms in interaction with their mothers. The girls in these studies are resisting oppressive traditional cultural norms, especially in regard to gender roles. In some cases, they transform traditional gender roles as a way to both resist and accept them.

The chapters show how girls are constructing identities and creating spaces in response to limits and negative expectations about who they should be. They are developing pride in their ethnic identity and building a bicultural identity that embraces and resists expectations from both cultures. The chapters also show how relationships are sources of both challenge and support for making decisions about sexuality.

Part 2: Overcoming Institutional Barriers

This part includes chapters by Lopez, Hyams, Rivera and Gallimore, and Marlino and Wilson that describe how Latina girls are actively engaged with their institutional and community contexts. The research describes the different ways that Latinas respond to expectations about their behavior in their schools, and how they seek out people and institutions to assist them to achieve their goals. In particular, the chapters show that Latina girls often have high aspirations for their education and career possibilities, see education as a path to upward mobility, and are able to seek out resources that can help them pursue their goals. These chapters also describe the ways in which helping others is a salient part of how they think about their futures. In addition, for some girls, sexuality is a site for negotiating institutional barriers.

Part 3: Accessing Institutional Support

This part includes three chapters that describe community- and school-based efforts to support Latina girls. Strategies to engage girls include critical reflection, nurturing cultural literacy, building on aspirations, and identity exploration. Harper et al. describe a program that encourages girls to challenge cultural and community norms about sexuality when they interfere with girls' ability to make healthy choices for themselves. The chapter by Reyes portrays a cultural literacy group in which Puerto Rican girls negotiate and learn about their histories. Finally, Fairlie and London describe the findings from a national study of computer and Internet access. Their data show a dramatic increase in Latina girls' use of technology in the last few years, and they highlight programs designed to increase the number of Latinas in the sciences, engineering, and technology. The authors of these three chapters show how Latina girls are avoiding risk by challenging gender stereotypes, accessing opportunities, and transforming out-of-school spaces into places of identity development, opportunity, and critique.

Part 4: Developing Initiative

The three chapters in this part describe the ways Latina girls maintain a positive view of their lives, even when faced with challenging circumstances. Developing initiative includes personal strategies (Larson, 2000) such as reframing other peoples' expectations of who they should be and making positive choices. The chapters provide examples of how Latina girls are confronted with expectations from adults and peers about who they should be and how to behave. In response, they develop strategies that include moving between languages and roles to succeed in and be a bridge to different social and cultural worlds. Girls also find strength in their cultural identity.

The chapter by Thakral and Vera focuses on subjective well-being and challenges the stereotype that poor Latinas are not happy or satisfied with their lives. Flores describes how Latina girls respond to pressure to engage in risky behaviors by drawing on cultural values and relationships and by developing identities that help them avoid engaging in sex and drug use. Russell and Lee reframe our perceptions of teen mothers to show how some Latinas have used the birth of their child as an opportunity to make positive changes in their lives.

Conclusion

To solicit chapters for this volume, we put out a national call for abstracts, through listservs and e-mail letters to researchers who have published on Latino/a adolescents. We targeted people in the fields of psychology and health that we know best, and we sought out researchers in other disciplines whom we had never met. As a result, the chapters in this book reflect much of the best social science research that focuses on the positive aspects of Latina girls' lives, but that pool of research is still quite limited. Most research still focuses on risks in Latina girls' lives, not on the ways these girls are succeeding. The reason for this lies in the lack of research funding to study girls' strengths. Some of those who do write about how Latinas succeed have had to fit this story within a larger study designed to address teen pregnancy, delinquency, or depression. The fact that we found fourteen chapters is testament to the creativity and commitment of those authors.

In the tradition of qualitative research, we consider it important to acknowledge the influence of our own histories and training. Jill was raised in a two-parent, middle-class family, the daughter of a Cuban-born, Jewish mother and two New York–raised parents. Her interest in Latina girls comes from being challenged to have a critical consciousness about gender and the role of privilege, as well as living in the state of California, where Latino culture is an increasingly dominant influence on the food, language, and attitude of the population. Bianca was born in Guatemala and immigrated to California as a young girl with her mother and younger brother. She has firsthand experience with what it is like to negotiate Latino culture and dominant U.S. mainstream culture. Bianca is clear that the process of transculturalism is dynamic and dialectical, providing a strong education in human behavior. Her interests in Latina girls stem from her commitment to give voice to their positive experiences as a way to create social justice for Latina women. In the last chapter of this book, we describe our position on this topic in relation to the book in more detail.

In conclusion, this book is about hope, or *esperanza* in Spanish. It is about our hope that Latina girls living in the United States will continue to succeed, and that the public will see beyond the cultural and gender stereotypes that are currently used to characterize Latina girls and restrict their opportunities. We offer this book with the expectation that by gathering an array of research studies into one volume, we will bring to the fore the experiences of the majority of Latina girls who are choosing positive and healthy behaviors and are working to improve their lives in tangible ways. We also believe the book will help to create a climate in which research is used to support girls in their quest to negotiate positive life pathways. Finally, we see this book as a space for girls' voices to be heard, so Latinas and non-Latinas alike can begin to recognize and repeat others' strategies to maintain their culture while resisting stereotypes and transforming systems of oppression.

This book was produced in the spaces between family (husbands, children, and other relatives), friends, and work (both paid and unpaid). During the time this book was being conceived and compiled, Jill gave birth to a daughter. As we submit this book to the publisher, Jill's daughter has just turned one year old. For the last six months, she has spent weekday mornings in the care of a woman named Esperanza, who gives her undivided attention and love, even while her own children are in the care of her sister. As Romero (1997) so beautifully articulates, we feel it is critical that this book does not obscure the social order that is constructed between the Latina women and the white women and children they care for. Clearly, this book would not have been possible without Esperanza and her family.

REFERENCES

Anzaldúa, Gloria. 1987. *Borderlands: La frontera.* San Francisco: Aunt Lute Books.

Bettie, Julie. 2003. *Women without class: Girls, race, and identity.* Berkeley: University of California Press.

Blum, Robert W., Beuhring, Trisha, Shew, Marcia L., Bearinger, Linda H., Sieving, Renée E., and Resnick, Michael D. 2000. The effects of race/ethnicity, income, and family structure on adolescent risk behaviors. *American Journal of Public Health* 90 (12): 1879–1884.

Bronfenbrenner, Uri. 1989. Ecological systems theory. *Annals of Child Development* 6:185–246.

Brown, Lyn M. 1998. *Raising their voices: The politics of girls' anger.* Cambridge, MA: Harvard University Press.

Coalition of Hispanic Health and Human Services Organizations. 1999. *The state of Hispanic girls.* Washington, DC: National Coalition of Hispanic Health and Human Services Organizations (COSSMHO) Press.

Cooper, Catherine R. 2002. Five bridges along students' pathways to college: A developmental blueprint of families, teachers, counselors, mentors, and peers in the Puente project. *Educational Policy* 16:607–622.

Cooper, Catherine R., Denner, Jill, and Lopez, Edward M. 1999. Cultural brokers: Helping Latino children on pathways toward success. *The Future of Children* 9:51–57.

Cooper, Catherine R., Jackson, Jacquelynne F., Azmitia, Margarita, and Lopez, Edward M. 1998. Multiple selves, multiple worlds: Three useful strategies for research with ethnic minority youth on identity, relationships, and opportunity structures. In Vonnie C. McLoyd and Laurence Steinberg (eds.), *Studying minority adolescents: Conceptual, methodological, and theoretical issues,* 111–125. Mahwah, NJ: Erlbaum.

Denner, Jill, Cooper, Catherine R., Dunbar, Nora, and Lopez, Edward M. 2005. Access to opportunity: How Latino students in a college outreach program think about obstacles and resources. *Journal of Latinos and Education* 4 (1): 21–41.

Denner, Jill, and Dunbar, Nora. 2004. Negotiating femininity: Power and strategies of Mexican American girls. *Sex Roles* 50 (5–6): 301–314.

Denner, Jill, Kirby, Douglas, Coyle, Karin, and Brindis, Claire. 2001. The protective role of social capital and cultural norms in Latino communities: A study of adolescent births. *Hispanic Journal of Behavioral Sciences* 23:3–21.

Dietrich, L. C. 1998. *Chicana adolescents: Bitches, 'ho's, and schoolgirls.* Westport, CT: Praeger.

Epstein, Jennifer A., Botvin, Gilbert J., and Diaz, Tracy. 2002. Gateway polydrug use among Puerto Rican and Dominican adolescents residing in New York City: The moderating role of gender. *Journal of Child and Adolescent Substance Abuse* 12 (2): 33–46.

Erkut, Sumru, and Tracy, Allison J. 2002. Predicting adolescent self-esteem from participation in school sports among Latino subgroups. *Hispanic Journal of Behavioral Sciences* 24 (4): 409–429.

Espín, Oliva. 1999. *Women crossing boundaries: A psychology of immigration and transformations of sexuality.* New York: Routledge.

Fine, Michelle, Weis, Lois, Weseen, S., and Wong, Loonmun. 2000. For whom? Qualitative research, representations, and social responsibilities. In Norman K. Denzin and Yvonne S. Lincoln (eds.), *Handbook of qualitative research,* 2nd ed., 107–132. Thousand Oaks, CA: Sage.

Fordham, Signithia. 1993. "Those loud black girls": (Black) women, silence, and gender "passing" in the academy. *Anthropology and Education Quarterly* 24:3–32.

Galambos, Nancy, and Leadbeater, Bonnie J. R. 2000. Trends in adolescent research for the new millennium. *International Journal of Behavioral Development* 24:289–294.

Gibbs, Jewelle T. 1998. High-risk behaviors in African American youth: Conceptual and methodological issues in research. In Vonnie C. McLoyd and Laurence Steinberg (eds.), *Studying minority adolescents: Conceptual, methodological, and theoretical issues,* 55–84. Mahwah, NJ: Erlbaum.

Granillo, Teresa, Jones-Rodriguez, Gina, and Carvajal, Scott C. 2005. Prevalence of eating disorders in Latina adolescents: Associations with substance use and other correlates. *Journal of Adolescent Health* 36 (3): 214–220.

Hurtado, Aída. 2003. *Voicing Chicana feminisms: Young women speak out on sexuality and identity.* New York: NYU Press.

Larson, Reed. 2000. Toward a psychology of positive youth development. *American Psychologist* 55:170–183.

Latina Feminist Group. 2001. *Telling to live: Latina feminist testimonios.* Durham, NC: Duke University Press.

Leadbeater, Bonnie J. R., and Way, Niobe, eds. 1996. *Urban girls: Resisting stereotypes, creating identities.* New York: NYU Press.

National Center for Education Statistics. 2001a. *Digest of education statistics.* Washington, DC: U.S. Department of Education.

———. 2001b. *Public elementary and secondary school districts in the United States 2000–2001.* Washington, DC: U.S. Department of Education.

Orellana, Margorie Faulstich. 2003. Responsibilities of children in Latino immigrant homes. *New Directions for Youth Development: Understanding the Social Worlds of Immigrant Youth* 100:25–40.

Ortiz-Torres, Blanca, Serrano-Garcia, Irma, and Torres-Burgos, Nélida. 2002. Subverting culture: Promoting HIV/AIDS prevention among Puerto Rican and Dominican women. *American Journal of Community Psychology* 28:859–881.

Phelan, Patricia, Davidson, Ann L., and Yu, Hanh Cao. 1997. *Adolescents' worlds: Negotiating family, peers, and school.* New York: Teachers College Press.

Phinney, Jean. S. 1996. When we talk about American ethnic groups, what do we mean? *American Psychologist* 51 (9): 918–927.

Pittman, Karin, Irby, Melita, Tolman, J., Yohalem, Nicole, and Ferber, Thaddeus. 2003. *Preventing problems, promoting development, encouraging engagement: Competing priorities or inseparable goals?* Washington, DC: Forum for Youth Investment.

Romero, Mary. 1997. Life as the maid's daughter: An exploration of the everyday boundaries of race, class, and gender. In Mary Romero, Pierrette Hondagneu-Sotelo, and Vilman Ortiz (eds.), *Challenging fronteras: Structuring Latina and Latino lives in the U.S.,* 195–209. New York: Routledge.

Romero, Mary, Hondagneu-Sotelo, Pierrette, and Ortiz, Vilman (eds.). *Challenging fronteras: Structuring Latina and Latino lives in the U.S.* New York: Routledge.

Sikes, Gini. 1998. *Eight ball chicks: A year in the violent world of girl gangsters.* New York: Doubleday.

Stanton-Salazar, Ricardo. 2001. *Manufacturing hope and despair: The school and kin support networks of U.S.-Mexican youth.* New York: Teachers College Press.

Suarez-Orozco, Carola, and Marcelo M. Suarez-Orozco. 2002. *Children of immigration.* Cambridge, MA: Harvard University Press.

Vazquez-Nuttall, Ena, Romero-Garcia, Ivonne, and de Leon, Brunilda. 1987. Sex roles and perceptions of femininity and masculinity of Hispanic women: A review of the literature. *Psychology of Women Quarterly* 11 (4): 409–425.

Weisskirch, Robert S., and Alva, Sylvia Alatorre. 2002. Language brokering and the acculturation of Latino children. *Hispanic Journal of Behavioral Sciences* 24 (3): 369–378.

Part 1

Negotiating Family Relationships

Chapter 2

Los Papas, La Familia y La Sexualidad

Bianca L. Guzmán, Elise Arruda, and Aida L. Feria

Research suggests that girls' sexual behavior is partly influenced by the family members and peers with whom they interact (Christopher, Johnson, and Roosa, 1993; Pistella and Bonati, 1998). In particular, parents play a major role in girls' sexual socialization (Dittus, Jaccard, and Gordon, 1999). Parents are readily accessible sources of information, and parents influence their daughters' intentions and actual sexual behavior directly by communicating their values about sexuality (Fisher, 1986b; Fox and Inazu, 1980; Lefkowitz, Sigman, and Au, 2000; Leland and Barth, 1993; Miller, Kotchick, et al., 1998; Moore, Peterson, and Furstenberg, 1986; Shoop and Davidson, 1994).

Currently, the majority of research on girls' sexual communication patterns examines the role that parents play in transmitting values and rules of sexual conduct. Most of the research done in this area suggests that parents do talk about sex to their adolescent children (Miller, Levin, et al., 1998). Females are also more likely than male adolescents to be the recipients of parental communication about sex (DiIorio et al., 2000; Jaccard, Dittus, and Gordon, 2000; Nolin and Peterson, 1992). Previous research conducted with ethnically diverse samples suggests that girls are more likely than boys to talk to their mothers about sex (DiIorio et al., 2000; Miller, Kotchick, et al., 1998).

Research also suggests that girls whose parents talk to them frequently about sex adopt their parents' values and beliefs about sexuality (Dittus, Jaccard, and Gordon, 1999; Fisher, 1986a). Adolescent girls who talk frequently about sex with their parents are less likely to be sexually active at an early age (DiIorio, Kelley, and Hockenberry-Eaton, 1999; Fisher, 1986b; Leland and Barth, 1993), have fewer numbers of sexual partners (Holtzman and Rubinson, 1998), report increase condom use once sexually active

(Fox and Inazu, 1980; Holtzman and Rubinson, 1998; Miller, Kotchick, et al., 1998; Miller, Levin, et al., 1998; Shoop and Davidson, 1994), and are more likely to talk to their sexual partners about safe sex (Shoop and Davidson, 1994). These studies suggest that parental-adolescent communication about sex sets the stage for the development of safe adolescent sexual behavior.

While much research exists on parental-adolescent sexual communication, especially among mother-daughter dyads, there is a shortage of work conducted specifically with Latina girls (Christopher, Johnson, and Roosa, 1993). The few studies that are conducted with Latina adolescent girls generally study high-risk populations such as psychiatric outpatient girls (e.g., O'Sullivan et al., 1999). Clearly, psychiatric outpatients are not typical of the average Latina adolescent girl, and therefore the findings currently in the research do not answer the question of how a normal population of Latina girls responds to parental communication about sex. The few existing studies indicate that Latina girls most often communicate with their same-sex parent, their mother (DiIorio et al., 2000; Miller, Kotchick, et al., 1998). Furthermore, research suggests that those Latinas who frequently discuss sex with their mothers are less likely to become pregnant (Adolph et al., 1995).

These studies, however, do not fully explain the process by which communication about sex impacts the sexual behavior of Latina girls. Because previous studies examine only the impact of parental-adolescent sexual communication, they provide a limited view of Latina adolescents' sexual discussion patterns.

Indeed, Latina girls may actually discuss sex with nonparental others more than adolescents of other ethnicities. As is stated over and over, Latinos place a high value on interfamilial bonds (Stycos, 1972) which often results in the formation of broad social networks of close friends and extended family members as a social support resource (Salgado de Snyder and Padilla, 1987). The notion of *familismo* highlights the important role these other individuals can play in the sexual socialization of Latina girls. The current literature focus on parental-adolescent communication leaves questions as to who else Latina girls may be accessing for sexual discussion, and how these others might influence their sexual behaviors. Why would these avenues of communication be important? If communication with parents reduces sexual risk for Latina adolescent girls, then communication with others may add protection beyond simply parental communication. Because many resources for communication exist as a large part of Latino culture, this may indicate that Latino culture could be a buffer for early sexual risk behaviors. These are the questions we will explore in our study.

Our Study

We collected data from 279 Latina girls who were part of a larger teenage pregnancy prevention project called the Community Awareness Motivation Project (CAMP). CAMP is a theater prevention project aimed at decreasing teenage pregnancy rates and increasing the safe-sex behavior of adolescents in the San Gabriel Valley of Los Angles County, California. A cast of young adults perform theater skits at school assemblies that provide educational messages and model behavior. The project is intended to be a first step in increasing adolescents' knowledge about risky sexual behavior. The intervention is also intended to increase adolescents' intentions with regard to abstinence and safe-sex behavior.

All eighth-grade teens who attended four middle schools in the San Gabriel Valley were invited to participate in the project. The schools that were targeted for the intervention had similar student demographics, that is, they had at least an 80 percent Latino enrollment rate, and at least 75 percent of all students were eligible to receive the free school lunch program (this was a measure of low socioeconomic status). All adolescents had the opportunity to participate, and their parents signed a consent form prior to their participation.

The evaluation component of the project consisted of collecting questionnaire data one day prior to the intervention and three days after the intervention. The participating teens completed both their pre- and post-test questionnaires in a group setting in their physical education or health education classes (for a complete discussion of the data collection procedure, refer to Guzmán, Schlehofer-Sutton, et al., 2003; Guzmán, Casad, et al., 2003). The data analyzed and reported for the present study are those collected on the female sample at baseline, prior to the implementation of the CAMP theater intervention.

Participant Demographics

The average age of the girls in this study was 13.65 years, and the sample ranged in age from 12.25 to 14.75 years. The majority of participants identified themselves as Mexican or of Mexican descent (93 percent). The rest identified as Central American, with the majority of this group reporting they were Salvadorian. With regard to their generational status, 75 percent of the participants were born in the United States, and another 24 percent were born outside of the United States. Seven percent either did not know where they were born or did not answer the question. The sixty-seven girls who were born outside of the United States listed the following countries as their place of birth: Mexico ($n = 60$), Guatemala ($n = 1$), and El Salvador ($n = 3$); three girls did not report their country of origin. The majority (60 percent) of the girls moved to the United States between the ages of two and five; 66 percent reported Spanish was their first language.

With regard to religion, we found that 84 percent reported being Catholic, and the rest of the sample reported Christian-based religions. These young women also reported that they attended church services at least twice a month, with 33 percent of the sample reporting that they attended church services on a weekly basis. Seventy-eight percent of the girls also reported that they were serious to very serious about their religion. Seventy-two percent of the girls also reported that they try not to get in trouble with their religion, and 67 percent reported that they try to follow the rules of their religion. Finally, 75 percent of the girls reported that they think that more people should go to church.

Overall, 95 percent of the girls in this study reported not being sexually active. The girls also reported that they had strong beliefs that individuals should not become sexually active until they are married. It is important to note that this finding may be due to the high level of religiosity practiced by the young women in our sample. The majority of these young women are not sexually active, and they have strong beliefs that they should not become sexually active until an older age.

Their Families

The girls in our sample reported that 82 percent of their mothers were not born in the United States. The majority of the mothers (72 percent) were born in Mexico, with the rest of the non–U.S.-born mothers being born in Central American countries. Most (82 percent) reported that their fathers were not born in the United States; the majority were born in Mexico

TABLE 2.1
*Parental Education**

	Mother (%) (N = 193)	Father (%) (N = 169)
Less than 8th-grade education	40.9	37.9
9th–12th grade	19.7	24.9
High school graduate	18.1	21.3
Some college	14.0	11.8
College graduate/postgraduate	7.3	2.6

* Due to rounding percentages, totals for some columns may not equal 100%.

(70 percent), with the rest born in Central American countries. The majority of the girls reported that both their mothers (97 percent) and fathers (77 percent) live in the family home. This information suggests that these young women come primarily from intact family units. The majority of the girls have at least one sister (75 percent) and one brother (73 percent) who live in the household. This information indicates that there is an average of five individuals in their immediate family unit.

We believe that our findings challenge popular beliefs that Latino households are filled with many extended family members. Only 10 percent of the participants in our study have grandmothers and 3 percent have grandfathers in the family home; 12 percent have aunts and 14 percent have uncles in the family home. Although several girls reported that there were extended family members living in the household, well over 85 percent of the sample had only five family members living in their household.

As can be seen in Table 2.1 with regard to parental education, the girls in our sample reported that 37.9 percent of their fathers and 40.9 percent of their mothers hand less than an eighth-grade education. Overall, 18.1 percent of their mothers and 21.3 percent of their fathers were high school graduates. This information leads us to believe that many of the parents of these young women did not have high levels of school attainment. Based on this low level of school obtainment, we believe that these young women come from families with poor economic resources. We also know from working in these communities that both parents work on average between ten and twelve hours a day. Despite the long hours that parents spend at work, the girls in our sample reported that they ate dinner with their parents at least five to six nights a week.

Our Results

Parental Communication

As can be seen in Table 2.2, 63.1 percent of the girls reported that they felt comfortable to very comfortable talking to their mother about sex. On the other hand, only 14 percent of the girls reported that they felt comfortable to very comfortable talking to their fathers about sex. Our results mirror previous research, which shows that girls feel much more comfortable talking with their mothers than they do with their fathers about sex.

Regardless of whether girls feel comfortable or uncomfortable about talking to their parents about sex, we wanted to examine the extent to which they actually did discuss sex with both their mothers and fathers. As can be seen in Table 2.3, more than half of the sample (53.9 percent) reported that they sometimes or frequently/always talked to their mother about sex. On the other hand, only 9.5 percent of the girls reported that they sometimes or frequently/always talked to their father about sex.

We were also interested in the content of the communication between parents and their adolescent daughters regarding sex. To explore this question further, we asked the girls the following questions: (1) How often do you talk to your mother/father about not getting pregnant? (2) How often do you talk about HIV/AIDS with mother/father? (3) How often do you talk about waiting to have sex until you are older with your mother/father?

TABLE 2.2
How Comfortable Are Girls in Talking with Parent about Sex?

	Very uncomfortable/comfortable		Comfortable		Very comfortable	
	N	%	N	%	N	%
Mother (N = 1,024)	101	36.9	100	36.5	73	26.6
Father (N = 994)	228	86.0	31	11.7	6	2.3

* Due to rounding percentages, totals for some columns may not equal 100%.

TABLE 2.3
Perceived Extent of Parental-Adolescent Communication by Parent

	Never/rarely		Sometimes		Frequently/always	
	N	%	N	%	N	%
Mother (N = 1,024)	128	46.0	121	43.5	29	10.4
Father (N = 994)	247	90.4	23	8.4	3	1.1

* Due to rounding percentages, totals for some columns may not equal 100%.

TABLE 2.4
*Frequency of Parental Discussion about Pregnancy, HIV/AIDS, and
Delaying Sexual Activity**

	Never/rarely		Sometimes		Frequently/always	
	Mother	Father	Mother	Father	Mother	Father
Pregnancy	41.3	82.6	27.1	9.1	31.6	8.3
HIV/AIDS	51.3	82.3	27.8	12.6	21.0	5.1
Waiting to have sex	32.4	76.6	27.7	10.9	39.9	12.4

* All figures are represented as percentages.

As can be seen in Table 2.4, the young women in our sample have different patterns of communication with their mothers than with their fathers. Overall, we find that these young women are less likely to talk to
their fathers than their mothers regarding pregnancy, HIV/AIDS, and
waiting to have sex until an older age. We find that 58.7 percent of the girls
talk with their mother about not getting pregnant, and 67.6 percent talk
about delaying sex until they are older. It is also important to note that
only 48.8 percent of the sample talk with their mother about HIV/AIDS.
The table also indicates that only 17.4 percent of girls talk with their father
about pregnancy, and another 23.3 percent talk about delaying sexual
activity until an older age. Once again, we find that 82.3 percent of these
young women rarely to never talk with their fathers about HIV/AIDS.

Communication with Friends and Others

To further understand the pathways in which communication acts as a
buffer and impacts Latina girls' intentions to delay sexual activity, we
examined communication with friends and other relatives. As can be seen
in Table 2.5 the girls reported that they feel very comfortable in talking
about sex with their friends (76.9 percent). When we asked the girls if they
planned to talk about sexual issues with their friends, 81.9 percent of them
stated that they probably to definitely will talk with their friends about
sex. When we asked the girls how often they talked to their friends about
not becoming pregnant, 67 percent of them reported that they sometimes
to always talk to their friends about not getting pregnant. With regard to
HIV/AIDS, 54.2 percent of them reported that they sometimes to always
talk to their friends about HIV/AIDS. Finally, 66.7 percent of the girls reported that they talk sometimes to always about delaying sexual activity
until an older age. As we examine the patterns of communication between

TABLE 2.5
Perceived Comfort during Sexual Discussion
by Recipient of Communication

	Uncomfortable		Comfortable	
	N	%	N	%
Friends (N = 1,005)	62	23.1	207	76.9
Others (N = 419)	18	14.4	107	85.6

TABLE 2.6
Relationship of the "Other" Recipient of
Sexual Communication

Relationship	N	%
Aunts	23	8.2
Brothers	4	1.4
Cousins	28	10.0
Grandparents	9	3.3
Sisters/sisters-in-law	43	15.4
Teachers/school counselors	4	1.4
Uncles	3	1.3
Miscellaneous others*	12	4.2
Did not specify relationship	153	54.8
Total	279	100.0

* "Others" included individuals for whom participants listed a name but not
a relationship.

parents and friends, we find that girls communicate with their mothers at about the same frequency that they communicate with their friends about sexual issues.

One hundred twenty-six girls in the sample (45 percent) reported that they talked with someone other than their parents or friends about sex. When we asked the young women how comfortable they felt about communicating with others, 85.6 percent of them reported that they felt comfortable doing so. When we asked the young women who else they communicated with, we found that sisters (15.4 percent), aunts (8.2 percent), and cousins (10 percent) were the primary recipients of sexual communication (see Table 2.6).

Finally, we asked these young women if they planned on talking about sexual issues with others and found that 86.1 percent of the sample who reported talking to others (N = 115) said that they would probably to definitely talk to others about sexual issues. Furthermore, 68.9 percent of the sample of girls who reported talking to another person said that they would talk with that person about not getting pregnant. With regard to

HIV/AIDS, 60.1 percent report that they talk to others about HIV/AIDS. Once again, when we explored who these others were, we found that they were sisters, aunts, and cousins.

Conclusion

As can be seen from the data presented in this study, many Latina girls are communicating with their parents, friends, and extended family members about sex. Overall, we found that Latina girls feel more comfortable in discussing sex and sexual issues with their mothers. This finding supports previous research suggesting that girls in general prefer to talk with their mothers about sex (DiIorio et al., 2000; Miller, Kotchick, et al., 1998). We also found that Latina girls do not feel comfortable discussing sex or sexual issues with their fathers, and they do not communicate frequently with their father about these topics. Once again, our findings mirror previous research that suggests that girls are less likely to talk with their fathers than with their mothers about sex.

Our findings are a contribution to the social science literature because they provide a picture of the other people (i.e., family members and friends) Latina girls talk to about sex and sexuality. We find that, indeed, Latina girls are talking with extended family members about pregnancy, delaying sexual activity, and HIV/AIDS. This important finding suggests that Latina girls have an extensive social network that they actively utilize for social support.

In conclusion, the Latina girls in our sample are actively engaging in negotiating their environment to seek out information that they can use to make decisions about their sexual behaviors. This is an indication of resiliency: seeking out what is needed for development. Contrary to research that suggests that these young adolescents are negatively impacted by their surrounding environment, we find that Latina girls have access to a family system that can potentially buffer detrimental environment influences. On a final note, we believe that Latina girls are taking the initiative and creating resiliency in their own lives.

Recommendations for Educators and Others Involved in Sexual Health Communication

We believe that the findings of our work are of great interest to educators and other individuals who work directly with adolescents in the areas of sexual health communication. First and foremost, the finding that Latina adolescents discuss sexual issues with a wide array of other individuals suggests that educators are one of many individuals who influence teen sexual decision making. Educators in the field of adolescent sexuality have long acknowledged the important role that parents play in adolescent sexual education (Kirby, 1985). However, the findings in this study suggest that nonparental others also strongly influence adolescent sexual behaviors. Therefore, it may be in the interests of educators to focus efforts on understanding nonparental sources of sexual information. As the current findings suggest, educators may want to include acknowledgment of these others in future interventions and programming by developing components that seek to educate adolescents about having comfortable sexual discussions with nonparental others.

Acknowledgments

We would like to thank Elsa Vasquez for her impeccable work with and dedication to Latina girls. We would also like to thank the adolescents involved in the CAMP project for their participation in this study, as well as the CHOICES staff, including the CAMP theater actors, for their hard work and commitment to the issues of adolescent sexual health.

REFERENCES

Adolph, Carol, Ramos, Diana E., Linton, Kathryn L. P., and Grimes, David A. (1995). Pregnancy among Hispanic teenagers: Is good parental communication a deterrent? *Contraception* 51:303–306.

Christopher, F. Scott, Johnson, Diane C., and Roosa, Mark W. (1993). Family, individual, and social correlates of early Hispanic adolescent sexual expression. *Journal of Sex Research* 30:54–61.

DiIorio, Colleen, Kelley, Maureen, and Hockenberry-Eaton, Marilyn. (1999). Communication about sexual issues: Mothers, fathers, and friends. *Journal of Adolescent Health* 24:181–189.

DiIorio, C., Resnicow, K., Dudley, W. N., Thomas, S., Wang, D. T., Van Marter, D. F., Manteuffel, B., and Lipana, J. (2000). Social cognitive factors associated with mother-adolescent communication about sex. *Journal of Health Communication* 5:41–51.

Dittus, P. J., Jaccard, J., and Gordon, V. V. (1999). Direct and nondirect communication of mother beliefs to adolescents: Adolescent motivations for premarital sexual activity. *Journal of Applied Social Psychology* 29:1927–1963.

Fisher, Terri D. (1986a). An exploratory study of parent-child communication about sex and the sexual attitudes of early, middle, and late adolescents. *Journal of Genetic Psychology* 147:543–557.

———. (1986b). Parent-child communication about sex and young adolescents' sexual knowledge and attitudes. *Adolescence* 21:517–527.

Forehand, Rex, Biggar, Heather, and Beth Kotchick. (1998). Cumulative risk across family stressors: Short- and long-term effects for adolescents. *Journal of Abnormal Psychology* 6 (2): 119–128.

Fox, G. L., and Inazu, J. K. (1980). Patterns and outcomes of mother-daughter communication about sexuality. *Journal of Social Issues* 36:7–29.

Guzmán, Bianca L., Casad, Bettina J., Schlehofer-Sutton, Michele M., Villanueva, Christina M., and Feria, Aida. (2003). CAMP: A community-based approach to promoting safe sex behaviour in adolescence. *Journal of Community and Applied Social Psychology* 13:269–283.

Guzmán, Bianca L., Schlehofer-Sutton, Michele M., Villanueva, Christina M., Dello Stritto, Mary Ellen, Casad, Bettina J., Feria, Aida, et al. (2003). Let's talk about sex: How comfortable discussions about sex impact teen sexual behavior. *Journal of Health Communication* 8:583–598.

Holtzman, Deborah, and Rubinson, Richard (1995). Parent and peer communication effects on AIDS-related behavior among U.S. high school students. *Family Planning Perspectives* 27:235–240.

Jaccard, J., Dittus, P. J., and Gordon, V. V. (2000). Parent-teen communication about premarital sex: Factors associated with the extent of communication. *Journal of Adolescent Research* 15:187–208.

Kirby, Douglas B. (1985). Sexuality education: A more realistic view of its effects. *Journal of School Health* 55:421–424.

Lefkowitz, Eva S., Sigman, Marian, and Au, Terry K. (2000). Helping mothers discuss sexuality and AIDS with adolescents. *Child Development* 71:1383–1394.

Leland, N. L., and Barth, R. P. (1993). Characteristics of adolescents who have attempted to avoid HIV and who have communicated with parents about sex. *Journal of Adolescent Research* 8:58–76.

Miller, K. S., Kotchick, Beth A., Dorsey, Shannon, Forehand, Rex, and Ham, Anissa Y. (1998). Family communication about sex: What are parents saying and are their adolescents listening? *Family Planning Perspectives* 30:218–222.

Miller, Kim S., Levin, Martin L., Whitaker, Daniel J., and Xu, Xiaohe. (1998). Patterns of condom use among adolescents: The impact of mother-adolescent communication. *American Journal of Public Health* 88:1542–1544.

Moore, K. A., Peterson, J. L., and Furstenberg, F. F. (1986). Parental attitudes and the occurrence of early sexual activity. *Journal of Marriage and the Family* 48:777–782.

Nolin, M. J., and Petersen, K. K. (1992). Gender differences in parent-child communication about sexuality: An exploratory study. *Journal of Adolescent Research* 7:59–79.

O'Sullivan, Lucia F., Jaramillo, Beatriz M. S., Moreau, Donna, and Meyer-Bahlburg, Heino F. L. (1999). Mother-daughter communication about sexuality in a clinical sample of Hispanic adolescent girls. *Hispanic Journal of Behavioral Sciences* 21:447–469.

Pistella, Christine L. Y., and Bonati, Frank A. (1998). Communication about sexual behavior among adolescent women, their family, and peers. *Families in Society: The Journal of Contemporary Human Services* 79:206–211.

Salgado de Snyder, Nelly, and Padilla, Amado, M. (1987). Social support networks: Their availability and effectiveness. In M. Gaviria and J. Arana (Eds.), *Health and behavior: Research agenda for Hispanics* (pp. 93–107). Chicago: University of Illinois at Chicago.

Shoop, Dawn M., and Davidson, Philip M. (1994). AIDS and adolescents: The relation of parent and partner communication to adolescent condom use. *Journal of Adolescence* 17:137–148.

Stycos, J., Mayone. (1972). Family and fertility in Puerto Rico. In Francesco Cordasco and Eugene Bucchioni (Eds.), *The Puerto Rican community and its children on the mainland: A source book for teachers, social workers and other professionals* (pp. 76–88). Metuchen, NJ: Scarecrow Press.

Chapter 3

Confianza, Consejos, and Contradictions
Gender and Sexuality Lessons between Latina Adolescent Daughters and Mothers

Jennifer Ayala

I begin this chapter with an abbreviated poem pieced together with actual quotations (along with my interpretations) from interviews with Latina adolescent daughters and their mothers. This poem begins with mother and daughter voices speaking in unison in order to represent the themes emerging from the study described in this chapter. The poem then splits into distinct mother voices and daughter voices, represented by separate columns, coming back together at different times in the poem. The stylistic movement between mother and daughter voices illustrated in this poem foreshadows the theoretical movement between what Villenas and Moreno (2001) have termed "mother-daughter pedagogies."

Together we weave a fabric of culture
With threads of respeto and love.

Como mama,	*Como hija,*
I will give you *confianza*	I will try to push the boundary outward.
Tell you my struggles and how it is	Find the limit you set and press it further,
Para que aprendas	learn from your contradictions
In a way that my *mami* never did,	and challenge you,
Though I hear her echoes in my soul.	even though it may hurt you as you did with your *mami.*

> Because *ella es muy fuerte,*
> *Si es mi mami.*
> *Muy fuerte de caracter,*
> In a way that I never could be . . .
> But perhaps I am.[1]

As the poem moves between distinct mother and daughter voices, shared vulnerabilities and strengths across generations of what Ana Castillo has called formidable women are revealed (1994; Villenas and Moreno 2001). Formidable is an appropriate designation, because women of color are mothering in the context of interlocking systems of oppression, fighting to survive while maintaining loving bonds and strong commitments to their communities (Collins 1990; Fine, Weis, and Roberts 2000; Villenas and Moreno 2001). The *cuentos* (stories) mothers tell serve a functional purpose; they are of "strategic, immediate value, giving historical perspective to current struggles, drawing out connections between oppressive conditions then and now" (Benmayor et al. 1987, 3; Fine, Weis, and Roberts 2000).

In the spirit of paying homage to our mothers, I initially investigated how these stories from mother to daughter persisted, shifted, or transformed among Latina mothers who had changed geographic and cultural contexts from Latin America to the United States. However, my initial conceptualization shifted as I heard mothers reference the strength of their daughters and the effect that had on their mothering. My work came to focus on the intergenerational negotiation of culture, gender, and social oppression between Latina adolescent daughters and their mothers.

Through personal contacts and snowball sampling techniques, in 1998 and 1999 I interviewed eleven Puerto Rican, Cuban, Ecuadorian, and mixed-nationality Latina young women who were nonmothers, aged fifteen to eighteen, and five of their mothers.[2] Participants resided in urban and suburban neighborhoods in New York and New Jersey. Daughters were U.S.-born (one was born in Puerto Rico), and mothers were born in Latin America, though they had significant tenure in the United States. Their mother-daughter narratives reveal how *mujer*-centered knowledge is constructed through the negotiation between generations, and not simply through a unidirectional process of transmission.

Mother and Daughter Voices

Espín (1997) has observed that "during the acculturation process sexuality becomes the focus of the parents' fears and the girls' desires" (175). In her interviews with immigrant mothers and daughters, she found that mothers passed on messages about sexuality and gender roles to their daughters not through structured lessons per se but through what they said about men and other women in the form of "half-muttered comments, behavior, by example and powerfully in their silences" (1999, 146). As they articulate deep concern about "their daughters' sexuality and their desire to do better than their own mothers" (146), mothers seem to deliver seemingly contradictory messages. These messages involve both critique and loyalty to women's cultural scripts. Villenas and Moreno (2001) have framed these perceived contradictions as complexities inherent in the process of mothering within structures of constraint,[3] shaped by what they call systems of racial domination and economic exploitation. The contradictions come from teaching daughters how to survive within the system while also finding ways of quietly subverting the system. Such is the nature of mothering in the borderlands (Anzaldúa 1999; Hurtado 2003).[4]

The daughters I interviewed also perceived contradictions in the messages mothers had passed on to them, and they built on these contradictions to teach their own mothers lessons. Mothers framed the messages they transmitted about culture, gender, and sexuality not as contradictions but as an effort to balance reality with possibility—the reality of gender oppressions and double standards, and the possibility of transcending them. In many ways, mothers and daughters would wear each other's roles, as daughter voices and mother voices emerged across the interviews. What I describe as mother voices or daughter voices involves more than just what they said about their individual experiences. For instance, daughter voices include what the mothers and daughters said about their respective daughter experiences, and what they heard/interpreted and reported on as the daughter experiences of their intergenerational counterparts.

Daughter voices critiqued gender arrangements at home and elsewhere and sung possibility, formulating visions of how things could be. Like their daughters, the mothers articulated a subtle critique of the gendered restrictions and responsibilities they experienced while growing up (Hurtado 2003). The restrictions consisted of not being allowed out of the house while their brothers were free to explore, following the rules of a *señorita,* saving her prized virginity for marriage, to a man, and dating only one person whom she would ultimately marry. Linked to the restrictions, the responsibilities involved the adult tasks of cooking, cleaning, caregiving, and often working to contribute to the family—a preview of their future lives working *"doble jornadas"* as wives and mothers (Fine, Weis, and Roberts 2000). The responsibilities they had to *la familia* at home were inextricably linked to the restrictions that were placed on their sexuality. As Souza (2002) has explained, "Parents confine adolescent women to the household like children needing supervision yet treat them like adults when it comes to certain reproductive matters within the household." One mother, Penny, describes her teenage years as

> extremely strict. . . . It was really staying home, doing your homework, cooking and cleaning. . . . They taught us how to grow so fast. We had to be adults so early. By sixteen, I had to be an adult and had to do chores . . . ironing and cooking, nothing about going outside and playing and a lot of things like that, that hold you back and made you grow up and want to leave your house . . . to worse things. To worse things because then you really cook and clean.

Not unaware of the privileges men were granted both at home and in the larger society in which they lived, mothers questioned some of these gender arrangements and described their responses to daughters indirectly through *cuentos:* how they cracked open opportunities to explore their sexuality and escape the restrictions, slipping through the culturally sanctioned passages of marriage or migration. Like Penny, Maribel, another mother, found that marriage was an escape from the watchful eyes of her parents: "Cuando yo era joven, pues, yo no sali mucho. . . . Cuando me case, entonces, pues, ya empezé a salir." Although as Penny noted, what they escaped to was not much different from what they escaped from. Other mothers found migration to the United States was a culturally acceptable way of achieving freedom from parental restrictions. However, their responsibilities multiplied as they found themselves having to be their own mother, with the adult responsibilities of sending money home, as well as supporting themselves and contributing to their sponsors here. Thus, the grip on their sexuality may have loosened a bit, but their gendered responsibilities tightened, and there was little time for the sought-after exploration.

Education, Independence, and Sexuality

The memories of their own daughter voices stayed with mothers as they raised their children. Reflecting on their experiences as daughters, mothers promised themselves they would do differently by their daughters. Raising their daughters became a way in which to realize the possible selves many had longed for, the selves that were spared the pain and the struggle, that had an education, that achieved independence from men, that were able to communicate with their mothers, *con confianza* (Hurtado 2003; Markus and Nurius 1986).[5] These characteristics embodied in the possible selves became the focus of the lessons mothers passed on to their daughters, lessons that were deeply connected.

One connection mothers emphasized in their lessons to daughters was that between education, independence from men, and sexuality. This connection is illustrated by the following passage from a poem by Ruth Behar (2001, 307):

> My mother taught me to be afraid
> Of *la cosa*
> Between your legs
> To run from it
> Like the plague
> Not to look in that direction
> Because that meant I wanted it.
> She wanted to be sure
> I got through school
> Became someone
> Before I let myself
> Go mad with yearning
> For *la cosa*
> Between your legs . . .

The first few stanzas of Ruth Behar's poem allude to her mother's concern that sexuality, specifically the possibility of getting pregnant, can get in the way of her daughter's educational and career goals. Many of the mothers I interviewed expressed similar sentiments. Josie explains the connections between education, economic opportunities, and patriarchy as she advised her daughter:

A woman today, without an education, without the knowledge, believe me, she'll fall into that man's world place. Okay? A woman has to be very captive, very intelligent, very ready to take on the world attitude, very bitchy to make it in the man's world. . . . I have always told [my daughter], and I've always shown her, "You don't need a man around to survive."

Like the women in Aida Hurtado's book *Voicing Chicana Feminisms* (2003), the mothers I interviewed underscore the link between education and independence from men, specifying that having an education could facilitate economic independence from men, cautioning, like Josie, that without one, "you fall into that man's world" (also see Lopez 1998). These are critical lessons because they represent active efforts on the part of mothers to interrupt the patriarchy of the larger society and within Latino culture. Mothers expressed intense concern over men's sexuality and their daughter's vulnerability. In the minds and experiences of mothers, sexuality represents missed opportunities and a deterrent from the goal of education, thereby ensuring economic dependence on men.

Mothers framed sexuality within a discourse of danger, violence, and victimization, pairing the heterosexual aggressiveness of men with the sexual vulnerability of women (Fine 1992). To protect their daughters from men's sexuality, mothers often opened up, or reproduced, the sexual silences they experienced growing up with explicit admonitions: "Don't let them touch you," "Keep your legs closed!" "Don't be coming home pregnant," or the coded vocabulary of sexuality, usually in Spanish, *"Tienes que darte a respetar," "Tienes que ser una señorita"* (Zavella 2003). They included in their definitions of a strong, independent woman the ability and courage to resist and defend themselves against male sexual advances. Thus, warnings to keep one's legs closed were often combined with warning to not depend on men—messages that were not contradictory in the minds of mothers but were congruent to the goal of independence (Villenas and Moreno 2001).

To protect their daughters from these dangers, mothers drew from the familiar survival strategies of restriction they had grown up with; for instance, keeping daughters at home was a way to protect them because home is considered a safe space, whereas outside is rife with danger. Daughters' requests for being allowed out, Souza (2002) points out, are often interpreted as "a desire to have unsanctioned, numerous sexual relations simply by wanting to go outside." Encouraging their daughters to stay home, not allowing them to be out alone without the protection of older brothers or cousins, insisting that they not have sex until marriage, to a man, mothers often used familiar strategies of gender restriction. They taught their daughters about the possibility of independence from men through education tempered with the reality that men are needed for their protection, as many daughters are allowed out only under the supervision of male relatives. In return, daughters often have to cook and clean for men. Thus, girls are asked to both care for and respect men while at the same time holding them suspect because of their predatory sexuality.

Contradictions as Learning Spaces

Daughters sometimes interpret the underlying messages embedded in these strategies as contradictory to the other messages of independence they receive. Jailene, one of the teens, observes, "[My mother] contradicts herself in a way, you know, because she's trying to be old school but trying to be like a nineties woman too." Jailene takes note of her mother's conflicting messages yet frames them as an effort at balancing values, tied more to generation than to Latino culture per se. Josie, a mother, also felt that she was delivering gender-empowering messages specifying independence from men while interweaving the cautions and protective behavior necessary for her daughter to achieve this possibility—messages that she felt were congruent and complementary. Yet her daughter Michelle interpreted some of her protective behavior as gender-oppressive, suggesting that the positioning of girls as vulnerable subordinates them, as well as entitling boys to maintain their heterosexually aggressive status. In the following exchange, Michelle illustrates the gender-based discrepancies in the application of social and household rules:

> *Interviewer*: Have you ever been treated unfairly because you're a girl?
> *Michelle*: Only with my mother. . . . She's always saying, like my brother can go out all the time, me, I have to tell her and I give the phone number of where I'm going, a list of things before I go out, beforehand, like I have to be home at a certain time and if I'm not there, she'll come out looking for me, only because I'm a girl.

These moments of contradiction, inherent to mothering and growing up in the borderlands (Villenas and Moreno 2001), were also spaces of learning and growth. Mothers moved between perceived realities (their concerns about sexuality) and possibilities (the desire to do better than their own mothers; Espín 1999). As these women raise their daughters with revisionist values they often are led to critical introspection and shifts in their own lives. For example, Penny, a mother, describes this process of reteaching herself as she teaches her daughter:

> I think now, as I teach her, I am reteaching myself. Sometimes, I catch myself, something that I used to do years back with my husband. I don't see why I have to iron his clothes. Like I don't see why, if you eat from that dish, I have to wash it. . . . But then as I teach her, I say hey, but this is what I am doing, right? And I am reteaching myself. . . . I teach her and I am learning to be different.

As Penny taught her daughter the importance of being in egalitarian relationships with men without the assumption of economic or domestic dependence (Fine, Weis, and Roberts 2000), she would catch herself not putting into practice what she was teaching her daughter. She came to realize that in her relationship with her husband, she was modeling something different from what she was trying to teach her daughter. She applied the critical consciousness she was imparting to her daughter to her own circumstances; thus, as she taught her daughter, she was learning to be different herself.

The daughters would push these gender/cultural/sexual borders further, as some directly drew attention to the perceived contradictions. Like their mothers before them, daughters formulated a critique of confining visions of sexuality and gender. In a way that their own mothers may not have dared to attempt, daughters tried to teach them lessons about sexuality and gender, reflecting their mother's teachings superimposed with their own observations, experiences, and generational lessons from peers.

Mothers spoke of guarding their daughters' sexuality as daughters encouraged their mothers to exert theirs—something that is difficult to imagine within traditional conceptualizations of Latino/a families that are characterized as strictly hierarchical and patriarchal. Yet both daughters who grew up in traditional two-parent families with the father as the head of the household and those in which both daughters and mothers were immersed in the dating scene described such instances to varying degrees. Jazmin, for instance, a fifteen-year-old daughter, described her upbringing as very strict. She was not permitted to have boys call her on the phone or to leave the house without the supervision of her brothers or cousins. In return for their taking her out, Jazmin had to cook and clean for her male family members. In a family dynamic where she may have felt as if she had little power as a respectful Latina daughter, Jazmin nonetheless clearly articulated how her mother learned from her and her underground moves toward changing the gendered division of labor at home. After describing the glaring silence about sexuality in her home, she recalled an occasion when she challenged her mother to confront the shame often surrounding women's sexual bodies, specifically regarding menstruation.

> She had this thing against like going to the store and like buying sanitary napkins. She was, like, very very shy about it. I remember once, you know, we were in the store and I was, like, "Oh please, mom [in a loud voice], you want this one or that one? You want Always with Wings or . . . ?" "Don't be shy about it. It's not like everybody doesn't buy it. What's the big deal about it?" That's what she's learned, so now she's like, still a little bit shy, she looks, if there's a guy in the aisle she won't go, but if it's a woman in the aisle, she'll go.

Jazmin challenges her mother to replace shame with pride in their bodies. She accomplishes this through a strategic confrontation; through Jazmin's loud announcement that they were buying sanitary napkins in a store, her mother was forced to publicly acknowledge her sexual body. Jazmin observes the results of her efforts as she sees her mother begin to overcome the shyness and shame she feels about her body. The dominant discourses of pathology and shame surrounding adolescent female bodies reverse in this situation, as Jazmin, a teenager, empowers her mother to come to terms with her woman's body and the shame surrounding menstruation.

Jazmin was also making subversive moves toward changing the gendered responsibilities. She saw her mother and father's insistence that she clean up after her brothers as disempowering, even detrimental, both to herself, for taking on most of this burden, and to her brothers. Because the young men in the family were not expected to clean or cook, they were being trained to be dependent on women. In Jazmin's view, this practice placed her brothers at a disadvantage. Therefore, Jazmin taught them, when her parents were not looking, how to care for themselves. She described taking them by the hand and walking them over to the kitchen

"See that shelf? Open it. That's where the plates are. Now come here, see that, that's where . . ." Jazmin framed this as gender-empowering lessons for the boys because she was, in essence, teaching them to be independent.

The Player Mode: Sexual Entitlements

As mothers taught their daughters about men's predatory sexuality, about the dangers, daughters also talked about acknowledging and asserting their needs and power, about the pleasures. For instance, many daughters expressed to their mothers their preference for casual exploration of romantic relationships with boys, as long as they did not admit to having sex.

Seventeen-year-old Jailene takes it a step further, as she responded "the player mode" to the question "What did you teach your mother?" She described how at first her mother did not approve of her casual stance toward dating, as she was encouraged to be loyal and self-sacrificing: "Your life has to be your husband." Jailene's mother warns potential dates that her daughter "is a player, has an attitude and wants everything her way," suggesting that her daughter possesses a sense of sexual entitlement or subjectivity that humble, self-sacrificing Latinas should not express. Such sexual entitlement is reserved for men (Souza 1995); therefore, potential male partners needed to be cautioned against Jailene's transgressions.

However, after a ten-year relationship did not work out for her mother, Jailene noticed that her mother's stance shifted. According to Jailene, she seemed to realize that she could be a sexual subject with the freedom to explore relationships that are rewarding for her as well as her partner. Although her mother had criticized her initially for engaging in the player mode, she eventually adopted the same strategy: "Now she's going out more with guys. . . . She's like going on dates here, going on a date there, you know, and she's like 'Mmmm, I see what you mean Jailene.' . . . She's like in a player mode too."

Thus, Jailene describes how her mother learned this strategy from her by observing her daughter's actions and attitudes toward boys and heterosexual relationships. Jailene seems to observe her mother, noting approvingly the changes she may have inspired in her, as she modeled for her mother a sexuality script that allows for her sexual subjectivity/entitlement.

These heterosexuality scripts are not located just within the women but are situated in a broader context of culture and structure. They contest/accept the Latino cultural script of virgin/whore dichotomies while also "grappl[ing] with their working-class origins, racialized bodies, traditional gender expectations, and sexual orientation" (Zavella 2003, 230).[6] Daughters are revising the cultural scripts, or templates, as Zavella (2003) has called them, that position Latinas as self-sacrificing and beholden to the needs of men. Being a player, in addition to introducing the danger of promiscuity, is threatening because it acknowledges girls' and women's sexual subjectivities. It implies that a woman acts in response to her own needs and desires, which conflicts with the idealized image of Latinas as self-sacrificing (Hurtado 2003). Thus, the power component of sexuality is implicit in these sexuality narratives, where virgen/puta binaries are being disrupted (Souza 1995).

The self-sacrificing aspect of Latina womanhood extends to domains outside of the home, including work and friendship spaces. Making their own modifications, daughters tried to teach their mothers how to maintain culture while challenging or shedding the aspects of it that hold women responsible for always sacrificing themselves for the good of others (Fine, Weis, and Roberts 2000). In line with what Taylor (1996) found, several daughters felt that their mothers' self-sacrificing tendencies or niceness often resulted in the women being stepped on or taken advantage of. Melissa, Penny's eighteen-year-old daughter, describes her mother this way:

> Like if she has something to do for herself, my mom will drop everything, for somebody else. And then that person wouldn't do it back for her, and that's why I've tried to teach her. . . . She can't never say no. . . . She is a sweetheart, but a lot of people take advantage of that today. . . . She lets a lot of people step on her.

Many daughters expressed concern over their mothers' self-sacrificing behavior, believing that it is an important cultural distinction in some ways, but often left them vulnerable to abuse by partners, friends, coworkers, and bosses. In response, daughters would try to protect themselves and their mothers from similar situations by learning to say no, refusing to neglect their own needs, and sharing this knowledge with their mothers.

Daughters are thus encouraging their mothers to revise the Latina cultural script in a way that leaves room for their own needs and desires, as they instill in their mothers or reinforce the idea that their own needs are worth nurturing. In moments of conflict and cooperation, they teach their mothers to say no; they remind their mothers that their own needs are worth considering and can be a priority—that they should do for themselves, have their own lives, be a player, and stand up for themselves. In these ways, daughters perhaps spoke as mothers, expressing concern about their mothers' vulnerabilities in relationships with friends, bosses, and partners, just as their mothers worried about daughters' vulnerable sexuality.

Conclusions and Implications

In moments of conflict, *consejos,* or *confianza,* mothers and daughters negotiated gendered restrictions and responsibilities, the pleasures and the dangers of heterosexuality, and race/class/ethnicity-based oppressions (Hurtado 2003). The mothers and daughters interviewed for this study described loving bonds even within contested spaces of gender/culture negotiations. Daughters deeply respected the strengths of their mothers even as they critiqued some of their practices. Mothers in turn acknowledged a strength in their daughters, as they listened to or let daughters teach them how to use the player mode and reminded themselves that they are *fuerte de caracter.*

As part of the sandwich generation (Hurtado 2003, 107), these mothers were maneuvering between layers of voices, those of their daughters and of their own mothers and upbringing. They raised daughters as best they could amid often risky or hostile environments, limited resources, and structural injustice. Some would say they raised resisters (Ward 1996), as they imparted and modeled for daughters "the ability to see freedom within restriction and the commitment to struggle within constraint" (Hurtado 2003, 77). What seemed to be contradictions in the messages they imparted to daughters in word and action, were, as Villenas and Moreno (2001) explain, a by-product of living in the psychological borderlands between U.S. mainstream and Latino/a cultures and generations.

Villenas and Moreno (2001) have aptly named the rich, complex lessons that mothers impart to daughters "mother-daughter pedagogies." What the present chapter adds to the literature is the idea that this *mujer*-centered knowledge does not simply flow down the generational chain. It is constructed by the negotiations between generations, allowing for the possibility that adolescent daughters are active producers of cultural knowledge. This counters assumptions of rigid patriarchy and hierarchical relationships within Latino families in the United States. This research suggests that practitioners who work toward promoting social change among young Latina women should do so using a strengths framework and an understanding of the multiplicity and fluidity of their culture and experiences. Practitioners and theorists can learn from and build upon the broader skills Latinas use in navigating the multiplicities of home, school, and work worlds. Several other findings are of use to practitioners: (1) that generation is an important dimension of diversity/difference within Latina groups, (2) that depictions of strict hierarchical arrangements within the family should not be assumed, and (3) that Latino/a culture is not a set of rigid prescriptions but by definition is shifting and fluid. Perhaps most important, this research illustrates that Latina young women are capable of (and are already engaging in) initiating social change in their communities as part of intergenerational partnerships. In fact, they are often change agents within the home space. This study invites another way of looking at mother-daughter relationships or pedagogies—as sites of cultural transformation. As such, they can be engaged as a powerful unit in broader social change efforts.

NOTES

1. Excerpted by permission of the publisher from Lois Weis and Michelle Fine, *Speed Bumps: A Student-Friendly Guide to Qualitative Research* (New York: Teachers College Press, (c) 2000 by Teachers College, Columbia University, all rights reserved), pp. 104–105.

2. A snowball sampling technique involves asking each participant to identify one or more additional people for the researcher to contact for the study. Burke Johnson and Larry Christensen, *Educational Research: Quantitative, Qualitative and Mixed Approaches* (New York: Pearson Education, 2004).

3. I use the concept of structures of constraint to describe in general terms the forces in society that constrain the choices available to, in this case, Latinas, through mechanisms such as race, class, or gender oppression. Theorists like Martin-Baro and Friere discuss structures of constraint in their writing. From a feminist/economics perspective, Nancy Folbre, in her book *Who Pays for the Kids? Gender and the Structure of Constraint* (1994), describes structures of constraint as being made up of societal rules, norms, asset distributions, and preferences that empower some groups and marginalize others.

4. In her pioneering book *Borderlands/La Frontera: The New Mestiza*, Anzaldúa explains the concept of borderlands as originating from the physical borders between the United States and Mexico. She indicates, however, that the "psychological borderlands, the sexual borderlands and the spiritual borderlands

... are not particular to the Southwest. In fact, the borderlands are physically present wherever two or more cultures edge each other, where people of different races occupy the same territory, where under, lower, middle and upper classes touch, where the space between two individuals shrinks with intimacy." I use the concept of borderlands within this framework—the understanding that Latinas in the United States live between different social, cultural, spiritual, and sexual worlds.

5. *Confianza,* loosely translated, is a mix of trust and familiarity. It was a mothering strategy some women had tried to incorporate in order to communicate with their daughters the lessons they had learned in life (Hidalgo 1998). Some interpret *confianza* as having a negative connotation, such as the accusation of having too much confidence or being *confiada,* meaning fresh or disrespectful. In this case, I found that mothers had reclaimed *confianza* as a way of reaching their daughters to discuss such issues as gender, sexuality, and what it takes to survive in a world of male privilege.

6. The *virgen/puta* (virgin/whore) dichotomy represents a patriarchal continuum, situated in a framework where women are positioned either as saintlike good girls who wait until marriage to have sex and, even then, only for the purpose of satisfying their husband's desires, or as bad, promiscuous women who sleep with multiple partners, flaunt their sexuality, are not taken as serious relationship partners by men and suffer the scorn of society (Zavella 2003, 248). Thrust into this binary, Latinas' sexuality is controlled, held as the basis for bringing honor or shame to the family. Zavella adds that some theorists suggest the history of Spanish conquest of indigenous people in Mexico set up the logic whereby sexual intercourse is viewed as the metaphorical conquest of women (248).

REFERENCES

Anzaldúa, Gloria. 1999. *Borderlands, la frontera: The new mestiza.* 2nd ed. San Francisco: Aunt Lute Books.

Ayala, Jennifer. 2000. Across dialects. In *Speedbumps: A student-friendly guide to qualitative research,* ed. Lois Weis and Michelle Fine, 102–105. New York: Teachers College Press.

Behar, Ruth. 2001. La cosa. In *Telling to live: Latina feminist testimonios,* ed. Latina Feminist Group, 307–308. Durham, NC: Duke University Press.

Benmayor, Rina, Ana Juarabe, Celia Alvarez, and Blanca Vasquez. 1987. *Stories to live by: Continuity and change in three generations of Puerto Rican women.* New York: Centro de Estudios Puertorriquenos.

Castillo, Ana. 1994. *Massacre of the dreamers: Essays on Xicanisma.* Albuquerque: University of New Mexico Press.

Collins, Patricia Hill. 1990. *Black feminist thought: knowledge, consciousness and the politics of empowerment.* Boston: Unwin Hymn.

Debold, Elizabeth, Marie Wilson, and Idelisse Malave. 1993. *Mother daughter revolution: From betrayal to power.* New York: Addison-Wesley.

Espín, Oliva. 1997. Race, racism, and sexuality in the life narratives of immigrant women. In *Latina realities: Essays on healing, migration and sexuality,* ed. Oliva Espín, 171–185. Boulder, CO: Westview Press.

———. 1999. *Women crossing boundaries: A psychology of immigration and transformations of sexuality.* New York: Routledge.

Fine, Michelle. 1992. Sexuality, schooling and adolescent females: The missing discourse of desire. In *Disruptive voices: The possibilities of feminist research,* ed. Michelle Fine, 31–59. Ann Arbor: University of Michigan Press.

Fine, Michelle, Lois Weis, and Rosemary Roberts. 2000. Refusing the betrayal: Latinas redefining gender, sexuality, culture and resistance. *Education/Pedagogy/Cultural Studies* 22:87–119.

Hidalgo, Nitza M. 1998. Toward a definition of a Latino family research paradigm. *International Journal of Qualitative Studies in Education* 11:103–120.

Hurtado, Aida. 2003. *Voicing Chicana feminisms: Young women speak out on sexuality and identity.* New York: NYU Press.

Latina Feminist Group. 2001. *Telling to live: Latina feminist testimonios.* Durham, NC: Duke University Press.

Lopez, Nancy. 1998. *Gender matters: Schooling among second-generation Caribbean youth in New York City.* Unpublished manuscript.

Markus, Hazel, and Nurius, Riula. 1986. Possible selves. *American Psychologist* 41: 954–969.

Souza, Caridad. 2002. Sexual identities of young Puerto Rican mothers. Mujeres! Special double issue of *Dialogo on Latinas* (online magazine), Winter/Spring, no. 6.

Taylor, Jill McLean. 1996. Cultural stories: Latina and Portuguese daughters and mothers. In *Urban girls: resisting stereotypes, creating identities,* ed. B. Leadbeater and N. Way, 117–131. New York: NYU Press.

Villenas, S., and M. Moreno. 2001. To *valerse por si misma* between race, capitalism, and patriarchy: Latina mother-daughter pedagogies in North Carolina. *International Journal of Qualitative Studies in Education* 14:671–687.

Ward, Janie Victoria. 1996. Raising resisters: The role of truth telling in the psychological development of African American girls. In *urban girls: Resisting stereotypes, creating identities,* ed. B. Leadbeater and N. Way, 85–99. New York: NYU Press.

Zambrana, Ruth. 1995. *Understanding Latino families: Scholarship, policy and practice.* Thousand Oaks, CA: Sage.

Zavella, P. 2003. Talkin' sex: Chicanas and Mexicanas theorize about silences and sexual pleasures. In *Chicana feminisms: A critical reader,* ed. G. E. Arredondo, A. Hurtado, N. Klahn, O. Najera-Ramirez, and P. Zavella, 228–253. Durham, NC: Duke University Press.

Chapter 4

La Casa

Negotiating Family Cultural Practices, Constructing Identities

Angela Gallegos-Castillo

This world is all hard and crazy.

—Patti, age sixteen

Patti is a young woman of Mexican origin who is in the process of finding her own identity within a family home culture that nurtures and supports while it also limits and subjugates her efforts at defining herself. When asked to characterize her experience making the transition from adolescence to womanhood, Patti sighs heavily and responds with the above comment that suggests that life is difficult.

Patti's life clearly has not been easy. She has had to contend with her mother's drug addiction, temporary placements in foster care, living with extended family members, and also coping with everyday adolescent challenges. While not all the young women in my study faced these particular experiences, Patti's sentiment reflects some of the other young women's feelings about growing up. Growing up working-class, Mexican, and female in an urban environment is, as Patti reflects, a challenging endeavor.

A common dissatisfaction shared by Patti and the other young women in my study is that Mexican family gender expectations are viewed as unjust and oppressive. Too often, family expectations conflict with these young women's desire for autonomy, discovery, and freedom. In seeking her young adult Mexican identity, Patti expresses and asserts her desire to break free of the rigid social and cultural practices imposed on her in the home. She chooses to assert her desires and personal expectations by challenging the gender expectations imposed in her aunt and uncle's household. Although far from traditional, her aunt and uncle hold many male-centered social norms that from Patti's perspective are unjust. In response to this gender injustice (Flores-Ortiz 2000), Patti, like other young women, develops strategies to guide her in her own development, ones that borrow from her American and Mexican culture. Developing these strategies is an attempt by Patti and other young women like her to establish norms that are more liberating and to retain social and cultural norms that maintain their working-class racialized and gendered identities.

Mexican Culture and Female Socialization

La familia, the family, is the primary socializing agent for all family members. It is *la familia* that imparts values, beliefs, traditions, and culture to each family member and directly influences how one experiences the world. For Latinos, *familismo,* the strong identification, loyalty, and attachment to family members, is considered one of the most important culture-specific values (Andrade 1980; Diaz-Guerrero and Szalay 1991; Marin and Marin 1991; Sotomayor 1991; Stanton-Salazar 1997). Family also defines what constitutes acceptable gender scripts, the way female and males should behave, and the role they should take on as gendered individuals.

Parents and the family system are especially important for Mexican youth because of their bicultural reality. As youth of color, Mexican young people must find ways to balance divergent cultural systems in the course of their psychosocial development. Unlike their European American adolescent counterparts, Mexican youth face challenges that necessitate developing social and cognitive skills to negotiate a racist society that undervalues their cultural identity (Boykin 1996; Keefe and Padilla 1987; Stanton-Salazar 1997, 2000). Moreover, if youth do not speak English, they are additionally challenged in developing a strong sense of identity given the discrimination and prejudice that come with speaking a language considered reflective of a devalued minority status (Espin 1997; Stanton-Salazar 1997). For monolingual Spanish-speaking youth, achieving school success, finding employment, and communicating in English are extra challenges to be negotiated in the adolescent process.

For Mexican-origin adolescent girls, the burden is accentuated by their female status. Patriarchal arrangements in Mexican culture privilege men over women, adding to women's oppression. How these male-centered cultural practices are played out and experienced is dependent on a family's socioeconomic status and material conditions. As poor, working-class youth, these young women experience urban poverty and all the social ills associated with it in gendered ways in the household. Young Mexican-origin women are socialized to adopt a strong work ethic and contribute to the household economy in specific ways by taking care of household tasks such as ironing, cooking, cleaning, and child rearing (Pesquera 1991). The social reproductive work young women perform, unfortunately, usually goes unacknowledged and is undervalued and unrecognized both inside and outside the family social unit (Souza 1995). In addition, the money young women earn through paid work outside the home is commonly used for household expenses and for their own personal expenses. In many households, the work young women do is vital to the maintenance and survival of the entire family system. Young Mexican-origin women are given enormous familial responsibilities yet are rarely given the corresponding increase in power or self-determination. Lacking recognition for their efforts and discontent over restrictive patriarchal home practices, many young women end up creating their own personal culture of resistance.

Participants

I explore the social worlds of twenty-two working-class Mexican-origin heterosexual women between fourteen and eighteen years of age in the Fruitvale District, an urban neighborhood of Oakland, California. I examine their home, school, and neighborhood life experiences and highlight the concerns and issues they face as they transition into womanhood. Furthermore, I explore how their gendered, working-class, and racialized experiences impact how they view themselves and their future identities.

Recruitment was conducted at the local public and private elementary and high schools, local community-based youth-serving agencies, and a summer employment program. To be included in the study, the young women had to have at least one Mexican parent, to have had resided in Fruitvale for at least three years, to have been socialized primarily in the United States, and to be from a poor or working-class background. Economic status was determined by parents' education and employment. The three-year residency criteria made it more likely that the young women would have been exposed to similar community experiences and be familiar with the social, cultural, and economic milieu of their community.

Seventeen young women came from a two-parent household, three came from a female-headed household, one young woman lived with her boyfriend, and another young woman lived with extended family. The majority of parents and caregivers (nineteen) were immigrants, whereas only three were born in the United States. Twenty-one of the twenty-two young women were born and socialized in the United States. The average age of the young women was sixteen years. Semistructured, open-ended interviews were conducted primarily in English, although code switching into Spanish occurred at various times throughout the interviews. Interviews were tape-recorded, transcribed, and analyzed for dominant themes and patterns. I utilized my own Chicana-informed viewpoint and first-hand knowledge of Mexican history, tradition, customs, and worldviews to guide the analysis. Using grounded theory (Strauss and Corbin, 2000) allowed me to take great care in providing an analysis that allowed the girls' perspectives to emerge, grounding the research in their life experiences while facilitating the emergence of their voices, thus enriching the intellectual enterprise and analysis (Delgado-Bernal 1998).

Community Context

The young women in this study come from an urban community known as the Fruitvale District, an ethnically, culturally, and economically diverse community that is predominantly Latino. Located in what are referred to as the flats of Oakland, Fruitvale is made up of a high concentration of poor and working-class residents who face the urban plights of poverty, gangs, crime, drugs, underresourced schools, and violence. Although Fruitvale suffers from these common urban social ills, it also counts on a variety of vibrant cultural, economic, and social institutions that help local residents negotiate everyday life and work. Fruitvale, for example, is home to approximately fifty community-based and grassroots organizations that work to improve the quality of life of its residents (Unity Council 2001). As a result, there is a strong Latino presence and identity in the area. This vast network of individuals and institutions helps residents with the basics such as finding jobs, obtaining health care, navigating bureaucratic systems, and finding daily food for survival. Until recently, Fruitvale had experienced blight, loss of jobs, and neglect by city officials; through community development projects such as the Fruitvale Transit Village, however, the area is slowly being revitalized. While revitalization efforts are now taking place, the social, economic, educational, and health needs of Fruitvale residents still remain high priorities. This is the community context in which these young women live—a vibrant cultural community with a strong Latino identity whose infrastructure is still in great need of resources and economic development.

Male Privilege

To place into context the ways in which the young women express their agency and resistance in creating their identities and consciousness as young Mexican-origin working-class women, I describe how they experience their home cultural practices. As female family members, young women realized early on that male privilege would impact their daily existence and would need to be negotiated. They learned their role in the family was (1) to provide services to others, (2) to obey and be subservient to men, and (3) to expect to be socially controlled.

At age fifteen, Libertad would often protest at having to perform household chores such as cleaning the house. Here, she recounts her conversation with her father about the subject:

> My dad, he says that I'm a woman and I should clean the house with no help or with the help of my mom. But like these past days, my mom works, so in the afternoons I should go and clean the house. But I tell him that my brothers don't want to help, and he says I'm a girl and I should do the cleaning.

Gabriela, who is seventeen, has learned that tending to *quehaceres* (chores) is her responsibility and an essential part of being a woman and future mother. Her displeasure at being pigeonholed solely in these terms is clear as she explains her family expectations: "I'm supposed to do the whole house . . . but sometimes I get mad. Do my bed and *recoger,* whatever *esta tirado recogerlo,* sweep and mop and vacuum and wash dishes. I mean, my little brother and my older could do it, too, you know, they're just sitting there. I'm responsible."

Brothers and fathers reap the benefits of entitlement and enjoy the privileges not granted to women in the home. Male privilege means that brothers, regardless of age, have the luxury of extra personal freedoms such as coming and going as they please without a chaperone; they are served first at the dinner table and are catered to by adult women and sisters. This varies by household, but most social reproductive labor still falls on women's shoulders. Few, if any, household responsibilities are assigned to men, who usually are responsible for weekly yard work, a task that is viewed as men's work.

Young women feel the most valued benefit of male privilege is the ability to hang out in public. Whether with friends or alone, boys experience far greater social freedom and fewer parental restrictions. Young women experience social restrictions far greater than their male siblings in any environment. Parents argue that the streets are dangerous and boys are better at defending themselves; however, this double standard creates tension between siblings.

The tension between brothers and sisters intensifies when brothers arrogantly assume their entitlement and goad their sisters in daily interactions. Brothers chide their sisters and remind them they are there to serve them. Many brothers seem to do this without reservation or apologies, often enjoying the interaction. Young men learn their privileged male status early on by watching the male-female interactions between their parents, other family members' households, and extended social networks. It is clear to the young women that brothers use this privilege to their advantage, expecting and demanding that their sisters cater to their needs. Fifteen-year-old Chela speaks to this attitude: "We argue about the phone a lot, and about things they [brothers] ask me to bring them . . . I'm always like, 'No, I'm not bringing you nothing.' . . . Like they're laying down and they want me, 'Go bring me a soda, or go bring me this' and 'No, I don't want to bring you anything.'" Chela continues, showing her exasperation:

> They don't do nothing! My mom tells them to, because that's not right. 'Cause I come home tired from work. And they still be like, "Oh, well, you have to, you know, you have to do the beds," or whatever. It's hard for me because I come [home] very tired. My mom tells them, but they say no, they don't want to do anything, so they really don't have any responsibilities.

Boys learn early on that women are there to serve them and that women can be ignored as well. When Magdalena's young brother receives more freedoms, the girl, who is sixteen, responds, "In a way it gets me upset because, that's like showing that he [Dad] trusts a thirteen-year-old more than a sixteen just because he's a boy. In a way, it makes me feel like he's putting down all the women, and I really don't appreciate that."

The critique of their families' cultural practices is a part of these girls' larger processes of questioning, negotiating, and creating their own identity within the family. In the following passage, fifteen-year-old Chela acknowledges her own values and hard work ethic while criticizing her family's practice of catering to her brother:

> I mean, I work, OK. I am working, I get home to my house and there is no food for me. I mean, I have to prepare it myself but . . . my brother comes home and everything for him. "Take him some food," or simply all he needs to do is sit. Then, I would remind them that I was also working. I think that we should have the same rights. We are the same. I wouldn't want to marry a man who thought the same [like my brother].

These young women are demanding that their efforts get recognized and rewarded. They do not have to wait until they are older to experience the second shift (Hochschild 1998). They already live it as racialized, working-class young women.

Because of their race, gender, and class position, young women make efforts at convincing their parents to change the unjust familial ways of being. Chela sees the inequities that exist in her home and criticizes them by saying, "I think that women should be treated equal," pointing out the potential social harm to her brother. She emphatically states that "no one will put up with him." Chela's analysis reveals her understanding of how sexism inevitably can hurt men as much as women.

Reading between the Lines

A mother's role in a young woman's quest for identity and self-empowerment is an interesting and often contentious one. Mothers are seen as both enforcers and resisters of the patriarchal family cultural practices these young women are trying to understand and negotiate. Mothers often give daughters contradictory messages, instructing them to follow traditional sexist cultural norms while simultaneously advising them to break free of them. While mothers might want their daughters to live a life different than their own, too few mothers know how to go about living differently.

Mothers primarily encourage their daughters to finish school, get a good job, and avoid being economically dependent on a man; however, the information needed to accomplish this is hard to come by. This is especially applicable to immigrant mothers, who may not have the knowledge necessary to pass on to their daughters how to navigate through a new cultural system. Daughters feel the pressure to acquiesce to the established family norms and yet hear the resistance message, too. Mona, aged eighteen, highlights this contradiction and confusion"

> I guess, sometimes I think she expects me to be a housewife. "*Cuando te cases,* you're going to be doing this, this and this, so you got to do it now." She's, like, "*Las mujeres son para andar en la casa no para andar en la calle.*" But sometimes she's, like, "*No, no te vayas a dejar.*" If you want to go do something, just do it. So, it's like balance, like *por fin.* What do you want me to do? Why do you keep on changing? I can't even understand what she's trying to say. *No la entiendo.*

Mona is trying to figure out whether she is supposed to resist, reinvent, or acquiesce. Mona's questioning behavior is a product of how mothers themselves are unclear about reinventing cultural traditions while liberating themselves. The answer is not to choose among the three options but to know when to utilize each. The conflicting messages young women receive and experience inform their emerging identity as someone who has the potential to change cultural traditions. This awareness creates an opportunity to make life-affirming decisions in relation to males in her life, as well as determine how she will socialize her own children and pave a more equitable cultural path for future generations. By vocalizing their opposition to the double standards and sexism experienced through male privilege, Mona and other young women are developing a different female consciousness and putting forth alternative and egalitarian practices that acknowledge women as full standing members of their family.

Fighting Back

In my study, young women's sense of gender injustice (Flores-Ortiz 2000) over their home cultural practices has caused them to contest these practices in a myriad of ways, including speaking out, creating conflict within the family, debating with parents, and breaking family rules. Young

Mexican-origin women in my study utilize strategies to liberate themselves from everyday chores and responsibilities imposed on them and used these strategies to create space to meet their own needs and foster their independence and autonomy—their personal cultures of resistance.

The young women voice to fathers, as well as mothers, their objection to the double standards. For example, Magdalena's insistence and her willingness to debate and engage in dialogue have made her father come to understand her position and see the contradictions. As she explains,

> Because I would say, I would complain about my brother. I would complain that my brother didn't do nothing around the house, and he would say, "Oh, well, he goes to work and you guys have to clean." And one time I was, like, I go to work, I go to school, I clean, I babysit! I was, like, so what. And I guess he got mad at me for telling him, but I guess finally he [dad] realized that I was right. So I told him, "If it's my job to be here and to clean, why bother going to school, or going to work?" He was, like—I guess he realized, I guess he was mad, but he realized it. So that was the situation and that lasted for a while.

Mona is the voice of reason advocating for a change in her home. She discusses these issues with her father and manages to make minor shifts in his consciousness; however, changes within her household come slowly. Young women learn that change does not come easily or quickly but that through persistence changes in their lives are possible. Negotiating their home cultural norms in order to define for themselves what it means to be a young woman in this time of changing perspectives on womanhood is one of the keys to their personal growth. Making sense of their cultural terrain and finding ways to gain autonomy, independence, and value for the work they do is a continuous enterprise. How much change occurs in the home depends on the degree to which a young woman's family, parents in particular, are open to cultural and gender norm changes.

Creating Suspended Space

Young women are their own personal advocates and create what I have come to term "suspended space," which is the space that young women create throughout their days to temporarily break free from the everyday responsibilities they are expected to fulfill, and that simultaneously suspend the social hierarchies constraining her persona and identity.

Fifteen-year-old Ester, for example, tired after working at a job, attending summer school classes, and working in the household all summer long, decides to take some personal vacation, as she fondly refers to it, the last week of summer. Instead of telling her parents that her summer employment has ended, she leaves the house at her usual hour and enjoys many of the summertime activities she has missed out on because of her work, school, and home responsibilities. As she describes it,

> I usually say I have to go to, like, when I would like want to go out? I've been saying that I'm going to work when I'm really not. I've been working the whole summer, so I haven't had a lot of time out . . . the summer went by really quick, and I haven't done a lot of things that I want to do. And if I would tell them that I'm not working, they would tell me to stay home, and I wouldn't be able to go out, so I'm taking this opportunity to go out.

Ester is conscious and purposeful about breaking the rules because she knows the restrictions that would be placed on her. Instead, she chooses to create time and space for herself, albeit clandestinely, that allows her to temporarily disconnect physically, emotionally, and psychically from her reality. On another occasion, Ester gets out of her cooking responsibility by arguing that there is not any food in the house, thereby releasing her from the responsibility of cooking for everyone and waiting for her mother to do the cooking. These acts of resistance, regardless of how small, reflect the strategies and cultures of resistance that free her from the accountability and responsibility assumed in her home life. Ester has found no other option that allows her to be in control of her time, body, mind, and spirit to nurture herself.

It is in these spaces that these young women have the potential for self-realization and awareness, exploring who they are and the possible selves to be. Unfortunately, this space also has potential negative consequences if the young women choose risky behaviors over positive ones. The key is to assist them to create these spaces openly so they can pursue their interests and support their process of self-realization and empowerment. Youth practitioners can educate and work with parents and schools to harness this energy and develop forums for young women to discuss issues openly with parents, friends, and peers. In addition, establishing female-specific programming that is guided by the young women themselves can foster constructive and positive development for young women.

Based on their comments, the intention of the young women in contesting and voicing their discontent around male privilege is to highlight and educate others about the injustices of family life and show the negative impact of male privilege and entitlement on their lives. The young women want to change familial arrangements to decrease their share of the household work, increase that of their brothers, and increase their personal time to pursue their own interests. These acts of resistance and creation of suspended space inform and lay the foundation for their developing Mexican-origin female consciousness and identity.

Consejos

Consejos, advice, is usually passed down from older and experienced individuals to those who are younger and less experienced. I invited the young women in my study to think about the type of advice they would give to other young women their age about preparing for and dealing with the transition into womanhood. The responses I received were varied, thoughtful, and extremely insightful. The young women welcomed the opportunity to share their personal realizations and cautionary guidance. They spoke frankly and honestly about the pitfalls and dangers of life, offering advice from a perspective of wanting to help other younger women like themselves understand how to become self-empowered and independent.

The advice focuses on three major themes: (1) the recognition that life is a struggle, (2) the importance of self-direction and independence, and (3) the value in developing strength, determination, and faith for a better tomorrow.

Life as a Struggle

A keen and fundamental awareness that life is a struggle is a strong message young women want to communicate. Living as a working-class Mexican woman in an urban environment is not easy and comes with its' hardships. The pressures of sex, alcohol and drug use, violence, and having to navigate the gang landscape are real and need to be carefully negotiated. Their advice is to steer clear of risky behaviors, ones that complicate life even more. As Xochitl expresses it, "I would recommend, then, to not live a bad life. Bad men, get into drugs, get into gangs, not to do anything, not even to try it at all. School right now is everything." And Catalina comments, "I would tell them they are going to face lots of things while they are growing up . . . and hopefully they will try and learn little by little." The young women advocate adopting a strong sense of perseverance coupled with a strong work ethic. This "don't give up" attitude is vital in negotiating safety, joy, and success in life. Using a common colloquial Spanish saying, one young woman suggests, "Never give up. El camaron que duerme se lo lleva la corriente." Another adds, "If you are persistent and work hard, you will in the end realize your goal." Another young woman notes, "Si le hechas ganas, vas a ganar lo que quieres." This advice entails seeking help from adult allies capable of finding resources to help achieve their personal goals. Having the determination and drive is important, but having a network of individuals to support and teach you the way is just as important.

Self-Direction and Independence

The young women emphasize the importance of placing themselves at the center of their lives and their decision-making processes. To recognize themselves as key players in their futures and taking themselves into consideration above anyone else speaks to the reality that too often girls place their boyfriends and peers ahead of themselves. The social pressure to conform to their peer group is extremely strong and often inhibits young Mexican origin women from following their own interests and educational goals. One young woman expresses this advice in the following manner: "Think about what you're gonna do and always think before you do anything. And to love yourself and to be proud of who you are."

Magdalena's advice also communicates to young women the importance of identifying personal goals and defining the steps to accomplish them. Failing at this endeavor brings regret:

> I mean you can trust, if you really trust somebody you can, but to always, always think about yourself before . . . but always make sure that you're okay before anyone else. And to think about what you're doing and to think about your future and to make sure that you're setting everything straight. Because sometimes you get to the future and you're, like, I wish I would've done this.

This quotation stands in sharp contrast to youth pop culture messages that portray young women as passive agents of their lives. Magdalena continues by saying, "When you let life go and you don't think about anything, you end up where someone else wants you, not where you want." She encourages young women to seriously think about, plan, and protect their own futures. In essence she is advocating for young women to take back their lives.

This notion of loving themselves by placing themselves at front and center is revolutionary given that women historically have been socialized and conditioned to care for others before themselves. Despite the heavy doses of romanticism and consumerism wrapped in sexy promotional media, young women are managing to see past the facade and realize the importance of steering their own life path and creating alternative messages. With this consciousness in hand, these young women, in their own way, can change both mainstream and Mexican home cultural practices into more just social spaces for young women.

Determination, Living a Future Fulfilled

Despite painful personal histories, the young women in this study possess a determination to not just survive but thrive to realize their dreams. This determination is fueled by faith, optimism, and hope. Comments such as "Don't look back," "Always go forward, not back," reflect the need to be strong and hopeful in the face of hardships. As Erica describes it,

> I guess for me, I have a lot of faith. . . . I have a lot of faith and I think that's what keeps me going. Like, I'll be like, well, tomorrow's another day, maybe it'll be better. And just be happy to wake up, go to sleep, wake up again, go to sleep, be okay. I'll be okay. And I guess in a way, all I have to do is think so.

Without hope there is nothing. These young women are determined and are optimistic that their lives will improve. Despite the odds, they are able to focus on the positive, to look at what they do have in order to see strength and resiliency in their lives and find value and beauty regardless of life circumstances. While life's journey for these young women is not over, the lessons they have learned thus far may be helpful to other young women starting on their own journey.

REFERENCES

Andrade, S. 1980. Family Planning of Mexican Americans. In M. Melville, ed., *Twice a Minority: Mexican American Women,* 17–32. St. Louis, MO: Mosby.

Baca Zinn, Maxine. 1975. Political Familism: Towards Sex Role Equality in Chicano Families. *Aztlan: Chicano Journal of the Social Sciences and the Arts* 6 (Winter): 13–26.

Boykin, A. W. 1996. The Triple Quandary and the Schooling of Afro-American Children. In U. Neisser, ed., *School Achievement of Minority Children: New Perspectives,* 57–92. London: Erlbaum.

Delgado-Bernal, Dolores. 1998. Using a Chicana Feminist Epistemology in Educational Research. *Harvard Education Review* 68:555–579.

Diaz-Guerrero, R., and Szalay, L. B. 1991. *Understanding Mexicans and Americans: Cultural Perspectives in Conflict.* New York: Plenum Press.

Espín, Oliva. 1997. *Latina Realities: Essays on Healing, Migration, and Sexuality.* Boulder, CO: Westview Press.

Flores-Ortiz, Yvette G. 2000. Injustice in Latino Families: Considerations for Family Therapists. In G. Carey, ed., *Family Therapy with Hispanics: Towards Appreciating Diversity,* 255–274. Boston: Allyn and Bacon.

Hochschild, Arlie. 1998. *The Second Shift.* New York: Viking.

Keefe, Susan E., and Padilla, Amado M. 1987. *Chicano Ethnicity.* Albuquerque: University of New Mexico Press.

Marin, Geraldo, and Marin, Barbara. 1991. *Research with Hispanic Populations.* Newbury Park, CA: Sage.

Pesquera, B. M. 1991. "Work Gave Me a Lot of Confianza": Chicanas' Work Commitment and Work Identity. *Aztlan* 20:97–116.

Sandoval, Chela. 1991. U.S. Third World Feminism: The Theory and Method of Oppositional Consciousness in the Postmodern World. *Genders* 10:1–24.

———. 2000. *Methodology of the Oppressed.* Minneapolis: University of Minnesota Press.

Sotomayor, M. 1991, *Empowering Hispanic Families: Issues for the 1990's.* Milwaukee, WI: Family Service of America.

Souza, Caridad. 1995. "Entre La Casa" and "La Calle": Adolescent Pregnancy among Puertorriquenas in a Queens Neighborhood (New York). Ph.D. diss., University of California, Berkeley.

Stanton-Salazar, Ricardo. 1997. A Social Capital Framework for Understanding the Socialization of Racial Minority Children and Youth. *Harvard Educational Review* 67:1–40.

———. 2000. The Development of Coping Strategies among Urban Latino Youth. In F. A. Villarruel, ed., *Making Invisible Latino Adolescents Visible.* 203–238. New York: Farmer Press.

Strauss, Anselm, and Corbin, Julie. 1994. Grounded Theory Methodology: An Overview. In Y. Lincoln, ed., *Handbook of Qualitative Research,* 273–285. Thousand Oaks, CA: Sage.

The Unity Council. 2001. *Community Profile: Get to Know Fruitvale.* The Unity Council. Available at www.unitycouncil.org/html/fruitvalehistory.html.

Chapter 5

Promoting Values of Education in Latino Mother-Adolescent Discussions about Conflict and Sexuality

*Laura F. Romo, Claudia Kouyoumdjian,
Erum Nadeem, and Marian Sigman*

Ecological models of development emphasize that adolescent developmental outcomes cannot be understood without considering the settings, or context, in which they occur (Bronfenbrenner, 1979, 1986). Some adolescents are raised in impoverished communities where the lack of quality schools may be a primary risk factor for teenage pregnancy (Kirby, 2002). Poor-quality school experiences among low-income youth contribute to pessimistic attitudes toward education, lack of school engagement, and high dropout rates. These factors have been identified as correlates of increased sexual behavior and teen childbearing (East, 1998; Kirby, 2002; Lederman, Chan, and Roberts-Gray, 2004; Lederman and Mian, 2003; Meschke, Bartholomae, and Zentall, 2002; Taylor-Seehafer and Rew, 2000). Because adolescent sexual activity and related consequences are influenced both by individual-level factors and by school and neighborhood issues (Small and Luster, 1994), adolescents in disadvantaged communities who attend low-quality schools might be served by pregnancy prevention programs that target academic achievement (Kirby, 2002).

Parents play a key role in endeavors to improve both sexuality and academic-related outcomes. Adolescents who engage in more conversations with their parents about their educational goals obtain higher levels of academic achievement (e.g., Muller, 1993). Similarly, across ethnic groups, positive family communication increases the likelihood that adolescents will engage in adaptive health-related behaviors (Jessor, 1993). With respect to Latinos, numerous studies show that sexuality communication between parents and adolescents is a protective factor against early sexual activity and unwanted pregnancy (Adolph et al., 1995; Baumeister, Flores, and VanOss Marin, 1995; Pick and Palos, 1995; Romo et al., 2002). Thus, improving communication between Latino parents and their adolescents has positive implications for multiple domains of adolescent well-being.

Nonetheless, many school administrators and teachers voice doubts about the extent to which low-income, immigrant Latino parents communicate with their children about the importance of education (Inger, 1992). An unsubstantiated notion put forth in the literature is that parental input discourages Latina girls from pursuing educational goals, placing them at risk for early childbearing (East, 1998). According to this understanding, Latina girls are purportedly socialized for child rearing and marriage at the expense of school-related roles, and such input may lead them to believe that they have limited future options (East, 1998). However, these notions contradict findings by others suggesting that immigrant families do value education for their children (e.g., Chavkin and Gonzalez, 2000; Segura, 1993). Cultural traditions that value *familismo,* a concept encompassing family closeness, obligation, and support, have positive implications for Latino adolescents' academic motivation (Cauce, Domenech-Rodriguez, and Paradise, , 2002; Fuligni, Tseng, and Lam, 1999; Fuligni, 2001; Gonzalez and Padilla, 1997; Zayas and Solari, 1994). As Marlino and Wilson (chapter 9, this volume) point out, mothers positively influence the aspirations and career paths that Latina girls expect to accomplish. For many Latina adolescents, succeeding in school is one of the best ways they can fulfill their sense of duty to the family (Suárez-Orozco and Suárez-Orozco, 1995).

We evaluate these contrary viewpoints regarding the nature of parental socialization about education through observational analysis of video-taped conversations between Latino adolescents and their mothers. The conversations are derived from an existing data set and focus on topics surrounding dating, sexuality, and conflict issues. We focus on whether or not the adolescents or their mothers spontaneously discussed the value of education, and what types of messages accompanied these statements. Although participants were neither prompted nor encouraged to talk about education-related themes, it was reasonable to expect that relevant topics would surface in these conversations. Discussions about dating and sexuality issues included expectations about appropriate behaviors for the sexes, which potentially include beliefs about educational goals. Moreover, homework issues were a key topic in everyday conflicts between adolescents and their parents (e.g., Gaines and Smetana, 1999).

A primary question was whether maternal years of education and immigrant status would influence the discussion of education-related matters. Given the literature suggestion that immigrant Latino parents care about their children's education (Chavkin and Gonzalez, 1995; Chavkin and Gonzalez, 2000; Marlino and Wilson, chapter 9, this volume; Trumbull et al., 2001), the extent to which immigrant Latino and U.S.-born Latino mothers discussed education was expected to be similar. However, it was possible that the content of these messages would be qualitatively different between the two groups. Interview and survey studies reveal that Latino immigrant parents play a critical part in their adolescent's "staying on the good path," which includes avoiding negative peer influences, valuing education and work, and becoming well-educated, or *bien educados* (Azmitia and Brown, 2002; Ceballo, 2004; Galindo and Escamilla, 1995; Gándara, 1982, 1994; Martinez, DeGarmo, and Eddy, 2004; Ramirez, 2003). The construct of *educación* carries strong cultural values related to the development of moral character in addition to the importance of scholarly attainments. We expected these values to be a common theme among immigrant mothers and their adolescents in discussions related to academic achievement and/or educational aspirations. For U.S.-born Latino mothers, who are better prepared to give direct forms of assistance (e.g., helping with homework), we expected that discussions with their adolescents about education would focus on specific issues related to course work and study habits. This hypothesis is supported by a study showing that acculturated Mexican American women who aspire to have challenging careers had a clear understanding of the specific behaviors needed to achieve their goals (Reyes, Kobus, and Gillock, 1999).

A major question of interest was whether or not girls communicate to their mothers about education in ways that are similar to those used by boys. We hypothesized that if Latina girls tend to be socialized around the importance of family and motherhood over education, then fewer mothers and their daughters would discuss the value of education than would mothers and sons. Moreover, because interview findings by Azmitia and Brown (2002) suggest that Latina mothers are more concerned about adolescent daughters succumbing to negative peer influences than they are for their sons, messages to girls about education would be linked to this concern. As a final analysis, we explored how relationship quality was associated with the likelihood that the pairs would discuss particular education-related themes, and how communication about education and relationship quality predicted academic achievement. For all ethnic groups, the negative effects of an emotionally distant parent-adolescent relationship impact adolescent achievement (Crosnoe, 2000), perhaps to a greater extent than socioeconomic disadvantage (Crosnoe and Elder, 2004). Thus, enhancing knowledge about the role of parental emotional support in adolescents' educational outcomes has implications for the design of parent communication training programs.

Participants

A total of 103 mothers of Latino descent and their adolescents, fifty-eight girls and forty-five boys, ranging in age from 10 to 15 years ($M = 12.6$, $SD = 1.4$) were included in this study. Participants were recruited through schools and community centers in the Los Angeles area to participate in a larger study that examined mother-adolescent communication about sensitive topics. The dyads were told that they would be videotaped conversing with each another about three issues, "AIDS," "dating and sexuality," and "conflicts."

The majority of the mothers were born in Mexico or other countries in Latin America (74 percent), with the remainder born in the United States (27 percent). Seventy-two percent of the foreign-born mothers and 28 percent of the U.S.-born mothers spoke mostly Spanish in the videotaped conversations, with the remainder speaking mostly English. The mothers ranged in age from 26 to 55 years, with foreign-born and U.S.-born mothers being comparable in age ($M = 38.5$, $SD = 6.0$). In general, family incomes ranged from less than $10,000 to more than $100,000, with the average in the $15,000 to $20,000 range. Maternal education varied greatly from 0 to 20 years, with an average of 9.8 years. The mothers differed by country of origin in average years of education completed (foreign-born, $M = 8.6$, $SD = 4.7$; U.S.-born, $M = 13.0$, $SD = 1.6$) and level of family income (foreign-born, $15,000–20,000$); U.S.-born, $30,000–40,000$) with foreign-born mothers reporting significantly lower levels of education and income than U.S.-born mothers.

Data Collection Procedures

Mothers and daughters were given the choice to participate at either a local community center, the adolescent's school, or a university laboratory.

The sessions lasted about two hours and were conducted by bilingual interviewers in the family's preferred language (English, Spanish, or a combination). Sessions began with an introduction to the activities and research procedures, followed by the opportunity to ask any questions.

The study procedure required that the mothers and adolescents participate in a warm-up activity and engage in three conversations about dating and sexuality, conflict, and AIDS. The warm-up activity helped the pairs feel comfortable in front of a camera before they engaged in the conversations. The order of the conversation topics was counterbalanced with the exception of the warm-up activity, which was always first. The researcher introduced each topic by saying, for example, "For the next seven minutes, I would like for you to discuss something you disagree about." The researcher then ensured that both parties felt comfortable in the environment, checking on the seating arrangement and answering any concerns. The researcher left the room and returned after seven minutes to introduce the next topic. For the purposes of the present study, only "dating and sexuality" and "conflict" conversations are reported. Because the "AIDS" topic was generally discussed in a neutral, impersonal manner (e.g., listing transmission facts), this conversation was omitted from these analyses.

After completing the conversation activity, the mothers and daughters were taken to separate rooms to fill out questionnaires in their preferred language. Translations were completed and then reviewed for agreement. Questionnaire responses were back-translated into English to provide a more accurate Spanish translation.

Measures

Demographic Questionnaire

All parties completed questionnaires about their personal information, including questions about age, ethnicity, language, income, years of education, and country of origin.

Adolescents' Grades

Adolescents reported on the grades that they had received the previous term in science, social studies, and math. The grades were converted to a scale ranging from 1 to 4 (1.0 = D, 4.0 = A) and averaged to obtain an overall estimate of grade point average (GPA).

Relationship Quality

The adolescents' perceptions of relationship quality with their mothers were measured using the ten-item Open Communication subscale from the Parent-Adolescent Communication Scale (PAC; (Barnes and Olson, 1986). The subscale assesses the extent to which adolescents and mothers perceive that they communicate openly with each another. Each question was answered on a 5-point Likert scale ranging from 1, "strongly disagree," to 5, "strongly agree." The openness scale contained questions such as "I don't think I can tell my [mother/child] how I really feel about some things."

Coding of Educational Messages

A computer program designed to code videotaped interaction was used to record information about the prevalence of education-related messages for the complete fourteen minutes of the videotaped data (i.e., the two seven-minute conversations). A coding system was developed by the second author to identify and classify the message types (Kouyoumdjian, 2004). This was done in accordance with traditional qualitative methods (e.g., Strauss and Corbin, 1998) in which the tapes are first reviewed to identify emerging themes and then relevant coding categories are developed. In reviewing the tapes, the researcher recorded all instances of education-related messages.

The messages communicated between the mothers and daughters were coded into 11 different categories: (1) avoid negative peer influences, (2) do homework regularly, (3) avoid or delay dating, (4) avoid or delay sexual activity, (5) complete educational goals (including plan for college), (6) avoid pregnancy and childbearing, (7) strive for good grades, (8) take relevant coursework, (9) have respect for school rules, (10) prioritize school and strive to succeed, and (11) study hard. An example of how the coding was applied is demonstrated using the following excerpt (M = mother; D = daughter):

M: *Qué metas tienes para el futuro?*
D: *Acabar mis estudios.*

M: *Y luego?*

D: *Agarrar un trabajo.*

M: *Qué vas a estudiar?*

D: *Voy a estudiar sicología.*

M: *Mmmm, . . . se puede, todo se puede, todo se puede hacer con mucha meta.*

D: *Si no, voy a ser doctora.*

(Translation)

M: What goals do you have for the future?

D: To complete my education.

M: And then?

D: Get a job.

M: What are you going to study?

D: I am going to study psychology.

M: Mmm, . . . it can be done, everything can be done, everything can be done with high aims.

D: If not, I am going to be a doctor.

This excerpt was assigned two codes, one for "complete educational goals" and the other for "strive to succeed." Two English-Spanish bilingual research assistants were trained to categorize instances of education-related messages in the videotaped conversations. Seven percent of the videotapes were coded by two people for training, and another 11 percent were coded independently for reliability purposes. The intraclass correlations between the two coders reached satisfactory levels.

Data Analysis

Our analytic strategy involved several steps. First, we computed a correlation matrix to examine the associations among the eleven educational message types. Second, we conducted a factor analysis to identify broader education themes among these variables. The resultant factors served as the communication variables of interest. Because the distribution was skewed, the communication variables were recoded into dichotomous variables (i.e., 1 = dyad discussed theme, 0 = dyad did not discuss theme). To see if we could explain why some pairs discussed a particular theme and some did not, we performed t-tests or chi-square tests on the demographic variables (mother's country of origin, mother's years of education, adolescent gender) and on level of relationship quality as reported by adolescents. Finally, we conducted multiple regression analyses to understand the influence of the demographic variables, relationship quality, and communication about education on adolescents' GPA.

Associations among the Types of Education-Related Messages

Table 5.1 presents the correlations, that is, the strength of relationships among the frequencies of the eleven message types. There were numerous significant positive correlations among the variables. For example, when "getting good grades" was discussed, there was a high likelihood that "respect school rules" was also discussed, which in turn increased the likelihood that "prioritize school" was part of the discussion. Messages to "avoid or delay sex" were linked to messages to "avoid pregnancy," and both of these were linked to "complete educational goals." "Avoid negative peer influence" was associated with messages that it is important to "avoid or delay dating." "Do homework regularly" was related to "take relevant courses." "Study hard" was positively associated with all variables with the exception of "avoid peer influence" and "prioritize school and succeed."

Because of the strong interrelationships between the eleven message types, we performed factor analysis to simplify the data. The four factors (and corresponding types of statements) are listed in order of their descending eigenvalues: (1) *pregnancy and its repercussions* (avoid or delay sex, avoid pregnancy and childbearing, complete educational goals); (2) *study habits* (do homework, take courses, and study hard); (3) *excelling*

TABLE 5.1
Correlations among Types of Messages about Education (N = 103)

Statements	1	2	3	4	5	6	7	8	9	10
1. Get good grades	—									
2. Study hard	.04	—								
3. Do homework regularly	.01	.52***	—							
4. Take relevant courses	−.01	.29**	.50***	—						
5. Respect school rules	.23*	.26**	.04	.13	—					
6. Avoid peer influence	0	.17	.08	−.04	.05	—				
7. Avoid or delay dating	.11	.41***	−.03	−.04	.07	.23*	—			
8. Avoid or delay sex	−.06	.39**	.02	.04	.09	.10	.13	—		
9. Prioritize school and succeed	−.01	.06	−.05	−.07	.31**	.02	.02	−.05	—	
10. Complete educational goals	.16	.26**	.08	−.04	0	0	.30**	.22*	.05	—
11. Avoid pregnancy	−.01	.34***	.03	.04	.09	−.03	.12	.30**	−.05	.34***

* p < .05; ** p < .10; *** p < .001.

academically (prioritize school and succeed, get good grades, respect school rules); and (4) *negative influences* (avoid peer influence, avoid or delay dating). Each of the eleven items loaded on a factor (between .49 and .83). The proportion of variance accounted for by factors individually was 21.93, 14.21, 12.37, and 10.39, respectively.

The number of messages associated with each of the four factor categories was summed for each dyad. As explained earlier, the distributions of the scores were highly skewed because the dyads discussed different combinations of these topics, with some dyads leaving out particular topics altogether. Each category was collapsed into a single dichotomous score by whether or not the dyad had discussed this topic (i.e., 1 = dyad discussed theme, 0 = dyad did not discuss theme).

Associations between Dyadic Characteristics and Communication about Education

Overall, 70 percent of the pairs discussed at least one education-related theme. Table 5.2 presents the t-tests and chi-square tests that were performed to assess whether we could identify characteristics of each dyad that explain whether or not its members discussed a particular theme.

Pregnancy and Its Repercussions

Presented at the top of Table 5.2 are the characteristics of the dyads by whether or not they discussed pregnancy and its repercussions. There were no differences in country of origin or in years of education between mothers who talked about pregnancy and those who did not, suggesting that this topic was relevant to Latina mothers from diverse backgrounds. Mother-daughter dyads were marginally more likely than mother-son dyads to discuss the importance of avoiding pregnancy and its repercussions, suggesting higher relevance for girls. Adolescent perceptions of openness in their relationship with their mother did not explain whether or not they talked about the importance of avoiding pregnancy.

Study Habits

The characteristics of the mother-daughter pairs by whether or not they discussed study habits are presented in the top half of Table 5.2. We

TABLE 5.2
Characteristics of Mothers and Adolescents by Whether or Not They Discussed Various Education-Related Themes (N = 103)

Characteristics	Discussed theme	Did not discuss theme χ²
Pregnancy and its repercussions (n)	*(n = 30)*	*(n = 73)*
% Foreign-born mothers 29	71	
% U.S.-born mothers	29	71
M (SD) maternal years of education	10.7 (4.1)	9.5 (4.7)
% Daughters	37	63†
% Sons	21	79
M (SD) relationship quality	38.6 (8.5)	36.5 (8.2)
Study habits (n)	*(n = 58)*	*(n = 45)*
% Foreign-born mothers	64	36**
% U.S.-born mothers	36	64
M (SD) maternal years of education	9.3 (4.9)	10.4 (4.0)
% Daughters	54	46
% Sons	59	41
M (SD) relationship quality	38.2 (7.6)	35.1 (8.2)*
Excelling academically	*(n = 45)*	*(n = 58)*
% Foreign-born mothers	40	60
% U.S.-born mothers	57	53
M (SD) maternal years of education	9.5 (4.4)	10.1 (4.7)
% Daughters	44	56
% Sons	46	54
M (SD) relationship quality	37.4 (6.7)	36.4 (8.9)
Negative influences (n)	*(n = 30)*	*(n = 73)*
% Foreign-born mothers	32	68
% U.S.-born mothers	21	79
M (SD) maternal years of education	8.2 (4.8)	10.5 (4.3)*
% Daughters	30	70
% Sons	29	71
M (SD) relationship quality	37.7 (9.6)	36.5 (8.2)

† $p < .06$; * $p < .05$; ** $p < .01$.

found that a higher percentage of the immigrant mothers than U.S.-born mothers discussed the importance of engaging in good study habits. Mothers' years of education was not related to whether they talked about study habits, suggesting that this topic was valued by all mothers regardless of their education backgrounds. Importantly, adolescent gender did not contribute to the likelihood of mothers discussing this topic. Mothers talked with their daughters and sons about study habits in equal amounts. Relationship quality did play a role in that adolescents who talked about the importance of study habits reported having a better relationship with their mothers than adolescents who did not discuss this topic.

Excelling Academically

In the center of Table 5.2 are the characteristics of the dyads, separated by whether or not they discussed the importance of excelling academically. A chi-square analysis revealed no significant difference in the percentage of immigrant mothers and U.S.-born mothers in whether or not they discussed this theme. Moreover, the t-tests revealed no differences in mothers' education and adolescent-reported relationship quality between the pairs. Consistent with the trend related to the discussion of study habits, the percentage of mothers who encouraged their daughters to excel academically was the same as for mothers and sons.

Negative Influences

The characteristics of dyads by whether or not they discussed negative influences are presented at the bottom of Table 5.2. The mothers differed only in terms of the numbers of education years completed. Mothers who discussed this theme had completed fewer years of education than mothers who did not discuss this theme, suggesting that socioeconomic status may have contributed to the likelihood of this topic being raised in the conversations. Messages to avoid negative influences were communicated equally to girls and to boys.

Communication and Relationship Quality Predicting Adolescent GPA

To evaluate the influence of communication about education, relationship quality, and various demographic variables (maternal years of education, country of origin, and adolescent gender) on adolescent GPA, we conducted a multiple regression analysis. As shown in Table 5.3, the adolescents' perceptions of relationship quality with their mothers, discussions about negative influences, and discussions about pregnancy reliably predicted GPA. Adolescents who perceived high relationship quality with their mothers tended to have good grades. We found that increased discussion about negative influences, and less discussion about pregnancy, predicted adolescents doing well academically. Communication about

TABLE 5.3
Regression Analysis Predicting Adolescent GPA from Relationship Quality and Communication about Education

	Adolescent GPA			
	B	SE B	ß	p
Adolescent gender	−.16	.19	−.09	
Adolescent-reported relationship quality	.002	.01	.36	.001
Maternal years of education	.002	.02	.15	
Mother's country of origin	.13	.24	.07	
Communication about education: pregnancy and its repercussions	−.46	.23	−.24	.05
Negative influences	.50	.22	.26	.03
Excelling academically	−.12	.20	−.07	
Good study habits	.27	.21	.15	

study habits and excelling academically did not significantly relate to GPA, nor did maternal years of education, country of origin, or adolescent gender.

Discussion

Contrary to popular notions that education is not valued in Latino culture, results from this observational analysis contribute to a growing body of literature (e.g., Chavkin and Gonzalez, 1995; Chavkin and Gonzalez, 2000; Marlino and Wilson, chapter 9, this volume; Trumbull et al., 2001) suggesting otherwise. About 70 percent of the mothers and their adolescents spontaneously discussed at least one education-related theme, although they were not requested to do so. Immigrant status was associated with more mothers talking about study habits, perhaps reflecting immigrant parents' values related to instilling a strong work ethic in their children (Lopez, 2001). There were no other differences in the content of these conversations by the mother's country of origin. Both immigrant mothers and U.S.-born mothers discussed the importance of excelling academically, regardless of years of education completed. Although low-income, immigrant parents may be limited in their capacities to advise their children in specific school-related matters due to lack of exposure to the U.S. education system, Latina mothers from varied backgrounds believe it is important for their children to succeed academically.

The themes that were discussed included prescriptions for proper behavior in addition to encouragement of academic success, reflecting values of *educación,* in which the development of moral character is viewed to be just as important as scholarly achievement (Azmitia and Brown, 2002). For example, discussions about excelling academically included advice about respecting school rules in addition to the importance of getting good grades and striving for success. Because values of *educación* encompass a broader definition than what is captured by the English cognate "education," the extent to which Latino families do communicate about education may be underestimated by school administrators and teachers.

As expected, family background variables were associated with the likelihood that values of *educación* would surface in the conversations. Mothers with less education were more likely to engage their adolescents in discussions about the importance of avoiding negative influences compared with mothers from more educated backgrounds. Given that mothers with less education were also of lower income, these messages may be due to concerns about living in disadvantaged neighborhoods where adolescents are frequently exposed to negative influences. More important, these messages were linked to positive outcomes, in that discussion about negative influences was associated with adolescents doing well academically as evidenced by high GPAs. This finding is a good example of how positive parenting is best understood when interpreted in the environmental contexts in which adolescents develop. For parents raising children in disadvantaged communities, protecting adolescents from negative influences is probably one of the best ways that they can be involved in their children's education.

A key question motivating this study was whether the spontaneous discussion of educational themes would be less evident among mother-daughter dyads than mother-son dyads. Such findings might indicate that Latina mothers view education as unimportant for girls, as suggested by East (1998). Interestingly, the themes that were raised by mothers and sons were similar to the ones raised by mothers and daughters. Furthermore, about a third of the dyads, mostly mothers and daughters, commented that avoiding pregnancy was critical for the adolescents to complete their educational goals. Taken together, we find no support for the notion put forth in the literature (East, 1998) that Latina girls receive parental support for marriage and childbearing at the expense of school-educated roles. In fact, girls explicitly receive messages that they should avoid or delay childbearing in order to finish high school and plan for college.

It is interesting that the mothers and adolescents drew a link between educational and sexual behavior outcomes in their conversations about dating, sexuality, and conflict. Increased discussion about avoiding pregnancy and its repercussions was related to lower GPAs among adolescents, perhaps because the mothers perceived that low-achieving adolescents were susceptible to engaging in risky sexual behaviors. This finding has implications for the design of pregnancy prevention programs. Most programs focus on increasing knowledge about self-protective behaviors or teaching assertiveness skills, all of which are valuable tools for reducing sexual behavior risks. However, because teen pregnancy rates are also associated with community factors such as limited access to quality schools, it may be necessary to broaden the content of pregnancy prevention programs to include strategies for overcoming educational challenges. Intervention programs focused on training Latino parents how to communicate with daughters about sexuality issues could be designed with a dual purpose of helping parents enhance the adolescents' educational aspirations.

The effectiveness of a dual-purpose communication training program is supported by our finding that the adolescents' reports of relationship quality with their mother best predicted their GPAs. Consistent with recent educational research (e.g., Crosnoe and Elder, 2004), the affective quality of the parent-adolescent relationship was associated with the adolescents' academic success. Likewise, with respect to sexual behavior, family connectedness positively influences adolescent sexual health outcomes. Teenagers who report having a close relationship with their parents tend to delay sexual activity (Jaccard, Dittus, and Gordon, 1996; Guzman et al., 2003; Resnick et al., 1997) and report less sexual behavior (Crouter et al., 1988). Thus, a close parent-adolescent relationship enhances resiliency among adolescents, protecting their well-being in multiple domains. Schools would do well to capitalize on values related to *familismo* and *educación* to improve the health and education outcomes of Latina girls who are at high risk for negative consequences.

Acknowledgments

This article is based on a master's thesis by the second author supervised by Laura Romo. This work was supported by National Institute of Mental Health Grant MH 54151 to Marian Sigman. We are grateful to Citalic

Briseño and Ana Soltero for their assistance with coding. We also thank the mothers and adolescents who dedicated time to this study.

REFERENCES

Adolph, Carol, Diana E. Ramos, Kathryn L. Linton, and David Grimes. 1995. Pregnancy among Hispanic teenagers: Is good parental communication a deterrent? *Contraception* 51 (5): 303–306.

Azmitia, Margarita, and Jane R. Brown. 2002. Latino immigrant parents' beliefs about the "path of life" of their adolescent children. In *Latino children and families in the United States: Current research and future directions,* ed. J. M. Contreras, K. A. Kerns, and A. M. Neal-Barnett, 77–105. Westport, CT: Greenwood.

Barnes, Howard L., and David H. Olson. 1986. Parent-adolescent communication. In *Family inventories,* ed. D. H. Olson, H. I. McCubbin, H. Barnes, A. Larson, M. Muxen, and M. Wilson, 33–48. St. Paul: University of Minnesota, Family Social Science.

Baumeister, Lisa M., Elena Flores, and Barbara VanOss Marín. 1995. Sex information given to Latina adolescents by parents. *Health Education Research* 10 (2): 233–239.

Bronfenbrenner, Urie. 1979. Contexts of child rearing: Problems and prospects. *American Psychologist* 34 (10): 844–850.

———. 1986. Ecology of the family as a context for human development: Research perspectives. *Developmental Psychology* 22 (6): 723–742.

Cauce, Ana Mari, Melanie Domenech-Rodríguez, and Matthew Paradise. 2002. Latino families: Myths and realities. In *Latino children and families in the United States: Current research and future directions,* ed. J. M. Contreras, K. A. Kerns, and A. M. Neal-Barnett, 3–25. Westport, CT: Greenwood.

Ceballo, Rosario. 2004. From barrios to Yale: The role of parenting strategies in Latino families. *Hispanic Journal of Behavioral Sciences* 26 (2): 171–186.

Chavkin, Nancy Feyl, and Dora Lara Gonzalez. 1995. Forging partnerships between Mexican American parents and the schools. ERIC digest. EDORC958 (Oct.): Report: EDO-RC-95-8. 4.

Chavkin, Nancy Feyl, and John Gonzalez. 2000. Mexican immigrant youth and resiliency: Research and promising programs. ERIC digest. ED447990 (Oct.).

Crosnoe, Robert. 2000. Friendships in childhood and adolescence: The life course and new directions. *Social Psychology Quarterly, Special The State of Sociological Social Psychology* 63 (4): 377–391.

Crosnoe, Robert, and Glen H. Elder Jr. 2004. Family dynamics, supportive relationships, and educational resilience during adolescence. *Journal of Family Issues* 25 (5): 571–602.

Crouter, Ann C., Judith H. Carson, Judith R. Vicary, and Janice Butler. 1988.

Parent-child closeness as an influence on the projected life course of rural adolescent girls. *Journal of Early Adolescence* 8 (4): 345–355.

East, Patricia L. 1998. Racial and ethnic differences in girls' sexual, marital, and birth expectations. *Journal of Marriage and the Family* 60 (1): 150–162.

Fuligni, Andrew J. 2001. Family obligation and the academic motivation of adolescents from Asian, Latin American, and European backgrounds. In *Family obligation and assistance during adolescence: Contextual variations and developmental implications,* ed. A. J. Fuligni, 61–75. San Francisco: Jossey-Bass.

Fuligni, Andrew J., Vivian Tseng, and May Lam. 1999. Attitudes toward family obligations among American adolescents with Asian, Latin American, and European backgrounds. *Child Development* 70 (4): 1030–1044.

Gaines, Cheryl, and Judith Smetana. 1999. Adolescent-parent conflict in middle-class African American families. *Child Development* 70 (6): 1447–1463.

Galindo, René, and Kathy Escamilla. 1995. A biographical perspective on Chicano educational success. *Urban Review* 27 (1): 1–29.

Gándara, Patricia. 1982. Passing through the eye of the needle: High-achieving Chicanas. *Hispanic Journal of Behavioral Sciences* 4 (2): 167–179.

Gándara, Patricia. 1994. Choosing higher education: Educationally ambitious Chicanos and the path to social mobility. *Education Policy Analysis Archives* 2 (1): 1–43.

Gonzalez, Rosemary, and Amado M. Padilla. 1997. The academic resilience of Mexican American high school students. *Hispanic Journal of Behavioral Sciences* 19 (3): 301–317.

Guzmán, Bianca L., Michele M. Schlehofer-Sutton, Christina M. Villanueva, Mary Ellen Dello Stritto, Bettina J. Casad, and Aida Feria. 2003. Let's talk about sex: How comfortable discussions about sex impact teen sexual behavior. *Journal of Health Communication* 8 (6): 583–598.

Inger, Morton. 1992. Increasing the school involvement of Hispanic parents. ERIC/CUE digest number 80. EDOUD923 (Aug.): Report: EDO-UD-92-3. 3.

Jaccard, James, Patricia J. Dittus, and Vivian V. Gordon. 1996. Maternal correlates of adolescent sexual and contraceptive behavior. *Family Planning Perspectives* 28 (4): 159–165.

Jessor, Richard. 1993. Successful adolescent development among youth in high-risk settings. *American Psychologist* 48 (2): 117–126.

Kirby, Douglas. 2002. The impact of schools and school programs upon adolescent sexual behavior. *Journal of Sex Research* 39 (1): 27–33.

Knight, George P., Jenn Yun Tein, Rita Shell, and Mark Roosa. 1992. The cross-ethnic equivalence of parenting and family interaction measures among Hispanic and Anglo-American families. *Child Development* 63(6): 1392–1403.

Kouyoumdjian, Claudia. 2004. Maternal messages of education among US born and immigrant Mexican mother-daughter dyads. Unpublished data.

Lederman, Regina P., Wenyaw Chan, and Cynthia Roberts-Gray. 2004. Sexual risk attitudes and intentions of youth aged 12–14 years: Survey comparisons of parent-teen prevention and control groups. *Behavioral Medicine* 29 (4): 155–163.

Lederman, Regina P., and Tahir S. Mian. 2003. The parent-adolescent relationship education (PARE) program: A curriculum for prevention of STDs and pregnancy in middle school youth. *Behavioral Medicine* 29 (1): 33–41.

Liebowitz, Stephen W., Dolores Calderon Castellano, and Israel Cuellar. 1999. Factors that predict sexual behaviors among young Mexican American adolescents: An exploratory study. *Hispanic Journal of Behavioral Sciences* 21 (4): 470–479.

Lopez, Gerardo R. 2001. The value of hard work: Lessons on parent involvement from an (im)migrant household. *Harvard Educational Review* 71 (3): 416–437.

Martinez, Charles R., Jr., David S. DeGarmo, and J. Mark Eddy. 2004. Promoting academic success among Latino youths. *Hispanic Journal of Behavioral Sciences* 26 (2): 128–151.

Meschke, Laurie L., Suzanne Bartholomae, and Shannon R. Zentall. 2002. Adolescent sexuality and parent-adolescent processes: Promoting healthy teen choices. *Journal of Adolescent Health* 31 (Suppl. 6): 264–279.

Muller, Mary E. 1993. Development of the prenatal attachment inventory. *Western Journal of Nursing Research* 15 (2): 199–215.

Pick, Susan, and Patricia Andrade Palos. 1995. Impact of the family on the sex lives of adolescents. *Adolescence* 30 (119): 667–675.

Ramirez, A. Y. Fred. 2003. Dismay and disappointment: Parental involvement of Latino immigrant parents. *Urban Review* 35 (2): 93–110.

Resnick, Michael D., Peter S. Bearman, Robert W. Blum, Karl E. Bauman, Kathleen M. Harris, Jo Jones, and Joyce Tabor, et al. 1997. Protecting adolescents from harm: Findings from the National Longitudinal Study on Adolescent Health. *Journal of the American Medical Association* 278 (10): 823–832.

Reyes, Olga, Kimberly Kobus, and Karen Gillock. 1999. Career aspirations of urban, Mexican American adolescent females. *Hispanic Journal of Behavioral Sciences* 21 (3): 366–382.

Romo, Laura F., Eva S. Lefkowitz, Marian Sigman, and Terry K. Au. 2002. A longitudinal study of maternal messages about dating and sexuality and their influence on Latino adolescents. *Journal of Adolescent Health* 31 (1): 59–69.

Romo, Laura F., Erum Nadeem, Terry K. Au, and Marian Sigman. 2004. Mexican-American adolescents' responsiveness to their mothers' questions about dating and sexuality. *Journal of Applied Developmental Psychology* 25 (5): 501–522.

Segura, D. 1993. Slipping through the cracks: Dilemmas in Chicana education. In *Building with our hands: New directions in Chicana studies,* ed. A De la Torre and B. Pesquera, 199–216. Berkeley: University of California Press.

Small, Stephen A., and Tom Luster. 1994. Adolescent sexual activity: An ecological, risk-factor approach. *Journal of Marriage and the Family* 56 (1): 181–192.

Strauss, Anselm, and Juliet Corbin. 1998. *Basics of qualitative research: Techniques and procedures for developing grounded theory* (2nd ed.). Thousand Oaks, CA: Sage.

Suárez-Orozco, Carola, and Marcelo M. Suárez-Orozco. 1995. *Transformations: Immigration, family life, and achievement motivation among Latino adolescents.* Stanford, CA: Stanford University Press.

Taylor-Seehafer, Margaret, and Lynn Rew. 2000. Risky sexual behavior among adolescent women. *Journal of the Society of Pediatric Nurses* 5 (1): 15–25.

Trumbull, Elise, Carrie Rothstein-Fisch, Patricia M. Greenfield, and Blanca Quiroz. 2001. *Bridging cultures between home and school: A guide for teachers—with a special focus on immigrant Latino families,* ed. Office of Educational Research and Improvement. Washington, DC: Erlbaum.

Zayas, Luis H., and Fabiana Solari. 1994. Early childhood socialization in Hispanic families: Context, culture, and practice implications. *Professional Psychology: Research and Practice* 25 (3): 200–206.

Part 2

Overcoming Institutional Barriers

Chapter 6

Resistance to Race and Gender Oppression
Dominican High School Girls in New York City

Nancy Lopez

Dominicans number over a million people and are the fourth-largest Latino group in the United States (Hernandez and Rivera-Batiz, 2003). A
third of Dominicans, like me, were born in the United States. It is estimated that by the 2010 census, the Dominican population will surpass the
Cuban population, and we will become the third-largest Latino immigrant
group after Mexicans and Puerto Ricans.

Among Caribbean immigrants to the United States, Dominicans are
the national origin group with the largest post-1965 migration. Like other
Caribbean immigrants, Dominicans are concentrated in the northeastern
United States, specifically New York City, where there are more than half a
million and they are the second largest Latino group after Puerto Ricans.[1]
In 2000, 24 percent of Dominicans in the United States were between the
ages of six and eighteen, representing 134,222 youth. In New York City
public schools, Latinos were the largest single group (37 percent); of these,
Dominicans were 10 percent and Puerto Ricans were 13 percent.[2] Among
eighteen- to twenty-one-year-olds, the city average for school/college enrollment was 63.4 percent of women and 57.8 percent of men.[3] Among
Latinas in this age-group, however, the average was 54 percent of women
compared with 43 percent of men. Yet among Dominicans 62.2 percent of
women were enrolled compared with only 50.8 percent of men.[4] The disparity in educational attainment among Dominicans in college is even
more pronounced. At the City University of New York, two of three (67.4
percent) of the Dominicans enrolled were women.[5] How can we unravel
the race-gender gap in education among Dominicans?

My research examines the race-gender gap among low-income second-generation Dominicans, Haitians, and Anglophone West Indians (Lopez, 2003). I found that one reason Dominican young women achieve higher levels of education than their male counterparts is their resistance to racial and gender oppression in schools. I found that women more than men actively voiced their social critique of substandard schooling by demanding an education.

On Operationalizing Race-Gender

It is important to clarify how I examine race and gender. Drawing on racial formation theory and matrix of domination theory, I define race and gender as a socially constructed process, whereby racial meanings are created, circulated, and enacted.[6] Omi and Winant (1994) have examined racial formation in the United States. They identify the various definitions and interpretations of racial dynamics, as well as attempts to redistribute resources along racial lines, which occur at both the level of policy and the level of lived experiences.[7] Collins's (2000) matrix of domination theory highlights how race and gender intersect by focusing on shifting domains of power such as race, gender, class, nationality, and sexual identity, among others. Each of these domains of power has a structural, disciplinary, hegemonic, and interpersonal component. Central to Collins's (2000:70) framework is the concept of individual subjectivity and resistance strategies that underscore the agency of social actors in any oppressive situation.[8] "Based on their personal histories, individuals experience and resist domination differently" (Collins, 2000:285).

   In my own race-gender framework, I examine race-gender experiences as the social interactions in which individuals undergo racial(izing) and gender(ing) processes (Lopez, 2003). Race-gender outlooks are life perspectives and attitudes about how social mobility is attained. Providing *dominicanas* and other Latinas who experience multiple oppression (race, class, gender) with counterhegemonic race-gender outlooks empowers them to resist those oppressions (Leadbeater and Way, 1996).

Socioeconomic Profile of Dominicans in New York City

Using the 2000 census, Hernandez and Rivera-Batiz (2003) found that Dominicans had a mean annual per capita household income of $11,065, half of what the rest of the country earned ($22,086). This was also lower than that of other Latinos ($12,483), non-Latino blacks ($14,516), Asians ($22,260), and whites ($25,187). Dominicans also had the highest poverty rate in New York City (32 percent); moreover, over a third of Dominican households were headed by women (38.2 percent), and of these half were poor. It is important to note that Dominican migration to the United States is predominantly female (Hernandez and Rivera-Batiz, 1995). This reality has important implications for the ways in which young women see themselves and their futures in terms of the migration of their mothers as a feminist act of self-determination.

Overall, Dominicans have low levels of educational attainment. Almost half of Dominicans twenty-five years or older had not completed a high school education at the time of the 2000 census, compared with only 20 percent of the general U.S. population (Hernandez and Rivera-Batiz, 2003). If we separate U.S.-born Dominicans from those born in the Dominican Republic, we find that there are stark differences. Only 19.4 percent of U.S.-born Dominicans aged twenty-five or older had not completed a high school education. Among Latinos, Dominicans have the largest number of people identifying as black (13 percent) and the lowest number who identify as white (24 percent).[9] The highest number of individuals identify themselves as "other" on the race question in the census (63 percent) and write in "Dominican" (Logan, 2003). This is important because unlike other Latino groups who have significant numbers of lighter-skinned people who can pass as white, most Dominicans are of discernible African phenotype and cannot easily partake of what Guinier and Torres (2000) term the "racial bribe," whereby lighter-skinned Latinos assume a white identity by denigrating blacks (see also Bonilla-Silva, 2002).

Although Dominicans are included as a Latino group in most analyses, in reality on many indicators we are more like other black groups. A study conducted by New York University School of Law found that throughout the 1990s, 34 percent of Dominicans, 22 percent of Caribbeans and Africans, and 27 percent of African Americans residing in New York City were living in apartments that suffered from rat infestation, lacked water or heat, and had no kitchen or bathroom.[10] In contrast, European immigrants from similar class backgrounds were able to obtain better housing. National studies of the contours of racial segregation across the United States continually find that African Americans and other groups of African phenotype, such as Latinos of African phenotype, experience extremely high degrees of residential segregation and that only groups subjected to the one-drop rule continue to do so (Massey and Denton, 1994; see Bonilla-Silva, 2002).[11]

Research Design

I chose to do my research at Urban High School (UHS) because it was 90 percent Latino, mostly Dominican.[12] Urban High School is representative of the schools attended by most Latinos in New York City. It is, de facto, a hypersegregated school in terms of race and class, and it suffers from many of the problems that afflict the city's public schools (Massey and Denton, 1994). The main building is severely overcrowded and dilapidated. Trailer classrooms have been placed in the baseball fields to accommodate the overcrowding. There is a visible security presence, including metal detectors and police officers on the campus ready to arrest any student involved in a fight, that makes UHS feel prisonlike and uninviting.

Only 52 percent of the teachers were fully licensed and permanently assigned to this school.[13] While the teacher population is predominantly white, the student population of nearly 3,000 is mostly Latino and mostly Dominican.[14] The remaining student population, which is categorized as black, includes second-generation youth from Haiti, the Anglophone West Indies, and Africa.[15] The enrollment of Asian and whites students is less than 1 percent.[16] Almost two-thirds of the students receive free school lunch, indicating that they come from very low-income families. About 25 percent of the students are immigrants who entered the school system during the last three years, and over half of ninth and tenth graders are overage for their grade. Only a quarter of UHS's students graduate within the four years it usually takes to earn a diploma, and of those students, most are women. Among graduates, less than 1 percent received the academic Regents diploma in 1998, while 6 percent received the general equivalency diploma. In addition, 85 percent of the students who graduated planned to attend college, but almost half of the class of 1998 were still enrolled, and a quarter dropped out of school.

I sought to uncover how day-to-day school practices and classroom dynamics were racialized and gendered and in turn shaped women's views about the role of education in their lives (Lewis, 2003; Bettie, 2003). In doing so, I combined my focus on the organizational structure and the concrete lived experiences of the young women. My research questions included the following: How were women's lived experiences linked to institutional practices? What role did classroom pedagogy play in women's attitudes toward education? How did women respond to schooling? Over a six-month period in 1998, I observed four classes three to four days a week. For this chapter I report on two of these classes: Ms. Gutierrez's American history classes for juniors and Mr. Hunter's global history course for sophomores.

On Feminist Identities

On a windy March morning Ms. Gutierrez began her American history class by challenging her students, mostly juniors, to analyze a cartoon she had distributed on the American Revolution: "What do you see represented here?" Rafelo called out: "Men who founded the nation." The cartoon depicted several European colonists aboard a ship spotting the North America territory after their long journey across the Atlantic Ocean. At the bow of the ship was the mascot—a sculpture of a scantly clad and buxom woman. Ms. Gutierrez pressed: "Who is missing from the cartoon?" Lissette, accompanied by a cacophony of young women, called out: "Women!" Smiling, Ms. Gutierrez asserted: "Although throughout history women have represented freedom, they have been treated unequally." Vindicated by Ms. Gutierrez's feminist discourse, exultant young women nodded in agreement.

Ms. Gutierrez is a fireball who never stands still. One morning she declared: "I'm tired of the assembly line." In an attempt to enhance student interaction, Ms. Gutierrez asked students to move their desks and chairs around to form a semicircle. As I helped rearrange the desks, I noticed that many of them were broken, chipped, and filthy—stuffed with gum wrappers, dusty paper, and grime—seemingly they had not been cleaned in months.

Students began writing the day's aim in their journals:

What is *your* aim? What do you hope for spiritually, physically, and materially? How far is your dream—the "American" dream—a house with a white picket fence, 2.5 children, a car, and a dog? What can prevent your dreams from coming true? Can the government help or stop you and your dreams from coming true?

After a few minutes of free writing, Ms. Gutierrez asked for volunteers to share their thoughts with the rest of the class. As always, Lissette, Analiza, and several young women shot their hands up in the air; however, Ms. Gutierrez called on Eduardo, who seemed distracted: "Tell us your dream." Eduardo boasted: "I want to be a millionaire, to be famous, to make history, like Michael Jackson; although I'm not going to be gay or anything." Of course the entire class burst out in laughter. Although seemingly playful, Eduardo's comments pointed to the underpinnings of hegemonic masculinity across the globe: wealth, power, fame, and heterosexuality.

Women gave differing visions of their goals. Beaming with a mixture of pride and restraint, Lissette raised her hand and volunteered her desires: "I want to go to a good college and become a lawyer so I can become a strong, independent woman." Lissette's assertion was not simply that she wanted to attend college, but a "good" college so that she could go on to law school, indicating that she had been planning for her future. Analiza said: "My dream is to become an independent woman. I will build schools for the homeless. I also want to have a family and children—at least one child." Traditional notions of motherhood and nontraditional notions of career women coexist as aspirations among these second-generation young women. Rooted in the experience of many of their mothers, aunts, and grandmothers, many of whom were the heads of their households, they did not assume a man was going to take care of them.

Roberto, who always wore a baseball cap to class, smirked and commented: "It's interesting that you mention one child. I want five children. My father had fourteen children." Betsy affirmed: "People don't have children because they are busy with their jobs. Women don't want to stay at home and take care of children." Ms. Gutierrez interjected: "The best birth control is education," while the young women nodded in agreement.

Ms. Gutierrez pressed, "Do you think your dreams would have been different if you had been born in the Dominican Republic?" She may have been alluding to some studies that posit that feminism among Dominican women is a by-product of assimilation into U.S. society; however, women in the class begged to differ (Pessar and Grasmuck, 1991). Lissette asserted, "All the women in my family have been independent." The young women spoke about coming from a legacy of strong and independent women, many of whom ran their households and provided for their families for generations in their home countries and now in the United States. These independent women do not subscribe to the traditional role of female; this orientation is not simply a by-product of assimilation but is rooted in a legacy of Dominican women's insubordination to patriarchy that dates to the colonization of the island (De Filippis, 2000).

Ms. Gutierrez continued, "Do you think that the government is involved in your dreams? How do you plan to go to college?" Roberto seemed skeptical: "Miss, you don't need a college diploma. You can work for a lot of offices and you don't need a college diploma." Carmela had a response that was grounded in educational aspirations: "Financial aid. Loans." Although these young people were juniors, it appears that the young women seemed more geared toward reaching their educational goals and more knowledgeable about the college application process.

Ms. Gutierrez nudged students to draw parallels between multiple forms of oppression: "Do we have slavery today?" Alex called out, "No. But we have racism." Ms. Gutierrez moved on to discuss the amendments to the U.S. Constitution and asked students, "Do we have equal protection under the law?" All students unanimously roared: "No!" Ms. Gutierrez rejoined, "What can we do about it?" Just before the bell rang, Ms. Gutierrez cited the civil rights movement and the women's rights movements, then ended the class by affirming: "Freedom is a struggle, not a privilege. The pen is mightier than the sword. Your education . . . no one can take that away from you." Through her classroom lessons and pedagogical practices, Ms. Gutierrez actively created spaces for social critique of racism, capitalism, and patriarchy and, most important of all, for the discourse of possibility and action.

Resisting Marginalization

During the five minutes that students are given to change classes, I barely had enough time to make it to Mr. Hunter's tenth-grade global history class, which was located on the fourth floor of the main building. Mr. Hunter usually opened his class by saying, "Guys, you have work to do; let's get going." The all-too-familiar "Do Now" list on the chalkboard read: "Why did the United States enter World War I? Define Neutral, Proclamation, Isolation, Read Page 435." Today, I was pleased to see an uncommon sight: textbooks. To my dismay, while distributing the books, Mr. Hunter added, "These are just for class, guys. You don't have to take them home." None of the classes I observed had textbooks on a regular basis.

Mr. Hunter called on Gustavo to read a passage from the book, but I noticed that the student was having trouble pronouncing some of the words. Yocasta, one of the most active participants in the class, who always sat in the front row, interrupted, "I'll read!" Upon finishing the passage, Yocasta boasted, "I'm doing my homework because I want to get a 99 in class. I'll do a report if that's what it takes to get a 99." Mr. Hunter then called on several young men who were talking to ask them to read, and they all declined. Next, Sandra volunteered but warned: "I am going to read, but no one else is going to interrupt me. I'm not going to read if there is constant chitchatting."

The next day the aim listed on the board read: "What did Mr. Hunter teach me about World War I?" Mr. Hunter began by whining, "Guys, why am I seeing more and more hats? You know that you are not allowed to wear them." I noticed that five young men had their baseball caps on. Yocasta retorted, "You know girls are allowed to wear them." Previously, I had asked Mr. Castellanos, the head of security, about the double standard regarding the prohibition of hats on the school premises; he reiterated the official regulations, which stipulated that no student, male or female, could wear a hat on the school premises; however, double standards prevailed, with the enforcement of no hats only for men.

Because young men continued chatting, Mr. Hunter urged, "Ricky, I like it when you sit up here." Mr. Hunter called on some of the young men who sat in the back of the classroom, but they shook their heads and refused to participate. The teacher warned, "Sosa, if you don't stop talking you're going to have to leave. It's rude." Yocasta commanded, "Separate them." Yocasta indulged in numerous disruptions throughout class, but she was never disciplined or sent to the principal's office.

Interruptions were a regular occurrence in Mr. Hunter's class. It seemed like twenty minutes went by before any academic work was done. Mr. Hunter finally began his explanation for the causes of World War I, "Austria is hungry for war . . ." Before he could finish his sentence, we had yet another disruption. Ms. Jones, a white teacher in her twenties, came by to show Mr. Hunter pictures of her last vacation to the Caribbean. To my surprise, Mr. Hunter suspended class and started giggling with Ms. Jones over the pictures. Seemingly annoyed by the disruption, Yocasta began distributing announcements for ASPIRA, an educational opportunity program for Latino students that provided tutoring and other academic support. Yocasta demanded, "Mr. H., why don't we start?" Annoyed by Yocasta's insistence, Mr. Hunter shot back: "Why don't you come up to the front of the class and teach the material if you know it so well?" Up for the challenge, Yocasta darted to the front of the classroom, while Mr. Hunter grudgingly took a seat next to me in the back of the classroom. Yocasta lectured adroitly, at times referring to the map while explaining the background and immediate causes of World War I. Throughout Yocasta's presentation, Mr. Hunter seemed distracted, constantly looking at his watch. Upon finishing her talk, Yocasta took her seat unscathed. Mr. Hunter ended class early, collected the books before the bell rang, and made informal chitchat with students.

On the day of the exam, Mr. Hunter quickly announced: "All my tests are from the Regents, and the final is cumulative. I made a mistake on number 4; there is no right answer." During the exam, I noted that while several young women left their seats to consult the map, none of the young men did so. Before the end of the class period, Yocasta called out: "Mr. H., come here. I'm finished!" Mr. Hunter grabbed her test, eyed it, and jokingly declared: "You failed!" Yocasta retorted: "I studied my ass off!" Sandra interrupted: "Mr. H., you know we only have eight more weeks of school. When are we going to have the review? What are we going to do tomorrow? This again?" "Yes," answered Mr. Hunter. "All right, we will finish tomorrow," declared Sandra as she marched off to her next class.

The women in this class, as well as in other classes I observed, always seemed more concerned about their learning than men. When Mr. Hunter asked for volunteers, it was the young women who read, often demanding silence before they continued. Women also handed in homework more consistently than men, and they were among the most active classroom participants sometimes volunteering to co-teach classes. It appeared that the girls were not interested in just doing enough to pass their classes. They strove for academic excellence and were proud to verbalize their efforts to study and earn good grades.[17] Moreover, in response to the low-curriculum tracks they were subjected to, women more often than men resisted their marginalization and demanded an education.

Another morning, Mr. Hunter's class welcomed an invited guest, Ms. Penner, a white woman in her fifties who was a health educator from the HIV Prevention Programs Clinic. She asked the class: "Are we protected against the HIV virus when we use any kind of birth control?" Jokingly, Mr. Hunter declared, "It's too late; many of you are already having sex." Ms. Penner rejoined, "Thirty percent of teens are not having sex. The 100 percent way of never getting HIV or getting pregnant is abstinence." When queried about the different methods of birth control, the young women in the class clearly knew more methods than did the young men. While the young men were busy fooling around and not taking the class seriously, young women were the first to mention condoms as a means of preventing the spread of HIV.

Conclusion

As we have seen, although the young men and young women in this study were members of the same ethnic group, attended the same high schools, and came from the same socioeconomic backgrounds, they had fundamentally different experiences in their school setting. Differing race-gender experiences at school are significant because they accumulate and eventually frame outlooks toward education and social mobility. Since young women were not seen as threatening, they were not disciplined as harshly as young men even when they engaged in the same type of school infractions (Lopez, 2003). In response to efforts to track them into certain classes, time and time again young women were the ones who were the most vociferous in demanding an education. These young women were also more active in extracurricular activities as the heads of student organizations. Overall these young women took pride in their academic excellence and strove to achieve their academic goals.

Another important factor in young women's experiences in school has to do with the teaching staff, which is primarily female. In the aftermath of the 1970s women's movement, schools are one social space where feminist ideologies are circulated and practiced.[18] A critical mass of women teachers impart a gender identity that is inextricably linked to feminist practices, namely, pursuing an education as a means of achieving independence. The presence of large numbers of women teachers in the public school system provides a space for feminist ideologies to be embodied and enacted. In these safe spaces, women carved feminist discourses on education, financial independence, and motherhood as coexisting rather than contradictory.

Finally, although much of the mainstream literature on Latina women's experience in the United States assumes that the development of feminist consciousness and practices among Latinas is a direct by-product of assimilation into U.S. culture, it is also important to consider how these young women are modeling their behavior after that of their mothers, many of whom are the heads of their households not only in the United States but also in the Dominican Republic. Feminism has historical roots in the home countries of second-generation women. Generations of Caribbean women are the heads of their households even before migration, and increasingly they are the breadwinners of their households in the United States (Safa, 1995). The Dominican Republic and the commonwealth of Puerto Rico have had women serve as vice presidents and as governors during the 1990s. Thus, in many respects feminism and the quest for women's self-determination have been facts of life in the Caribbean and Latin American countries even among those who do not migrate to the United States. To ignore the legacy of women's feminist practices and insubordination to male domination in their home countries would be an unfortunate omission in understanding the historic and burgeoning feminism among Latinas and Dominican young women in particular (Lopez, 2003).

It remains imperative that those doing research on Latinas recognize the importance of investigating the variations in distinct national origin groups (Ybarra and Lopez, 2003; Kerlee, 2005). While there are many commonalities among Latinas (language, religion, mores, etc.), there are also substantive differences in terms of their racialization, terms of incorporation, citizenship, immigration status, generation, class backgrounds, family structures, cultural practices, and resistance strategies. To gloss over these real variations in lived experiences and outlooks by speaking of a generic "Latina" or Dominican girl misses the diversity among Latinas. This is important to understand as we craft meaningful approaches and programs to foster success for Latina youth within these populations.

NOTES

1. The 2000 census counted 9,314,235 people living in New York City. Of these, a third (34 percent) are foreign born, and close to half of the population speaks a foreign language (45 percent; Logan, 2003).

2. Hernandez and Rivera-Batiz, 2003.

3. Ibid.

4. Ibid.

5. What is most remarkable is that of these enrolled Dominicans, 63 percent came from households with household incomes of $20,000 or less, compared with 39 percent for the overall population at City University of New York (Hernandez and Rivera-Batiz, 2003).

6. These approaches to studying race are markedly different from the essentialist perspective of difference, which tends to see race and gender differences as genetic and innate characteristics. It is also quite different from the ethnicity

paradigm—the hegemonic approach to race relations, which continues to give primacy to ethnicity or cultural differences as the main explanatory variable in assessing the schooling outcomes of distinct "ethnic" groups (Portes and Zhou, 1993).

7. Racial logic is ubiquitous and constitutive of our individual identities, psyche, lived experiences, social interactions, societal institutions, laws, social movements, and cultural representations (Omi and Winant, 1994).

8. "The experience of oppressed people is that the living of one's life is confined and shaped by forces and barriers which are not accidental or occasional and hence avoidable, but are systemically related to each other in such a way as to catch one between and among them and restrict or penalize motion in any direction" (Frye, 2000:190). A macroscopic view of oppression enables one to see "a network of forces and barriers which are systemically related and which conspire to the immobilization, reduction and molding of women and the lives we live" (Frye, 2000:193).

9. In contrast, Cubans have the highest number of people who identify as white (85 percent); only 5 percent describe their race as black (Logan, 2003). Half of Mexicans identify as white (49 percent), and only (1 percent) identify as black; among mainland Puerto Ricans 8 percent identify their race as black, and nearly half describe their race as white (49 percent; see Logan, 2003).

10. Schill, Friedman, and Rosenbaum, 1998.

11. Massey and Denton, 1994.

12. The names of all participants and schools have been changed to preserve their anonymity.

13. The majority of the teachers at Urban High School had been there for less than five years. The "revolving door" phenomenon was increasingly common among teachers in overcrowded, undersupported neighborhood schools.

14. In New York City, 10,000 of the 75,000 teachers in the public education system have not been certified to teach, compared with 500 for the rest of the state (Molotsky, 1999).

15. Although the Board of Education of the City of New York categorizes Dominicans as Hispanics and West Indians as blacks, Dominicans and West Indians are often indistinguishable from one another in terms of phenotype (i.e., skin color, facial features) and therefore are subjected to the one-drop rule, whereby anyone of discernible so-called African ancestry is categorized as "black" and racially stigmatized.

16. During the course of fieldwork, I never encountered a single white or Asian student at Urban High School.

17. Valenzuela (1999) also found that among both Mexican-born and U.S.-born high school students, women were the purveyors of social capital in the form of wider social networks and resources than their male counterparts.

18. Arnot, Weiner, and David, 1999:73.

REFERENCES

Arnot, Madeleine, Gaby Weiner, and Miriam E. David. 1999. *Closing the Gender Gap: Postwar Education and Social Change.* Malden, MA: Blackwell.

Bettie, Julie. 2003. *Women without Class: Girls, Race and Identity.* Berkeley: University of California Press.

Bonilla-Silva, Eduardo. 2002. We Are All Americans? The Latin Americanization of Racial Stratification in the USA. *Race and Society* 5 (1): 1–17.

Collins, Patricia Hill. 2000. *Black Feminist Thought: Knowledge, Consciousness, and the Politics of Empowerment.* 2nd ed. New York: Routledge.

De Filippis, Daisy, ed. 2000. *Documents of Dissidence: Selected Writings by Dominican Women.* New York: Dominican Studies Institute, City University of New York.

Frye, Marilyn. 2000. Oppression. In *The Meaning of Difference: American Constructions of Race, Sex and Gender, Social Class, and Sexual Orientation,* 2nd ed., ed. Karen E. Rosenblum and Toni-Michelle C. Travis, 190–194. Boston: McGraw Hill.

Guinier, Lani, and Gerald Torres. 2000. Whiteness of a Different Color? In *Off-White: Readings on Power, Privilege and Resistance,* 2nd ed., ed. Michelle Fine, Lois Weis, Linda Powell Pruitt, and April Burns, 411–430. New York: Routledge.

Hernandez, Ramona, and Francisco Rivera-Batiz. 1995. *Dominican New Yorkers: A Socioeconomic Profile, 1990.* New York: Dominican Studies Institute at the City University of New York.

———. 2003. Dominicans in the United States: A Socioeconomic Profile, 2000. New York: Dominican Research Monographs, the City University of New York Dominican Studies Institute.

Kerlee, Ime. 2005. Transnational Dreaming: The Impact of Migration Experience on Concepts of Race, Class, and Gender in Dominicanidad. Research proposal, Institute for Comparative and International Studies. Emory University. http://www.icis.emory.edu/programs/vm/kerlle%20proposal.htm. Retrieved May 31, 2005.

Leadbeater, Bonnie, and Niobe Way, eds. 1996. *Urban Girls: Resisting Stereotypes, Creating Identities.* New York: NYU Press.

Lewis, Amanda. 2003. *Race in the Schoolyard: Negotiating the Color Line in Classrooms and Communities.* Piscataway, NJ: Rutgers University Press.

Logan, John. 2002. *Separate and Unequal.* Albany, NY: Lewis Mumford Center for Comparative Urban and Regional Research, University at Albany.

———. 2003. *How Race Counts for Hispanic Americans.* Albany, NY: Lewis Mumford Center for Comparative Urban and Regional Research, University at Albany.

Logan, John, and Glenn Deane. 2003. *Black Diversity in Metropolitan America.*

Albany, NY: Lewis Mumford Center for Comparative Urban and Regional Research, University at Albany.

Lopez, Nancy. 2003. *Hopeful Girls, Troubled Boys: Race and Gender Disparity in Urban Education.* New York: Routledge.

Massey, Douglas, and Nancy Denton. 1994. *American Apartheid: Segregation and the Making of the American Underclass.* Cambridge, MA: Harvard University Press.

Molotsky, Irwin. 1999. White House Will Propose Public School Choice Plan. *New York Times,* 19 May, 6A.

Omi, Michael, and Howard Winant. 1994. *Racial Formation in the United States: From 1960s to 1990s.* New York: Routledge.

Pessar, Patricia, and Sherri Grasmuck. 1991. *Between Two Islands: Dominican International Migration.* Berkeley: University of California Press.

Portes, A., and M. Zhou. 1993. The New Generation: Segmented Assimilation and Its Variants. *Annals of the American Academy of Political and Social Science* 530: 74–96.

Safa, Helen. 1995. *The Myth of the Male Breadwinner: Women and Industrialization in the Caribbean.* New York: Westview.

Schill, Michael, Samantha Friedman, and Emily Rosenbaum. 1998. The Housing of Immigrants in New York City. Center for Real Estate and Urban Policy and New York University School of Law, Working Paper 98(2).

Valenzuela, Angela. 1999. *Subtractive Schooling: U.S.-Mexican Youth and the Politics of Caring.* Albany: State University of New York Press.

Ybarra, Raul, and Nancy Lopez. 2004. *Creating Alternative Discourses in the Education of Latinos and Latinas: A Reader.* New York: Peter Lang.

Chapter 7

La Escuela

Young Latina Women Negotiating Identities in School

Melissa Hyams

"Pay attention in class . . . [and] don't get pregnant." This formula for success was stated by a fourteen-year-old girl of Mexican descent and iter-
ated, occasionally challenged, but mostly accepted by all the young Latina
women who participated in the research presented here. This formula,
however, posed a tremendous challenge to them. The young women shared
their conviction and concern that completing (or failing to complete) high
school, with all that represented in terms of future success, depended on
their behavior and sexual morality. They also felt certain, however, that
young men, who "have a way of talking you into things" and gain in status
if they do so, controlled sexual intimacy. From this precarious position,
they felt themselves to be singularly responsible for both their academic
diligence and bounded sexuality in order to succeed as young women in
high school and realize their goals as adult women beyond high school.

This chapter addresses two interrelated questions raised by this formula
for success. First, how do gender and sexual identity formation intersect
with institutional and interpersonal social and spatial practices and
processes in school? Second, what are the implications of these gender and
sexual identities, and how do these identities lead young Latina women to
succeed academically? I consider these questions and interpret the Latinas'
experiences from a feminist social geographic perspective.

Theoretical Perspectives

Contemporary geographies of young people reveal practices and processes of inclusion and exclusion that shape local places and the social and

spatial boundaries of individual and group belonging (Aitken, 2001; Skelton and Valentine, 1997). For some feminist geographers, gender, sexuality, race, and ethnicity are key organizing principles (in conjunction with class) that shape places and belonging. Much of their work, including this research, looks into the subtle, noncoercive workings of group categorization and normalization. The work presented in this chapter includes gender, sexual, and academic representations, symbols, discourse, and practice that inscribe unequal social positions, delineate spaces of inclusion and exclusion, and perpetuate unequal social positions (Bondi et al., 2002; Pratt, 1998, 1999). Such an analysis can also offer the possibility for change through rethinking the terms in which we formulate the world (Young, 1990).

In locating the processes and practices of gender and sexual identity and belonging in an urban high school, I do not suggest that the high school is a system of social and spatial relations and practices bounded by the school's fences. Spatial relations reach farther than the space in which they are presented (Massey, 1994). I argue that it is both in school and through schooling, constituted as a "spatiality of protection," through formal and informal representations, symbols, discourses, and practices, that these young women reproduce, rework, and resist gendered and sexualized academic identities.

Methodology

The school in this study was located in a low-income, highly segregated Latina/o neighborhood of Los Angeles. It was chosen because of its predominantly second-generation Mexican-descent student body. Of the thirty-four Latina participants, twenty-five were born in the United States, nine lived and were educated in the United States from early childhood. They ranged in age from thirteen to eighteen years old; the majority were between fourteen and sixteen years of age.

The main purpose of my research was to examine the process of meaning-making: how places get invested with meaning and, in turn, the role place plays in how self and other are experienced and self-understandings are known. I used a convenience sample; the young women were recruited from social studies and physical education classes only. I solicited volunteers from the students in these classes and brought together eight friendship groups ranging in size from three to eight members. The participants were enrolled in honors, the University Preparatory Program (UPP),[1] and regular classes.

My principle method of data collection was to audiotape in-depth group discussions, each organized around a particular place-based theme (Burgess, Limb, and Harrison, 1988a, 1988b) followed by semistructured, in-depth interviews of individual participants. Individual interviews were also done with school personnel and community members.

My data analysis used a grounded theory technique in which the audio-taped group discussions and written notations regarding group dynamics were used to modify subsequent discussion topics (Strauss and Corbin, 1990). This refinement aimed at enabling the participants to articulate what was important to them (Kitzinger, 1994). The discussions became the basis for a qualitative analysis of the interactive, intersubjective construction of meaning and identity among the group members.

Categorically Bound: The Conflict

Adolescent women in contemporary, post–sexual revolution America are caught in a "double bind" (Luker, 1996). The number of years between being physically capable of sex and childbearing and the generally accepted age of marriage has increased in this century. At the same time, social norms regarding premarital sex have changed to where acceptable sex is that which is closely linked to serious and monogamous heterosexual relationships moving toward marriage (Luker, 1996). As Kristin Luker persuasively argues, adolescents are in a double bind because they are *categorically* too young and immature to get serious and contemplate marriage, whereas engagement in age-appropriate short-term intimate relationships for pleasure, not procreation, are deemed immoral. Among young Latinas, this double bind is conceived of in terms of a choice between being either a smart or a mature girl.

Becoming a Female High School Student

The majority of study participants were beginning their first or second year of high school. In our group discussions, they spoke about the tremendous pressure they experienced in becoming high school students and the dilemma they faced in managing their own needs and desires and satisfying others' expectations.

Carmen spoke for the majority of the young women by saying the following:

> I don't know, it's like just concerning—how can I put this? . . . you're a girl in high school—going to high school, sometimes means more guys. . . . Know what I mean? Like that kind of pressure. You have to act more mature, sometimes. You have to calm down. Well for me being more mature in high school is . . . doing homework, like studying, putting my whole concentration on schoolwork. Not going fooling around.

Alexandra explained:

> Pressure from parents. To get good grades, to do good in school because they want you to go to college. And like they want you to be somebody in life. . . . I don't like the pressure. 'Cause my mom she's always telling me that I should pay attention in class and do good and not to—well, in high school is where most girls end up pregnant and all of that disease and anything. That's what my mom tells me to take care of myself, and I think I'm a smart girl and I wouldn't do something stupid like that.

These young women are experiencing themselves becoming sexual subjects, that is, both desirous of and the object of desire in intimate relationships with boys. However, this sexual identity is regulated through discursive and disciplinary practices mediated and meted out by numerous authorities, in this particular example, their parents. They feel pressured by their parents to make the most of the opportunities that a U.S. education has to offer. In local terms they perceive a choice between being mature (e.g., avoiding intimate relationships with boys, doing well in school, and having a successful life) or being immature (e.g., having a boyfriend, getting pregnant, and enduring a life of poverty).

Their choices, however, are mediated by a wider set of social norms. When asked specifically why young women who are knowledgeable about and have access to birth control become pregnant, their explanations were twofold: victimization and loss of control. In their representations, ordinary adolescent girls who want to conform to society's expectations of mature girls and smart girls get pregnant because they are victims of male deception and self-deceit. When female desire is imaginable, it is only in terms of a complete loss of control. In their discussions there is a total absence of the young woman who, desirous of sexual intimacy, engages in *consensual* sexual relations using, or perhaps misusing, birth control.

The discourses of desire (Fine, 1992), preparedness, and responsibility (Luker, 1996) are missing in the social construction of young women who want to be mature. As Luker (1996:146–147) has suggested, the young, un-married woman "tend[s] to be culturally handicapped by society's expec-tations of appropriate female sexual behavior . . . she is culturally enjoined from looking too 'ready' . . . [and] forced to rely on the goodwill and moti-vation of her partner." Ironically, then, being unprepared for and over-come by sexual desire, resulting in pregnancy, is not incompatible with being a mature girl and smart girl and intending to succeed in school. For mature girls, however, when such cultural constraints result in preg-nancy, young motherhood appears incompatible with actually being able to succeed.

Becoming a Latina Woman

The dominant representations of mature girls and smart girls may be shaped by and give shape to specific material and symbolic possibilities and constraints regarding *Latina* (self)-control and protection of female sexuality. Within Catholic Latina/o religious and cultural ideology, turning fifteen symbolizes the life-course transition to womanhood and is cele-brated by the *quinceañera.* Lilliana and Sandra explained the pressures of becoming a woman as follows:

> *Lilliana*: Like, I'm going to church right now, every Saturday. . . . And then you talk to the priest about . . . what's right, what's wrong. You're changing from a little girl to a woman. And you need to take care of yourself.
>
> *Interviewer*: So if we relate your *quinceañera* and the lessons that you're learning back to school, does any of your life in school get affected by this?
>
> *Lilliana*: Always go the right way, not the wrong way.
>
> *Interviewer*: Can you tell me what the right and wrong way is 'cause those are words that have a lot of meaning?

Sandra: There are a lot of teenage girls that they're barely fourteen and they have babies already.

Interviewer: That's the wrong way?

All: Yah, that's the wrong way.

Sandra: The right way is to go, to finish their high school, go to college, get a good job. And then when they're ready to have kids, to have them.

The constraints and possibilities embodied in the *quinceañera* are tangible in the young women's day-to-day lives. This transitional age to womanhood is twofold: from the selfishness of childhood to a life of service to her family and community, and as a nonsexual to a sexual person. As a sexual person, however, she is to be seen as available for courtship but not desirable as an object of passion (Davalos, 1996; Horowitz, 1993). In her daily life, the fifteen-year old is expected, on the one hand, to take on more responsibilities and to become increasingly self-directed and self-reliant in the provision of services to others and in providing for her self. On the other hand, increased freedoms do not necessarily accompany increased responsibilities (Napolitano, 1997). In Latina/o culture and Western culture more generally, when a young girl "becomes a woman," the maintenance of sexual purity necessitates an increase in internal and external control over her social interactions, spatial mobility, appearance, and bodily comportment. For U.S. Latinas, this process of change is sanctioned at age fifteen and intersects with institutional and interpersonal processes and practices of becoming a high school student.

Sexually Bound: From "Hoochie" Mamas to Las Mexicanas

High school is the "pre-eminent [space] where adolescents come together during their initial period of sexual identity development" (Lesko, 1988: 123; see also Epstein and Johnson, 1998). Learning about their responsibility for modesty and chastity is central to these young women's experience as high school students. I analyzed the daily negotiations of normative femininity, masculinity, and academic achievement made compulsory through representations, symbols, discourses, and practices regarding appropriate dress and displays of affection on campus. I offer here an interpretation of these as constraining and disabling and provide examples of how some young women reproduce dominant normative identities and others rework and resist the terms and conditions of disablement.

Dress Code

The school's dress code is implicated in the normalizing practices of a "spatiality of protection" in and through which these young women negotiate their gendered and sexualized academic identities. Adults say the dress code helps to protect students both on and off campus. Although not explicitly geared toward regulating female dress, everyone understood that the rules that did not target gangster fashion targeted female fashion, specifically, female clothing that "do[es] not cover the body adequately."

Institutionalized in the school's policy and practices regulating female dress is a moral critique of female sexuality as problematic. As the dean of students explained:

> The whole purpose of [the dress code] is all based on experience. . . . The last fifteen years, there's been at least three occasions where . . . our girls have, um, been attempted to rape them [have been subject to rape attempts] on the way home from school, on the way to school. . . . And there's been at least six to eight times we've had . . . flashers cruising around the school stalking certain girls. So we keep telling the girls, "If you don't attract attention, you're increasing your chances of getting home safe." But some of the girls wear very short skirts, some of our fifteen-, sixteen-year-olds look twenty-three. . . . Everything's come about as a result of our experience in trying to protect them. Make their walk to school, or from school [to] home, safer.

Fashion is critical in the negotiation of feminine gender and heterosexual identities as a signifier of moral virtue (Tseelon, 1995). As evidenced in the following conversations, the young Latinas were continually engaged in positioning themselves and others in terms of gender and sexual identity and moral virtue according to adherence to the dress code.

> *Sabrina*: Some girls, you know how sometimes they wear a bra top, a little longer than a bra . . . it's getting attraction to the guy, then saying "Yah, I'm easy," "I want you" or "Come here. Look at what I have. Touch it."
> *Michelle*: Yah, 'cause if you dress like that it's just an invitation to get raped. . . . Some people just ask for it.

This most extreme noncompliance with the dress code was attributed to "hoochie" mamas, whose appearance marked them as morally suspect and compelled uncertainty about their sexual activity:

Sportie: It's like a girl who's been around. Not been around, but—
Betty: Shows too much of what she's got.
Nikki: She wears short, short skirts, high heels.
Betty: Her breasts are about to fall out when she bends over.

Everyone characterized hoochie mamas as popping out everywhere. This construction was institutionalized in the enforcement of the dress code. The following story told to me by the dean illustrates this point. Two sisters came to school wearing identical shirts. On one of the girls, the big-busted one, this top exposed her cleavage. She was sent home from school. The other sister did not attract the attention of the authorities. In response to a complaint by their mother, the dean said he thought the young woman knew that the top was too small for her and needed to be more responsible about how she dressed. I would argue, however, that hoochie mamas are not young women who "show too much of what they have" but, rather, have too much to show. They are young women who represent, in the quintessential sexualized female form, the embodiment of danger and desire.

The relatively protected environment inside the school gates offers some young women the opportunity to rework the terms of a disabling gendered, sexualized academic subjectivity. I saw school personnel ask young women of all shapes and sizes to cover themselves up. Inside the school gates, they had the opportunity to "try on and take off" sexualized clothing or identities in the day-to-day negotiation of gender and sexual identities and safely resist the visual mastery that boys and men have over them which compels them to be invisible (Koskela, 1997).

A few of the participants contested the meanings attached to certain styles, and a couple of them challenged the moral critique of female fashion. Conflicting discourses provide other categorizations in which they can position themselves within acceptable and safe bounds. For example, Maria felt the fashion was appropriate because it was feminine. She challenged the dress code's definition of feminine through the authorization of the fashion industry: "It's like the new style. Today, you know, like little short things." In order to wear these feminine clothes, Maria, Pilar, and many others were compelled by the dress code to wear something over these outfits. Many girls wore zipper-fronted sweatshirts that covered their upper bodies and their upper thighs. They strategically zip closed in order to conceal or zip open in order to expose their midriffs, cleavage, and/or thighs, thereby maintaining some autonomy in self-representation.

Although there was a consistency among most of the young people and school personnel in the stigmatizing of hoochie mamas, some girls resisted categorization and challenged the name's negative attributions. Lucy is a case in point. She explained, "Like if [you're] dressed all hoochie they also think you're dumb. They think you waste all your time . . . in the mall or something." Lucy was a graduating senior with a 3.5 grade point average and perfect attendance and dressed in a way that was perceived as hoochie.

Although most of the participants challenged the dress code in minor ways, very few challenged the moral critique of overtly sexualized feminine dress. None of the young women challenged the notions of gender, sexuality, and age that reinforced the norms of heterosexual and male-dominant social relations. Regardless of the clothing they wore in order to conform to or resist the dress code, they fashioned themselves as "feminine," sexually desirable to and desired by boys. At the same time, they struggled to be seen as and to see themselves as managing their vulnerability.

The dress code prohibitions at once sexualize adolescent female bodies and discipline that sexuality. Girls who do not conform to the dress code are marked as sexually immoral and destined for teenage pregnancy and academic failure. Further, the moral critique of female dress makes girls responsible for their own victimization. In and through schooling, these young women learn the lessons of sexual boundedness, that is, modesty and chastity. For each young woman, her body, in her sartorial display and display of affection, is the principal site of this learning experience.

Displays of Affection

In their day-to-day interactions in school, these young Latinas are also subjected to normalizing and vilifying practices instituted in the school's code of conduct. This code prohibits engagement in "exaggerated public expression of affection, that is, kissing, embracing, caressing." As the dean explained:

> Again, we go back to protection. . . . What we end up seeing sometimes, you know, guys with their hands on the girl's butt. Girls sitting between the guy's crotch. . . . I say, "You were in a sexual position. By law I have to call your mom. This is considered a form of sexual harassment." She says, "But he didn't force me. I wanted to." I say, "I understand. But the law's the law."

There have been situations where these necking couples have got into argu-
ments and then the guys become very abusive with the girl. So, again, it's a
question of protection.

He assured me that boys who engage in this behavior are punished in a
similar manner to the girls. He said:

I call the mother and say, "Your son's over here putting his tongue in this
girl's mouth." Because, you know, most of the guys have sisters, you know.
And I say, "Would you let your sister make out with a dude like that?" [They
say,] "No, I'd kick his ass!" And I say, "Oh. But you can do it, though, right!"
[They say,] "Uh, uh, uh . . ." So sometimes I get both the parents in there,
and that stops it.

The sexuality of both young women and young men is subjected to
adult regulation by parents and school personal in loco parentis. However,
a level of autonomy seems to be afforded boys, whereas girls are constructed as the object of protection/control in each of the dean's examples.
In discursively subtle ways, boys are authorized to assume the position of
controlling girls' sexuality in comments such as "he didn't force me," "the
guys become abusive," or "his tongue in this girl's mouth." In not-so-subtle
terms, young men as brothers are authorized to control their sisters' sexuality. As the administrator said, "Most of these guys have sisters," or, said
another way, "Most of these girls have brothers" who police their sexual
behavior in school.

The terms of violence used to represent sexual activity contribute to the
construction of young adolescent women as subordinate in the prevailing power relations and objects of protection and control. Moreover, they
deny female agency and desire. In each example, young men are "doing
stuff" to young women, who are the victims of sexual exploitation and
abuse. In the example in which a young woman is reported as "wanting
to," her desire is pathologized: in citing legislative norms concerning sexual harassment, her judgment about desiring engagement in such behavior is questioned (Butler, 1993).

The relations of power that give shape to and are shaped by a "spatiality
of protection" inside the school gates can also produce an opening for
the possibility of reworking or resisting disabling norms through parody,
hyperbole, and/or reversal of meaning. For young women who, as they

report, have limited access to public space, school can provide them with the only *relatively* unregulated space to be with a boy. As Sportie explains:

> I can't go out on a date with the boy alone until I'm sixteen. . . . I have a boyfriend, I wouldn't mind going to the movies with him or going to the park with him. I'm not going to do anything bad, you know, just to spend time with him. . . . Well, like in the mornings we meet. . . . I leave at 7:00 in the morning and I'm here like by 7:15 and we meet and we just talk until the bell rings.

Sportie assumes a position of maturity, that is, she will not do anything bad that might put her in a position to be sexually exploited. However, she is also a girlfriend. The "spatiality of protection" inside the school gates allows her to resist vulnerability and reverse the terms of the sociospatial relations of power. School provides an autonomous space away from adult control in which to spend time with her boyfriend. In the space of the following group discussion, Sportie and her friends Betty and Nikki also rework disabling terms of female incompetence and dependence through parody:

> *Sportie*: I just think that girls are better than guys. Guys are always saying, "I can beat you in this. You can't run as fast as I can." Just 'cause they're boys and they're more athletic . . .
> *Nikki*: It's because they're stronger.
> *Betty*: Strength isn't anything.
> *Nikki*: No, it's usually you use your head.
> *Sportie*: So you mean if there's like a hundred pounds sitting right there on the table and between the guy and the girl to lift it, the guy's not gonna lift it and the girl is?
> *Nikki*: The girl's smarter. She can get something else to lift it!
> *Betty*: The girl thinks. She can analyze.
> *Nikki*: She can get like a shopping cart or something.
> *All*: (Laugh)
> *Betty*: Yah, she'll push it with her foot or something. With her high heels.
> *Nikki*: But then she'll get tired. With a shopping cart she can move it a mile.

Confronted with the local limitations on independence from boys, Sportie and her friends liberate themselves in a parody of conformity to gender inequality by conceding to inferior strength but claiming intellectual superiority and resignifying symbols of female subordination: high heels and shopping carts.

Despite girls' apparent awareness that they are being framed as dependent (and their resistance to this view), the school policy on displays of affection promotes a sense of female victimization, loss of control, and dependency. Through formal and informal policies and practices in school and through schooling, these young women learn that boyfriends can behave toward them both benevolently and malevolently. They also learn that to a large degree they themselves are responsible for eliciting this behavior. Positioning themselves as young ladies by acting appropriately does not always guarantee the desired safety, security, and respect. Vulnerability and its associative risks—of playing leading to being grabbed, of necking leading to abuse, of kissing leading to pregnancy—are the lessons girls learn in school, above and beyond the school's academic curriculum (Fine, 1992).

The Mexican Ideal

In sharp contrast to their own local experiences, Mexico is a place where a young woman's modesty, in appearance and bodily comportment, and her chastity guarantee her the safety, security, and respect she bargains for within the constraints and possibilities of "being a girlfriend." In conversations about the similarities and differences between their lives and those of their counterparts in Mexico, the girls all agreed with the following representation of how boys and girls behave around one another.

> *Nikki*: Guys respect girls. Girls are always in a dress. They're always neat; they're never dirty or anything. They have respect for themselves. They never flirt with anybody. 'Cause they all know each other so they all respect each other.
>
> *Betty*: The boyfriends and girlfriends do not be hiding behind trees, scamming [kissing].
>
> *Interviewer*: Where do they scam?
>
> *Nikki*: They don't.
>
> *Betty*: They really respect each other, and the guy just goes to her house and just talks. He's sitting on one side; she's sitting on the other. They don't even hold hands or anything. Just talk. Her mom knows that that's her boyfriend.

Victimization and loss of control are absent from the descriptions of the romantic experiences of these girls' Mexican counterparts. Young Mexican women dress and behave in accordance with normative conceptions, and consequently Mexican boys and men behave benevolently in the extreme. Their Mexican counterparts represent the ideal that is, by definition, unattainable. This unattainability is reinforced when their own position as "Americans" undermines any possibility of sharing in the experiences of their Mexican counterparts. As Michelle explained, "One guy told me 'We don't take you American girls serious. . . . Yah, when you guys come over here we just play around with you. You guys think that we really like you, but we don't. . . . We only take the Mexican girls serious. We'd marry them and not the Americans.'"

The impossible idealization of Mexican girls reiterates gender and sexual norms that position them as vulnerable and out of control. However, here, too, a space of ambiguity is opened within which disabling terms of subjectivity may be reworked. In affirming the attribution of ideal dress, bodily comportment, and displays of affection to Mexican girls, they reinforce young Mexican women's embodiment of modesty and chastity. In this way, the Latinas position themselves, geographically and socially, out of reach of living in strict obedience to the dominant norms of appropriate feminine and heterosexual attitudes and behavior in the sociospatial context in which they live and learn.

In summary, within the heterosexual-dominant and female-subordinate protected space inside the school gates, differences in dress and displays of affection provide the substance from which determinations are fashioned about sexual morality and academic diligence. Within this moral economy, hoochie mamas mark out the lower limits of the moral economy: victimization and loss of control leading to academic failure and ruined lives. The upper limits of the moral economy, modesty and chastity, are marked out by their counterparts in Mexico, who, although literally and metaphorically beyond their reach, are integral in the networks of social relations and understandings in and through which they negotiate gender and sexual identities in school.

Conclusion

As we have seen, high school is not a gender-neutral stage in the life course but one that is embedded in society's expectations of and anxieties about adolescent women. This anxiety gives rise to and is shaped by the social space of high school. In school and through school regulations of female dress and displays of affection, young women learn consciously and unconsciously about their positions as victims and the lessons of self-control and external control of their sexuality. In the attention to dress and displays of affection, a young woman's body instead of her mind becomes the locus of meaning in the negotiation of a gendered and sexualized academic identity.

Although academic achievement among U.S. Latina/os is comparatively low, the problem with achievement is not what the young women fear most. Teenage pregnancy is more often a result, not the cause, of academic failure (Luker, 1996; Legischool Project, 1995). In struggling against disabling subject positions, some young women are able to rework the terms and gain a sense of themselves as competent and autonomous, while others' engagement with these feminine gender and heterosexual norms inculcate feelings of vulnerability, lack of control, and passivity.

The implications of this study for those who work in educational institutions are to look critically at the discourses and practices shaping individuals and spaces of education. A veteran New York City high school teacher I know suggested that as a teacher she can begin to gain insight by "looking at the students in a way that may help me to see how and what they see so that I can unlock the window to their world . . . to see that another way exists, let alone accept it as a choice." I agree that hearing the young Latinas' voices is indeed crucial to unlocking windows to their experiences and the meanings they attribute to those experiences. I caution, however, that we should not distinguish between their world and our world and attribute to them too much free choice. In our classrooms we need to engage young people in critical analyses of institutional and interpersonal representations, symbols, discourses, and practices that inscribe unequal social positions, delineate spaces of inclusion and exclusion, and perpetuate unequal social positions. We need to look critically at how our world is implicated in shaping their world: how the ways in which young Latinas' "abilities and knowledge about themselves [as gendered and sexualized] are gently and quietly shaped in a gentle, caring institution" (Marshall, 1990:15). Their choices, particularly their words and acts of resistance, can be very educational.

N O T E S

An earlier version of this chapter appeared in *Environment and Planning A* 32 (2000): 635–654.

I am indebted to the young women who participated in this research project and to my adviser, Sarah Radcliffe, my family, and Susan K. Passler for their total support. I am grateful to the Economic and Social Research Council for its financial support; this research was funded by award number R00429734503. 1.

1. University Preparatory Program (UPP) is a California State University, Los Angeles (UCSLA) university–high school partnership to increase the number of underrepresented minorities who graduate from college, preferably with degrees in mathematics, science, engineering, and technology. UPP focuses on the middle-achieving students.

R E F E R E N C E S

Aitken, Stuart. 2001. *Geographies of young people: The morally contested spaces of identity.* London: Routledge.

Bondi, Liz, et al. 2002. *Subjectivities, knowledges, and feminist geographies: The subjects and ethics of social research.* Lanham, MD: Rowman and Littlefield.

Burgess, Jacqueline, Melanie Limb, and Carolyn Harrison. 1998a. Exploring environmental values through the medium of small groups: 1. Theory and practice. *Environment and Planning A* 20:309–326.

Burgess, Jacqueline, Melanie Limb, and Carolyn Harrison. 1988b. Exploring environmental values through the medium of small groups: 2. Illustrations of a group at work. *Environment and Planning A* 20:457–476.

Butler, Judith. 1993. *Bodies that matter: On the discursive limits of "sex."* New York: Routledge.

Davalos, Karen. 1996. La quinceañera: Making gender and ethnic identities. *Frontiers: A Journal of Women's Studies* 16:101–127.

Epstein, Debbie, and Richard Johnson. 1998. *Schooling sexualities.* Buckingham: Open University Press.

Fine, Michelle. 1992. *Disruptive voices: The possibilities of feminist research.* Ann Arbor: University of Michigan Press.

Horowitz, Ruth. 1993. The power of ritual in a Chicano community: A young woman's status and expanding family ties. *Marriage and Family Review* 19:257–280.

Kitzinger, Jenny. 1994. The methodology of focus groups: The importance of interaction between research participants. *Sociology of Health and Illness* 16:103–121.

Koskela, Hille. 1997. "Bold walk and breakings": Women's spatial confidence versus fear of violence. *Gender, Place and Culture* 4:301–319.

Legischool Project. 1995. *How will we care for our children? Adolescent pregnancy and public policy in California.* Collaborative project of the California State Legislature and California State University. Sacramento: Center for California Studies.

Lesko, Nancy. 1988. The curriculum of the body: Lessons from a Catholic high school. In *Becoming feminine: The politics of popular culture,* edited by Leslie Roman, 123–142. Philadelphia: Falmer Press.

Luker, Kristin. 1996. *Dubious conceptions: The politics of teenage pregnancy.* Cambridge, MA: Harvard University Press.

Marshall, James. 1990. Foucault and educational research. In *Foucault and education: Disciplines and knowledge,* edited by Stephen Ball, 11–28. London: Routledge.

Massey, Doreen. 1994. *Space, place and gender.* Cambridge: Polity Press.

Napolitano, Valentina. 1997. Becoming a mujercita: Rituals, fiestas and religious discourses. *Journal of the Royal Anthropological Institute* 3:279–296.

Pratt, Geraldine. 1998. Inscribing domestic work on Filipina bodies. In *Places through the body,* edited by Heidi Nast and Steve Pile, 283–304. London: Routledge.

———. 1999. Geographies of identity and difference: Marking boundaries. In *Human geography today,* edited by Doreen Massey, John Allen, and Philip Sarre, 151–168. Cambridge: Polity Press.

Skelton, Tracey, and Gill Valentine, eds. 1997. *Cool places: Geographies of youth cultures.* London: Routledge.

Strauss, Anselm, and Juliet Corbin. 1990. *Basics of qualitative research: Grounded theory procedures and techniques.* Newbury Park, CA: Sage.

Tseelon, Efrat. 1995. *The masque of femininity: The presentation of woman in everyday life.* London: Sage.

Young, Iris. 1990. *Justice and the politics of difference.* Princeton, NJ: Princeton University Press.

Chapter 8

Latina Adolescents' Career Goals
Resources for Overcoming Obstacles

Wendy Rivera and Ronald Gallimore

This chapter explores the career goals and the resources that are associated with the career development of low-income, Latina adolescents. Previous studies suggest that Latina girls aspire for careers that require a higher education and that they are knowledgeable about the requirements for their desired careers (DeLeon 1996; Reyes, Kobus, and Gillock 1999). However, there is little research on the career and educational paths of Latina girls, or what resources help them meet their goals.

This research is critical because in 2001 only 53 percent of the Latino students who graduated from high school in the United States enrolled in a junior or four-year college (National Center for Educational Statistics, 2001). This chapter examines the educational and career paths of adolescent Latinas and how resources provided by family, peers, educational personnel, and community members influence postsecondary outcomes.

Background

Widely employed career development models (e.g., Super, Tiedman, and Borrow, 1961) were formulated based on studies of middle-class white populations and focus on the role of individual development and resources as determinants of career choices. Applying such models to non-white and/or poor populations is problematic on two grounds. First, extension of these models to nonwhite populations may not sufficiently address or incorporate issues of race, gender, socioeconomic status, and discrimination. Second, it may be problematic to apply career models that are focused on individual decision making. Latinas often incorporate family, peers, and other forms of social capital into their decisions (Stanton-Salazar, 1995).

Parent education plays a role in children's career aspirations. Latino parents communicate their career aspirations to their children and encourage them to pursue higher education and professional careers (Cooper et al., 1994; Reese et al., 1995). However, Latino parents who hold semiskilled or unskilled jobs and who view education as a means to social mobility (i.e., higher education or white-collar jobs) might not have access to information about the proper steps and requirements (Reese et al. 1995). They do, however, display other forms of involvement and support. For example, immigrant Latino families who are not familiar with the educational system in the United States may use teachers and other adults as institutional brokers to promote careers that require higher education and provide information on college entrance criteria and financial aid resources (Cooper, Denner, and Lopez 1999).

Peers may also play a crucial role for youth with limited institutional resources. Students who share their career goals and ideas with their peers are more likely to explore and commit to careers (Felsman and Blustein 1999). Disclosure and sharing of ideas allows them to explore possible careers and acquire the information needed to attain these careers. Peers may play an especially valuable role for youth who are limited in the social capital needed to obtain information required to effectively explore professional careers.

Objective

The specific questions guiding this study are as follows: (1) What were the girls' desired and expected career objectives when they were in high school? (2) What academic and career paths do Latina girls take to reach their career objectives after high school? (3) What is the availability and part played by role models and institutional brokers in the lives of these girls? And (4) How do resources such as family, peers, and school and/or community personnel affect the girls' academic and career outcomes two years after high school?

Participants

In 1989, 121 participants and their families were recruited from thirteen kindergarten classrooms in two Los Angeles area school districts. In 2003, 82 participants (38 females) and their families were still taking part in the study. There were no differences in socioeconomic status or gender between retained and lost participants.

Parents of the thirty-eight students who participated in the study reported here had an average of 6.7 years of formal education (the range was 0 to 12.5 years). They typically reported employment as laborers or in the service industry and came predominantly from Mexico (86 percent) or from Central or Latin America. However, most of the girls (79 percent) in this study were born in the United States.

Procedure

The thirty-eight female students were interviewed nine times beginning in tenth grade and ending when they had been out of high school for two years. In eleventh and twelfth grade, they were asked to specify their desired and expected career, whether they knew people in their specified career, and if they knew what preparation or steps were necessary to attain their expected job (see Appendix A). School transcripts were used to obtain cumulative grade point averages (GPAs).

Desired and expected occupations reported by the students were coded for the required education or training, using guidelines defined by the Bureau of Labor Statistics (2001). Two categories were used: community college/trade school versus four or more years of college.

Two years after completing high school, the working students described their jobs, why they were working, whether they liked their jobs, if they would stay in this line of work, and their future work plans. Those still in school were classified into three mutually exclusive groups based on academic and career outcomes two years after high school. The three groups were (1) four-year college, 2) community college/vocational (includes recent vocational graduates), and (3) nonacademic/career track (not enrolled in any formal school, or working in a job the participant considered to be nonpromising or a career).

The grounded theory method was used to identify emergent themes, and the interviews were coded for presence of those themes (Miles and

Huberman, 1994). Themes included teacher instrumental support, teacher emotional support, peers, and families. Persons were counted as a resource if the student said that he or she had obtained instrumental or emotional support from them. Interrater reliability was established by coding 10 percent of the data; there was 93 percent agreement between the two independent coders (see Appendix B for codes).

Results

Academic and Career Paths

Two years after high school, 48 percent of the students were enrolled in a community college or vocational school (hereafter CC/VS track). The rest of the students in the study were at a four-year college (hereafter four-year track; 26 percent) or in a nonacademic/career track (hereafter NA/C track; 26 percent).

Academic Performance

There were significant differences between groups in their high school GPA ($F(2, 37) = 19.29, p < .001$). The average high school GPAs were as follows: students in the four-year track: 3.7 ($SD = .37$); students in the CC/VS track: 2.4 ($SD = .72$); and students in the NA/C track: 2.0 ($SD = .65$).

Desired and Expected Career Objectives

During the twelfth grade, all the students were asked about their most desired careers. Twenty-one percent of the 38 students chose a teaching occupation. The remaining students (79 percent) chose a wide range of careers. Four-year-track students aspired for careers such as medical doctor, forensic scientist, editor, film producer, and investment banker. Some of the careers the CC/VS and NA/C track students chose included teacher, secretary, police officer, and entertainer. Most (67 percent) of the students aspired to careers that required a college education, regardless of their academic track at the time of the interview.

When asked about their expected (more realistic) career, 88 percent of the students attending a four-year college described a career that required at least an undergraduate degree. In contrast, only 58 percent of the students attending CC/VS and 37 percent of the students in the NA/C track named careers that would require a college degree. These differences were not statistically significant.

Role Models and Institutional Brokers

In twelfth grade, 43 percent ($n = 30$) of all the students knew someone in their desired careers. Students in both the NA/C track (62 percent) and the CC/VS (46 percent) track were more likely to know someone who worked in a career that they desired. In contrast, only 22 percent of the four-year college students knew someone in their desired careers. However, the difference between groups was not statistically significant.

Resources for Academic and Career Outcomes

When asked if anyone encouraged them to pursue their specified careers, all students said they felt encouraged to pursue their desired careers regardless of their academic standing during high school. Students who were attending a four-year college were the least likely to report encouragement to pursue their desired careers (33 percent compared with 78 percent of those in a CC/VS and 60 percent of those not in school. However, the difference across groups was not statistically significant.

Peer Resources

Forty-two percent of all the students said that their friends were a source of encouragement or information. Seventy percent of the students who were attending a four-year college and 44 percent of those in CC/VS reported that their peers were a resource in their academic and career endeavors. However, only 10 percent of the students who were not in school reported their peers as a resource, a difference that was statistically significant ($\chi^2(2, N = 38) = 7.46, p < .05$).

The experiences of a specific student illustrate this finding. Ramona was a high-achieving high school student who aspired to be a physical therapist.[1] Two years after high school, Ramona was attending a four-year college. In her interview, she described how her friends supported her future educational plans while they were in high school. She explained,

"They are excited about college and stuff and are all into the applications and everything, so I figure I can talk to them about stuff." The interviewer asked if they had all worked on their applications together, and Ramona said yes. "They would come over, and we do some online and some by hand and stuff like that."

Students who were out of school two years after high school were more likely to have friendships that did not center around school-related issues and at times served as negative influences. For example, Miriam performed poorly during high school but was able to obtain her general equivalency diploma at a continuation school. During high school she stated that she aspired to become a teacher, but she had not been encouraged by anyone to pursue this career. Two years after high school, she was working as a hostess in a restaurant but did not have plans to continue at this job because she did not find it interesting. However, she was contemplating attending community college but needed "time off first." When she was in high school, she responded to the question "How would you describe your friends?" in this way: "The gangsters, I like have friends, some are greasers, some are rebels, some are all mixed up. [My parents don't like my friends] 'cause of the way they dress. . . . Like they say that if like I'm with him that they might shoot me in like a drive-by or something . . . mostly 'cause like he got caught with drugs and stuff."

Relationships with School Personnel as a Resource

Overall, 42 percent of the students said that people at school were a source of encouragement or information. Only one girl out of ten (10 percent) who were not in school reported receiving support from school personnel or described school as an emotional or institutional resource, compared with 80 percent of students in a four-year college. Less than half (39 percent) of the students who were enrolled in community college or vocational school said school personnel gave them support to reach their academic and career goals or served as a resource when they were in high school. The difference between the groups was statistically significant (χ^2 $(2, N = 38) = 10.19, p < .05$).

Data from the interviews show how students think about their relationship with school personnel. In the following account, Miriam discusses one of her last positive experiences with a teacher:

My seventh-grade teacher, I think. He always was there when you needed him. And I was having a problem with my family, and he always tried to help me out as best as he could and made me see things. . . . 'Cause I used to think that basically everything was wrong or whatever, and he made me look at it in another way . . . so that's cool.

Students in a four-year college were more likely to have had a close relationship with school personnel during high school.

Family Support as a Resource

Overall, 81 percent of the students said that their family served as a resource in choosing in their academic and career paths. All the students who were attending a four-year college and 89 percent of those attending a community college reported their family as a resource. This includes being emotionally supportive, providing direct encouragement to pursue their goals, and providing information or protective tactics. The girls in the nonacademic group were significantly less likely to report family as a resource (χ^2 (2, $N = 38$) = 9.53, $p < .05$). For example, Rosalia was behind on credits but worked very hard in order to graduate. Throughout high school she stated that she was interested in careers in the medical field, such as a pediatrician or a registered nurse. When she was in twelfth grade, she stated that she expected to be a medical assistant, reflecting a lowered career aspiration. However, Rosalia reported receiving encouragement from her older brother. She asked:

Hey, what do you think is better, practitioner nurse or registered nurse? And he goes, "Go for the registered nurse because my cuñada's [in-law] mom, she is a registered nurse. Go for the registered nurse because they make a lot of money, you get vacation and sick days." He said, "Do whatever you want, and I am behind you."

While her brother did not describe the required steps to become a nurse, or the expected duties, he did communicate his support in the career of *her choice.* However, only half of the students who were not in school saw their family as a resource who tried to steer them away from risks (e.g., negative peer influences).

Family support was salient for some of the students who attended junior college or a vocational school after high school. Five of these students had fallen behind in their high school credits and might not have been able to graduate from high school without family support.

For example, Gabriela describes the various ways her parents motivated her to do well in school. In high school, Gabriela had poor grades and expected to attend "some type" of vocational school. However, she aspired to obtain a bachelor's degree. During her twelfth-grade year, Gabriela became highly motivated to make up class credits to graduate from high school. Two years after high school, Gabriela was attending junior college and was exploring her career options. As she explained, "[My parents] tell me that if I don't raise my grades up I won't be going out. And that the only reason I'm going to school is for myself, not for them, and to get a good job because my mom's like you don't want to [be] working at Jack in the Box." When asked what happens when they ground her, she replied, "I can't go out or talk on the phone. [When I get good grades] they hug me, you did [a] good job, if you want anything just tell us."

The Lack of Resources

The students who were enrolled in a four-year college, junior college, or vocational school two years after high school shared the characteristics of having family, peers, and school personnel as resources. However, students who were not enrolled in school had been behind in high school credits due to failing courses. They were also more likely to ditch school and engage in risky behavior. As the preceding results demonstrate, they were also less likely to perceive resources or support, and their risky behavior outweighed their protective factors when they were in high school (χ^2 (2, $N = 38$) = 11.57, $p < .01$).

Discussion

Most students in this study aspired to careers that required higher education, a finding that parallels previous research (DeLeon 1996; Reyes, Kobus, and Gillock 1999). This is a higher rate than the national average (53 percent) for Latino high school graduates enrolling in a two- or four-year college (National Center for Educational Statistics, 2001). The Latinas in the study were taking various paths en route to their career objectives. Some were on the four-year college path, and an equal number were on a nonacademic or career track, but most were enrolled in either a community college or vocational school.

For this sample, however, there was a disconnect between career expectations and knowledge of educational requirements. Only 50 percent of those in junior college and 22 percent of those not enrolled in school knew the educational requirements for the career goals they hoped to pursue. Moreover, students in these two groups primarily identified teaching as their career goal, yet they could not describe the educational credentials a teaching career requires. Despite being in frequent contact with teachers who know the steps required for a teaching career, it is surprising so few students knew what they needed to do.

The students' perceptions of school personnel may partially account for the gap between career expectations and knowledge of requirements. Those attending community college or not in school were the least likely to perceive teachers or school personnel as a resource for academic and career objectives. Students on the four-year or community college track had higher grades and were more likely to describe teachers as a resource. However, they, too, were uninformed about how to reach their desired careers. Perhaps these Latino students did not seek out teachers and other available adults because of a lack of trust or *confianza,* as suggested by some research (Stanton-Salazar, 2001).

Family members played an important role in the students' academic and career choices. Many of the students reported family-based emotional encouragement, information, and/or protective tactics.

Parental support and family commitment are known to predict greater career commitment (McWhirter, Hackett, and Bandalos, 1998). Thus, it is not surprising that the Latina students who described their family as a resource were more likely to be pursuing their educational and career objectives. At times, parents may emphasize the importance of having individual goals, even though Latino families are typically described as emphasizing goals that benefit the family unit. For example, one parent told her daughter to do well in school for "herself" and mentioned a job in a fast-food restaurant as a negative outcome.

Another source of support was peers. Students who were pursuing their academic and career objectives in a four-year college, community college, or vocational school were more likely to identify their peers as a source of encouragement and as a resource. The students' peers encouraged them, and together they built a community and sense of camaraderie as they went through the endeavors of reaching careers that require a post–high school degree. The roles that peers play may be more crucial for first-generation immigrant Latina students as they encounter the unfamiliar process of planning and strategizing for academic and career objectives.

Students on the four-year college track were the least likely to report encouragement for their career choice from any source. This might be a function of their greater likelihood of expecting professional careers, for which information is not widely available in their community. Their choice of careers that require higher education might have affected the amount or types of encouragement they were able to receive, since the people in their immediate communities are less likely to be familiar with requirements and pathways to those careers.

The finding that most of the students did not know how to obtain their career objectives regardless of their academic performance and desire to become educators demonstrates that there is a gap in the transfer of information that promotes the attainment of white-collar occupations. The fact that the girls in four-year colleges desired careers that required the greatest amount of formal education whereas they received the least amount of encouragement is also alarming. The data suggest that the students receive various forms of encouragement from their families and community. However, along with emotional encouragement they also need instrumental knowledge and reassurance from family members that they are on the right path to obtaining their desired career objectives. These specific needs may not always be met when few members of their communities have actually obtained such occupations, and school personnel fail to transfer relevant information.

Regardless of the obstacles that were present in the students' paths toward their career objectives, most of them have persisted with their original career objectives and are pursuing careers that require a post–high school education. The most plausible explanation for this persistence is the emotional encouragement that the students receive from their families and peers. Family members encouraged them to strive for careers that would lead to social mobility as a means for a better life. Some of the students reported that this was the only source of encouragement they had and that it motivated them to finish high school and continue their education. Although those in a four-year college reported receiving the least encouragement, they were more likely to build school-focused relationships with their peers. This showed their ability to be resourceful and get their needs met outside the home and in spite of the lack of teacher support.

Implications

Two findings reported here provide information about how programs and research can build on girls' stated aspirations. First, it is clearly important to improve career counseling for Latinas. School personnel should play an even bigger role in the students' career paths by linking them to role models and providing information to the students and their families about the education and training required for various careers. Many of the girls said they wanted to be teachers, and for them a ready source of information on how to enter the profession is potentially available every school day. Second, further research should incorporate the interpersonal aspects of development that involve school personnel, family, and peers into career development models. For career development models to be useful for understanding poor and nonwhite populations, they must address issues of race, gender, socioeconomic status, and discrimination. These models should reflect the fact that although many of the students in this study did not limit their career aspirations based on their parents' education and socioeconomic status, most reported having some emotional rather than instrumental support to achieve their goals.

NOTES

1. All names were changed to protect the students' identities.

REFERENCES

Bureau of Labor Statistics, U.S. Department of Labor Statistics. 2001. Retrieved November 18, 2002. from the Bureau of Labor Statistics Web site, http://data.bls.gov/servlet/oep.noeted.servlet.ActionServlet?Action=empoccp.

Cooper, Catherine R., Azmitia, Margarita, Garcia, Eugene E., Ittel, Angela, Lopez, Edward M., and Rivera, Lourdes. 1994. Shifting aspirations of low-income Mexican American and European American parents. In *Environments for socialization and learning: New directions in child development,* edited by Francisco A. Villaruel and Richard M. Lerner, 272–315. San Francisco: Jossey-Bass.

Cooper, Catherine R., Denner, Jill, and Lopez, Edward. 1999. Cultural brokers: Helping Latino children on pathways toward success. *The Future of Children* 9:51–57.

DeLeon, Brunilda. 1996. Career development of Hispanic adolescent girls. In *Urban girls: Resisting stereotypes, creating identities,* edited by Bonnie Leadbeater and Niobe Way, 380–398. New York: NYU Press.

Felsman, Debra, and Blustein, David. 1999. The role of peer relatedness in late adolescent career development. *Journal of Vocational Behavior* 54:279–295.

Fuligni, Andrew, and Pedersen, Sara. 2002. Family obligation and the transition to young adulthood. *Developmental Psychology* 38:856–868.

Hackett, Gail, and Byars, Angela. 1996. Social cognitive theory and the career development of African American women. *Career Development Quarterly* 44: 322–341.

Hernandez, Thomas, and Morales, Nestor Enrique. 1999. Career, culture and compromise: Career development experiences of Latinas working in higher education. *Career Development Quarterly* 48:45–58.

Honora, Detris. 2002. The relationship of gender and achievement to future outlook among African American adolescents. *Adolescence* 37:301–316.

Leong, Frederick, and Serafica, Felicisima. 2001. Cross-cultural perspective on Super's career development theory: Career maturity and cultural accommodation. In *Contemporary models in vocational psychology: A volume in honor of Samuel J. Osipow,* edited by Leong Frederick and Azi Barak, 167–205. Mahwah, NJ: Erlbaum.

Lopez, Gerardo. 2001. The value of hard work: Lessons on parent involvement from an (im)migrant household. *Harvard Educational Review* 71:416–437.

Lundberg, David, Osborne, Larry, and Miner, Claire Usher. 1997. Career maturity and personality preferences of Mexican-American and Anglo-American adolescents. *Journal of Career Development* 23:203–213.

McWhirter, Ellen Hawley, Hackett, Gail, and Bandalos, Deborah. 1998. A causal model of the educational plans and career expectations of Mexican American high school girls. *Journal of Counseling Psychology* 45:166–181.

Miles, Matthew, and Huberman, A. Michael. 1994. *Qualitative data analysis.* 2nd ed. Thousand Oaks, CA: Sage.

National Center for Educational Statistics. 2001. Retrieved July 27, 2004, from the National Center for Educational Statistics Web site, http://nces.ed.gov/programs/digest/d01/dt184.asp.

Reese, Lesllie, Gallimore, Ronald, Goldenberg, Claude, and Balzano, Silvia. 1995. Immigrant Latino parents' future for their children. In *Changing schools for changing students: An anthology of research on language minorities, school and society,* edited by R. Macias and R. Garcia, 205–223. Los Angeles: Regents of the University of California.

Reese, Leslie, Garnier, Helen, Gallimore, Ronald, and Goldenberg, Claude. 2000.

Longitudinal analysis of the antecedents of emergent Spanish literacy and middle-school English reading achievement of Spanish-speaking students. *American Educational Research Journal* 37:633–662.

Reyes, Olga, Kobus, Kimberley, and Gillock, Karen. 1999. Career aspirations of urban, Mexican American adolescent females. *Hispanic Journal of Behavioral Sciences* 21:366–382.

Stanton-Salazar, Ricardo. 1995. Information networks and social reproduction of inequality. *University of California Linguistic Minority Research Institute* 4.

———. 2001. *Manufacturing hope and despair: The school and kin support networks of U.S. Mexican youth.* New York: Teachers College Press.

Super, Donald, Tiedman, D., and Borrow, H. 1961. Vocational development: A symposium. *Personnel and Guidance Journal* 40:11–25.

U.S. Census Bureau. Fact Finder. Retrieved July 27, 2004, from the U.S Census Bureau. http://factfinder.census.gov.

Appendix A

Interview Questions

GRADE 10

What are your educational aspirations?

Why?

What are your educational expectations?

Why?

What are your resources for reaching school success?

What are your thoughts about the future?

What are some important things about your future?

GRADE 12

What is your dream job?

Who encouraged you to pursue your dream job?

Do you know someone who does your dream job?

What is your expected job?

Who encouraged you to pursue your expected job?

Do you know someone who does your expected job?

Do you know what preparation you need for your expected job?

What kind of job do you think your parents would like you to have?

Did your parents have certain career expectations because of your gender?

Appendix B

Codes for Resource Assessment

Family Protective Factors:

1 = Student mentioned family members as sources of support and utilized (acknowledged) them

2 = Student does not mention family members as sources of support or, if they do, they do not utilize them (e.g., does not talk to them about school, goals, or problems)

School Protective Factors:

1 = Student mentions a school mentor, role model, close connection with school personnel

2 = Student does not mention a school mentor, role model, close connection with school personnel

Peer Protective Factors:

1 = If they mention peers that provide instrumental help or encouragement toward their educational and career goals

2 = If the above is not mentioned

Chapter 9

Career Expectations and Goals of Latina Adolescents

Results from a Nationwide Study

Deborah Marlino and Fiona Wilson

On a brisk spring day we sat with a group of Latina adolescents in a Chicago high school. Although we were barely five miles from the heart of downtown and the Magnificent Mile, this area was a world apart. These girls lived in economically disadvantaged neighborhoods where college education is the exception, not the norm. However, they are determined to be different—to get a good education and to find financially rewarding professional careers. They want to use their success to give back to their families and make their communities stronger. We were inspired by the goals of these young women, in that they want to do well and also want to do good. By exploring the motivations underlying their ambitions, we hope to better understand how public policy, schools, and community organizations can work together to help ensure that their aspirations are fully realized.

According to 2002 census data, more than 80 percent of employed Latinas are working in nonmanagerial/nonprofessional occupations. Of these, 37 percent are working in technical, sales, and administrative positions. While many Latinas are attaining positions that require responsibility, skills, and training, only 8 percent of full-time Latina workers are earning more than $50,000 per year (U.S. Census Bureau Current Population Survey 2002, Tables 10.1 and 11.1).

Two important trends are changing the face of the labor pool of tomorrow. First, the rapid influx of women into the paid workforce in the last several decades and the accompanying breakdown of gender roles in career expectations have dramatically increased the presence of women in all job categories. At the same time, the proportion of the U.S. population classified as Latino is growing steadily and is expected to reach almost 20 percent by 2025 (U.S. Census Bureau Statistical Abstract of the United States 2001, Table 10; Women of Color 2003). As a result of these changes, we can expect continued growth in the number of Latinas actively participating as members of the paid labor pool.[1]

Today's adolescents are a significant economic and social force for the future. It is important to understand what types of careers will be sought by this coming generation of younger women so that educators and policy makers can best support them in their choices and future contributions to the workforce. How are these choices shaped by their aspirations and motivations, and by their perceptions of their own skills? What influences their career expectations?

We asked the Latina girls with whom we spoke these questions as part of a larger nationwide study of teen girls and boys undertaken in spring 2002 (Marlino and Wilson 2003). The primary purpose of our study was to examine how teen girls see business as a career and life opportunity, with the underlying goal of encouraging educational, community, and social organizations to develop programs that would actively enable girls to pursue their career interests.

Recognizing that adolescence may be a crucial period in the formation of career interests and life goals, we surveyed Latinas between the ages of twelve and eighteen in twenty-nine middle and high schools spanning four geographic areas.[2] We measured aspirations and goals for their education and careers, self-perceptions of abilities in different skill areas, attitudes toward different careers, and the sources seen as useful for career advice. We also gathered data on activities and on selected demographic and socioeconomic factors for comparison purposes. In addition, we carried out a limited number of focus groups.

Our respondents were 530 adolescent U.S. girls who self-identified as being of Spanish/Hispanic/Latino origin. Most attended urban public schools in California, Texas, or Illinois and lived in communities with median household incomes of under $50,000 (see Table 9.1 for predominant sample characteristics).[3]

Study Results

What do Latinas in their middle and high school years expect and want in their career and educational futures? What motivations underlie these goals? The girls' responses to our surveys helped us answer these questions.

TABLE 9.1
Respondent Characteristics

Key Characteristics of Sample (n = 530)	%
Grades 7–9	49.6
Grades 10–12	50.4
California resident	55.7
Texas resident	20.0
Live in urban area	74.3
Attend public school	77.5
In household with total income under $50,000	90.9

TABLE 9.2
Educational Goals of Respondents and Parents

Educational Aspiration	%
High school or lower (grades K–12)	10
College	49
Graduate school	41

Parent's Education	%
Mother: high school or lower (grades K–12)	73
Father: high school or lower (grades K–12)	69

Educational and Career Goals

First, we know that Latina adolescents have strong educational aspirations. In our study, more than 40 percent expect and want to attend college and graduate school. While similar ambitions may have been held by earlier generations, the reality is that most of the parents of these young women did not advance beyond high school (see Table 9.2). Results from our focus groups suggest that the girls' educational ambition is driven both by parental aspirations and by teens wanting to be more successful than their parents. Many Latinas are keenly aware of the fact that their parents have to work extremely hard, often juggling multiple jobs, and that they often do not enjoy what they do. Latina adolescents appear determined to create a different reality for themselves and their own families. As one explained, "They do it because they have to . . . they don't like what they do. . . . I don't want to be stuck at something and then hate it as much as they do." Another said, "We don't want to have to get up in the morning and know that we're going to a job that we don't like. Something we're stuck with. . . . That's my biggest fear."

TABLE 9.3
Future Career Expectations

Expectations of Financial Support	%
Support both self and family	86
Support self only	12
Others will support me	2

Expectations of Job Status	%
Full-time job	79
Part-time job	20
No job	1

Job Expectations after Children	%
Work after children	37
Quit temporarily after children	52
Quit permanently after children	1
Not planning to have children	6

Following their education, the girls expect to be employed as adults. As Table 9.3 illustrates, 98 percent said they expected to support themselves or themselves and their families, and most believe that they will hold full-time jobs. If they have children, the majority expect to leave work while they are raising them. They feel that their role as mothers and the role of family in general are of high importance; however, like most young women, they feel their break from work will be only temporary. As one girl explained, "I kind of have this thing about taking care of my kids when they're young, and seeing them kind of grow up and grow accustomed to me. So I'll probably be out of work for a while with my kids, and then I'll get back to work."

The career expectations of the Latina adolescents in this sample are consistent with their educational ambitions. When we asked them, using an open-ended question, to specify the careers or jobs they would like as adults, the majority—more than 70 percent—listed professional careers. The most popular choices included medicine (most often listed), education, law, and government. Another 7 percent wanted careers in science, technology, or engineering. Only 23 percent listed nonprofessional careers (e.g., fashion, entertainment, and cosmetology). This information is in direct contrast to the jobs held by their parents, approximately 70 percent of whom were in nonprofessional occupations.

In addition to this open-ended question, we asked these young women directly about their interest in fifteen specific careers using a 5-point scale

(1 = definitely not interested to 5 = extremely interested). As expected, overall interest levels for all listed careers were higher when direct questioning was used. As Table 9.4 illustrates, the young women did not express high levels of interest in management careers, even when prompted with a question that forced them to indicate interested they were in a certain a career choice.[4] Indeed, many appeared to hold quite negative feelings about business/management as a career path. Our focus groups with Latina adolescents suggested that their aversion may in part be connected to their impressions of "big" business based on their parents' experiences of inequality and injustice from management, as well as their impression that big business does little to contribute to positive social change. One girl commented, "Most businesses are about money, tax, profits, and everything. [People in business] usually have a lot of power over other people, and they do a lot of (bad) stuff."

In contrast, entrepreneurship ("starting a business," which was listed rarely as a response to the open-ended question) received the highest rating of *all* careers given on the survey when the girls were asked directly, with just under half rating themselves as extremely or somewhat interested. We also noted this interest in focus group discussions, in which Latinas, when prompted, often expressed highly positive feelings about being entrepreneurs, especially in terms of independence and control. In other words, while starting a business did not come readily to mind as a career choice, unlike other careers such as being a doctor or lawyer, it was of

TABLE 9.4
Top Career Choices

Career Choice	Unprompted (open-ended question) (% listings as free choice)	Prompted (direct question) (% somewhat or extremely interested
Business (all)	6.1%	n/a
Manager	2.7%	27.9%
Starting/owning own business	0.6%	48.9%
Science/technical/engineering (all)	7.2%	n/a
Computers	5.1%	39.0%
Other professional (all)	61.0%	n/a
Medical/health care	22.7%	48.6%
Lawyer	9.2%	35.8%
Teacher	12.5%	34.7%
Art/graphic design	6.1%	38.9%
Nonprofessional (all)	23.4%	n/a
Cosmetology	4.5%	n/a
Fashion	2.9%	n/a
Police/fire/etc.	3.5%	n/a

TABLE 9.5
Career Goals

Top personal goals for Latinas in their careers	Percent rating goal as one of three most important
Having enough time for family/friends	60
Enjoying what I do	57
Making lots of money	50
Helping others	35
Being respected	35

great interest when brought up as an option. As one girl noted, "And actually when you have your own business, you feel stronger . . . you know?"

Motivations Related to Family and Community

To explore the motivations behind these career or job choices, we asked the girls to rate the personal importance of different job characteristics and career goals (1 = not at all important to 5 = extremely important). Next we asked them to choose the three most important characteristics and goals from the full list (see Table 9.5). The young women in our sample felt that respect for others and job enjoyment were highly desirable in a future job. Most important, however, was a career that allowed them to have time with friends and family. Financial security was also seen as very important but was balanced by a strong belief in the value and importance of making a positive contribution to their communities. Helping others in a career was also rated highly. The desire for a career in which one could be financially secure and at the same time help others likely explains the girls' strong interest in careers like medicine, as well as their preferences for the types of professional jobs not typically seen in their own families.

Consistent with these results, we found that the Latinas in our focus groups were passionate in their ambitions to escape what they perceived as the dead-end jobs held by their parents. In addition, they expressed strong desires to make things better not just for themselves but also for their families and their communities. In short, these Latina girls value professional and financial success as well as helping others, and they feel that these goals are compatible. As one girl explained:

> My family hasn't always had a lot of money, and I always see them struggling for money. And obviously people need money to live, to live well. And

it's like if you don't have money, you're always going to be worried about the next thing, like how you're going to get your money to live. It's like money is important, but it's not the most important thing. Of course family is more important.

Another said, "My hope is to be a lawyer . . . because I've always wanted to help people. And it's like I saw that as a way of helping other people . . . but I'm only going to have specific cases, like immigrant cases."

Self-Perceptions of Skills

In addition to exploring motivations behind career choices, we also examined self-confidence in different areas by asking these young girls to rate themselves in relation to their school peers on their abilities in a number of skill areas related to leadership in management.[5] Comparing themselves with their classmates, Latina adolescents rated themselves as relatively strong in areas such as being a good listener, working in teams, and making decisions and relatively weak in working with numbers, solving problems, and overall leadership. Latinas also expressed relatively lower levels of confidence in their verbal and written communication skills. And, when we asked about their favorite and least favorite school subjects, mathematics was given as the least favorite by almost half of the Latinas in our sample (46 percent), with English/literature being the most popular subject area (24 percent), followed by a mix of areas.

As expected, we found a strong connection between self-ratings on areas seen as important for success in management and interest in management or entrepreneurship as a career (see Wilson, Marlino, and Kickul 2004 for additional analysis on this topic). In other words, the girls who believed they had the necessary skills to succeed in management were more likely to be interested in a career in this area. We did not gather data that would allow us to extend this analysis to interest in other careers. However, the self-ratings given by Latina adolescents on working with numbers and problem solving, coupled with a dislike of math as a school subject, may help to explain the low level of interest in careers in science or technology. Certainly the evidence on the development of "math phobia" among teen girls nationwide, and its negative impact on career choices in math or science, is well established and appears to be a factor for the participating girls in this study (How Schools Shortchange Girls 1995).

TABLE 9.6
Sources of Career Advice

Top Sources of Career Advice	%
Mother	60
Father	37
Teacher	42
Guidance counselor	37
Internet	77
Print media	44
School programs	43
Workplace visit	41

Sources of Career Advice

We asked girls where or from whom they would seek career information and advice by asking them to indicate sources of career information from a list of options. Mothers emerged as the most important source of personal influence, well ahead of fathers (see Table 9.6). The majority also view the media, especially the Internet, as a critical resource. We also found that teachers and guidance counselors, as well as school programs, are highly influential sources of career advice for these girls.

In addition to home- and school-based sources, girls may also use experiences through their participation in clubs, teams, or jobs to gain knowledge about different career paths and to make connections with adult workers. However, only 38 percent of the Latina girls we interviewed belonged to any clubs or teams, and only 18 percent held jobs outside their homes.

Discussion

The girls' responses provide a compelling picture of the career aspirations and motivations of Latina adolescents. Overall they have strong aspirations and goals. They want to go to college and beyond, and to pursue professional and financially lucrative careers. They are driven by a strong desire to contribute in positive ways to their communities and the world around them.

Although limited, existing studies on the career aspirations of Latina adolescents support their interest in professional careers (Phinney, Baumann, and Blanton 2001). In particular, previous research on the career choices of Latina girls (using open-ended responses) reports that their strongest career interests are in medicine and law (Reyes, Gillock, and Kobus 1999).

These results are similar to ours when the results of open-ended questions were examined; however, the use of direct questioning in our study elicited a high level of interest in entrepreneurship not captured through the use of open-ended questioning. This interest in starting and owning a business reflects a growing trend in the Latina population overall (Women of Color 2003). Our focus group research indicates that one reason for this interest is that girls see business ownership as more flexible, and hence more compatible with having children and being with family. They may also feel that the power of business ownership allows them to contribute more actively to their communities, a career motivator that has been demonstrated to be important to professional women in general (Women on Work 2004).

Previous research has demonstrated that career choices are strongly tied to feelings of self-confidence in the ability to perform well in a given task domain, or self-efficacy (Bandura et al. 2001). Research also provides evidence that gender, in general, is an important variable in understanding this relationship, such that girls who hold less traditional and more inclusive gender attitudes demonstrate higher educational achievement, greater self-efficacy, and more ambitious, nontraditional career goals (Betz and Hackett 1981; Nevill and Schlecker 1988). Results of studies examining relationships between self-esteem, gender role attitudes, and career aspirations specifically of Latina teens further corroborate these findings (Valenzuela 1993; Reyes, Gillock, and Kobus 1999). Together with our own findings, this body of work concludes that assisting Latina adolescent girls to develop their self-efficacy in a broad range of areas will encourage them to consider a wider set of educational and career choices.

Additional research on self-efficacy also suggests that the development of confidence in specific task domains is strongly affected by mastery experiences or, simply put, learning by doing (Bandura 1992). Hence, a lack of access or opportunity to experience in the workplace may contribute to lower feelings of self-efficacy and to less ambitious career goals. As our results indicate, access to such mastery experiences outside of school and home may be limited for some Latina adolescents. Results from the Latino Home-School Research Project help explain this finding (Gallimore, Goldenburg, and Reese, ongoing study, accessed September 2004). In this study, some parents actively discouraged outside activities for their daughters because of cultural norms or based on the hazards inherent in living in urban neighborhoods. In the same study, the presence of fewer extracurricular activities among teens was correlated with lower success rates in school. Given the importance of learning by doing, the lack of opportunity for engaging in extracurricular activities may contribute to lower self-efficacy and lessened career aspirations.

Not surprisingly, mothers emerged as one of the key sources of career advice, supporting earlier research that demonstrates the power that Latina mothers have over their daughters' education and career choices (Tinajero, Gonzales, and Dick 1991). However, the same research indicates that many mothers, due to their own gender stereotypes, may discourage their daughters from their professional ambitions. Moreover, many Latina mothers, the majority of whom hold nonprofessional jobs, may not know how to access information on the professions aspired to by their daughters (Behnke, Piercy, and Diversi 2004).

In addition to directly offering career advice, parents also exert influence over the career choices of their daughters indirectly, through their presence as role models. Teen girls interested in professional careers also seek role models outside their homes, most notably in female-oriented organizations and clubs. Both Girl Scouts and the YWCA, among other organizations, actively seek to provide opportunities to connect with professional women and offer professional development programs directly targeted to teen girls.[6] However, as we have discussed previously, a minority of Latina adolescents are involved in these organizations. Hence, their access to these role models and potential mentors is limited. This, too, has been tied to decreased self-efficacy among Latina adolescents (Equity and Careers 2002; Weiler 1997).

Our results are consistent with other research that finds teachers are critically important in enabling and encouraging ambitious goals among Latinas (Weiler 1997). However, teachers sometimes reinforce past stereotypes of Latinas as having low potential (Hernandez 1995). In some schools, Latinas may be routinely tracked into noncollege courses or vocational programs (Romo 1998), or they may lose the confidence in their abilities to achieve their goals as they move forward in the school system (Shortchanging Hispanic Girls 1992).

Almost half of the Latinas in our sample listed school programs as another important source of career information. How effective are these programs? Previous research has argued that school programs that are most successful in promoting educational and career achievements not only focus on academic assistance but also increase self-efficacy and self-confidence and encourage high expectations through exposure to successful professionals (Equity and Careers 2002). These are precisely the areas in which current career development programs in middle and high schools serving Latina populations can potentially strengthen their interventions (Romo 1998).

Researcher Patricia Gándara sheds further light on the factors leading to high levels of educational and career achievement. Gándara (1994) studied fifty highly successful Latino/a professionals, all of whom were from family backgrounds of poverty and little school achievement. Her study results indicated that, for this group, standardized measures purporting to assess intellectual ability did not predict career success as much as parental (especially maternal) support and encouragement, personal persistence and drive, and the opportunities afforded by high school programs. Specifically, successful Latino/as came from families in which reading and intellectual inquiry, hard work, and ambition were modeled and rewarded. In their high schools, most had been tracked into college preparatory courses, sometimes due to their own persistence and in spite of previous judgments by the educational system that they did not have college potential. This educational path in turn increased and validated their self-confidence and aspirations and exposed them to special college recruitment programs and financial aid opportunities. Gándara's research supports further the role of self-efficacy, the importance of maternal encouragement, and the potential of improved and targeted school programs.

Conclusions

We have found that many Latina adolescents expect to continue on to college and/or graduate school and to pursue financially and personally rewarding professional careers as adults. They are actively seeking more fulfilling jobs than those held by their parents. They see their mothers as key career advisers, along with the Internet and school resources.

As they look to the future, these girls hope for personal balance—careers that provide them with time for their friends and their families. While understanding the value of their own economic empowerment, they also have a strong commitment to finding opportunities that will allow them to positively contribute to their communities and the world around them. Starting their own businesses or becoming medical practitioners seems to them to be consistent with these multiple goals and are of special interest to them.

This research suggests areas in which we can better nurture these aspirations, including increasing access to role models and mentors in professional careers, and improving career development programs in middle and high schools. Equally important is the encouragement of positive self-efficacy in nontraditional domains such as mathematics and problem solving.

We, along with others, endorse the development of school-based programs that draw on social cognitive career theory (Equity and Careers 2002; Browne and Lent 1996). Key components of these programs would include school-based initiatives designed to develop the self-efficacy of girls with full consideration of the interactions of gender, culture, and ethnicity (Kerka 1998). As part of these initiatives, the skills of both educators and teens in identifying and dealing with bias and negative stereotyping must be developed. Entrance requirements for college preparatory courses should be reconsidered so that they are based not primarily on academic testing or grades but also on other student characteristics related to motivation and aspiration, and such courses should be available across all schools (Gándara 1994). Successful career guidance initiatives should provide accurate and current information on different careers, preparation, and training. Outreach efforts that draw in families and communities toward the goal of helping girls achieve must be encouraged. Role models of successful Latinas, especially those in nontraditional careers, should be provided, as well as mentors and opportunities for girls to learn by doing that might include internships or school-based collaborations with businesses. Finally, these programs must start in middle school or earlier, before math phobia and other negative trends in self-efficacy that limit girls' career choices can take hold. Through initiatives and structural changes such as these, we can better support Latina girls as they develop and pursue their educational and career aspirations.

NOTES

1. Latinas have contributed significantly as part of the economy and labor force in the United States for many years as undocumented workers. The numbers cited here reflect the documented labor force according to U.S. census data.

2. Students from schools in Massachusetts, New Hampshire, Connecticut, Illinois, California, Texas, Florida, and Tennessee participated in this study.

3. Nonprobability sampling was used in collecting these data; therefore, results cannot be seen as representative of the population.

4. Table 9.4 should be read as follows: When asked to list their career interests, 2.7 percent listed a management career first (unprompted). When asked to rate their interest in a management career on a scale of 1 to 5 (prompted), 27.9 percent rated it as a 4 (somewhat interested) or 5 (extremely interested). N/A indicates a category or career interest that was not included in the set of direct or prompted questions. The "management" category included several job titles or descriptions as sorted by the researchers.

5. The inventory of leadership skills was developed in consultation with senior executives. A full discussion can be found in Marlino and Wilson 2003.

6. For example, the Girl Scouts of the USA and the Hispanic Chamber of Commerce Foundation cosponsor the national "Bizfest," a business training and scholarship competition for Latina youth interested in entrepreneurship. These initiatives and others are described at www.girlscouts.org.

REFERENCES

Bandura, Albert. 1992. Exercise of Personal Agency through the Self-Efficacy Mechanism. In *Self-Efficacy: Thought Control of Action,* edited by Ralf Schwarzer, 3–38. Washington, DC: Hemisphere.

Bandura, Albert, Claudio Barbaranelli, Gian Vittorio Caprara, and Concetta Pastorelli. 2001. Self-Efficacy Beliefs as Shapers of Children's Aspirations and Career Trajectories. *Child Development* 72 (1): 187–206.

Behnke, Andrew, Kathleen Piercy, and Marcelo Diversi. 2004. Educational and Occupational Aspirations of Latino Youth and Their Parents. *Hispanic Journal of Behavioral Sciences* 26 (1): 16–35.

Betz, Nancy, and Gail Hackett. 1981. The Relationship of Career-Related Self-Efficacy Expectations to Perceived Career Options in College Men and Women. *Journal of Counseling Psychology* 28:399–410.

Browne, Steven, and Robert Lent. 1996. A Social Cognitive Framework for Career Choice Counseling. *Career Development Quarterly* 44 (4): 354–367.

Equity and Careers: Progress and Promise. 2002. *WEEA Digest.* WEEA Equity Resource Center at EDC, www.edc.org/WomensEquity/resource/alldigest/index .htm, September 2002.

Gallimore, Ronald, Claude Goldenberg, and Leslie Reese. Latino Home-School Research Project. UCLA/NPI, http://cultureandhealth.ucla.edu/latinohsproj/ GeneralInformation.html, September 2003.

Gándara, Patricia. 1994. Choosing Higher Education: Educationally Ambitious Chicanos and the Path to Social Mobility. *Education Policy Analysis Archives* 2 (8), http://epaa.asu.edu/epaa/v2n8.html.

Hernandez, Arthur. 1995. Do Role Models Influence Self-Efficacy and Aspirations in Mexican American At-Risk Females? *Hispanic Journal of Behavioral Sciences* 17 (2): 256–264.

How Schools Shortchange Girls. 1995. AAUW and Wellesley College Center for Research on Women, New York: Marlowe and Company.

Kerka, Sandra. 1998. Career Development and Gender, Race and Class. *ERIC Digest,* ED421641, www.eric.edu.gov.

Marlino, Deborah, and Fiona Wilson. 2003. *Teen Girls on Business: Are They Being Empowered?* Simmons School of Management and The Committee of 200, www.simmons.edu/som.

Nevill, Dorothy, and Debra Schlecker. 1988. The Relation of Self-Efficacy to Willingness to Engage in Traditional/Non-Traditional Career Activities. *Psychology of Women Quarterly* 12 (1): 91–98.

Phinney, Jean, Kathleen Baumann, and Shanika Blanton. 2001. Life Goals and Attributions for Expected Outcomes among Adolescents from Five Ethnic Groups. *Hispanic Journal of Behavioral Sciences* 23 (4): 363–377.

Reyes, Olga, Karen Gillock, and Kimberly Kobus. 1999. Career Aspirations of Urban, Mexican American Adolescent Females. *Hispanic Journal of Behavioral Sciences* 21 (3): 366–382.

Romo, Harriett. 1998. Latina High School Leaving: Some Practical Solutions. *ERIC Digest,* ED423096, www.eric.edu.gov.

Shortchanging Hispanic Girls: An Analysis of Hispanic Girls in the Greenberg-Lake Survey of Self-Esteem, Education and Career Aspirations among Adolescent Boys and Girls in the United States. 1992. Academy for Educational Development. *ERIC Digest,* ED387557, www.eric.edu.gov.

Tinajero, Josefina, M. Gonzales, and F. Dick. 1991. Raising Career Aspirations of Hispanic Girls. *Fastback 320.* Bloomington, IN: Phi Delta Kappa Educational Foundation, at www.eric.edu.gov.

U.S. Census Bureau Current Population Survey. 2002. U.S. Census Bureau, Ethnic and Hispanic Statistics Branch, Population Division, http://www.census.gov/population/socdemo/hispanic.

U.S. Census Bureau Statistical Abstract of the United States. 2001. U.S. Census Bureau, http://www.census.gov/prod/2002pubs.

Valenzuela, Angela. 1993. Liberal Gender Roles and Academic Achievement among Mexican-Origin Adolescents in Two Houston Inner-City Catholic Schools. *Hispanic Journal of Behavioral Sciences* 15 (3): 310–323.

Weiler, Jeanne. 1997. Career Development for African-American and Latina Females. *ERIC Digest,* ED410369, www.eric.edu.gov.

Wilson, Fiona, Deborah Marlino, and Jill Kickul. 2004. Our Entrepreneurial Future: Examining the Diverse Attitudes and Motivations of Teens across Gender and Ethnic Identity. *Journal of Developmental Entrepreneurship* 9 (3): 177–198.

Women of Color: Their Employment in the Private Sector. 2003. U.S. Equal Employment Opportunity Commission Report, http://www.eeoc.gov/stats/reports/womenofcolor/, July 2003.

Women on Work: Is There a Generational Divide? 2004. Simmons School of Management research note, Simmons College, www.simmons.edu/som.

Part 3

Accessing Institutional Support

Chapter 10

Latina Adolescents' Sexual Health
A Participatory Empowerment Approach

Gary W. Harper, Audrey K. Bangi,
Bernadette Sanchez, Mimi Doll,
and Ana Pedraza

Condoms Protect Your Body, Not Your Heart

Marisol was a shy fourteen-year-old Mexican American girl who came to the SHERO's sexual health program wearing tight jeans, a baggy shirt, and heavy makeup. Early on it was clear that Marisol was trying to "act tough" in front of the other participants in order to gain acceptance, often talking about how she liked to flirt and "make out" with gangbangers. She insisted that she was not yet ready to have sex but admitted she enjoyed the attention she got from these gang members. When Marisol was thinking of having sex with her boyfriend, she turned to Ana, the coordinator of the SHERO's program. Marisol's boyfriend told her that they did not need to use a condom when they had sex because "girls can't get pregnant the first time they have sex." Ana told her the facts about condoms, sexually transmitted infections, and pregnancy and also discussed the emotional aspects of having sex. She reminded Marisol that "condoms protect your body, not your heart," encouraging her to think about whether she was ready for the feelings she may experience after having sex. After this conversation, Marisol decided that she needed more time. It was nearly two years after this conversation that Marisol decided to have sex, and again she talked with Ana about her motivations and appropriate forms of protection beforehand. Later Marisol shared that she was glad she waited to have sex because she was more mature and ready to handle the physical and emotional aspects of being sexually active.

Marisol went from being a shy but "tough-acting" young woman to one who is not embarrassed to talk about sex and to access the resources that are needed to remain sexually healthy. The SHERO's program was a safe and nonjudgmental place to talk openly with other young Latina women about her body, her sexuality, and her life. After graduating from the program, Marisol volunteered with the group by helping with outreach and special projects, and even cofacilitated some of the sessions. Although she is now a certified phlebotomist and working her way through college, Marisol continues to volunteer with the SHERO's program. Known affectionately in her neighborhood as the "Project VIDA girl," she has become an advocate of sexual health for other young Latina women by distributing condoms to those who are too embarrassed to get them on their own.

The Sexual Health Needs of Latina Adolescents

The majority of sexual health interventions for adolescents in general, and young Latinas in particular, have taken a deficit approach. In general, they have failed to utilize a health promotion philosophy that capitalizes on young Latinas' individual and cultural strengths. For example, interventions have emphasized the negative consequences of sexual activity (e.g., disease acquisition), the relationship between sexual risk and other risk behaviors (e.g., drug use), and the consequences of having limited knowledge about sexual health knowledge (Anaya, Cantwell, and Rotheram-Borus, 2003; Rew, Chambers, and Kulkarni, 2002). Unfortunately, most interventions have neglected to address how the strengths of young women and Latino/a culture may promote sexual health.

Culturally distinct constructs such as *marianismo and machismo* (female and male gender roles) and *familismo* frequently have been studied in terms of how they lead to risk instead of how they advance health (Baumeister, Flores, and Marin, 1995; Gomez and Marin, 1996). Rather than attending only to the negative or risky aspects of culture, it is imperative to recognize that Latino/a culture possesses strengths that interventionists can utilize in promoting sexual health. In addition, researchers, interventionists, and young women themselves have called for a reconceptualization of *marianismo* and *machismo* (Beattie, 2002; Koss, 1997; Ortiz-Torres, Serrano-Garcia, and Torres-Burgos, 2000; Torres, Solberg, and Carlstrom, 2002). They have noted that researchers must update conceptualizations of male and female gender roles to reflect the current culture and context and must recognize that gender roles are multifaceted constructs. In addition, conceptualizations of gender roles are further complicated by cultural issues such as migration and urbanization.

Both young women and health interventionists have the power to create personal, community, and cultural narratives that depart from traditional values that may have oppressed and limited Latina female adolescents' capacity to promote their own health (Harper et al., 2004; Koss, 1997; Ortiz-Torres, Serrano-Garcia, and Torres-Burgos, 2000). It is not acceptable to merely acknowledge inequalities as part of a cultural belief system and work to bolster young women's resilience in the face of these inequities (Ortiz-Torres, Serrano-Garcia, and Torres-Burgos, 2000). Sexual health educators bear a responsibility to challenge and change these power imbalances in an effort to truly promote young women's health and well-being. One way to accomplish this is to employ a participatory empowerment approach when developing interventions. By incorporating the voices and lived experiences of Latina adolescents regarding their familial, peer, and sexual relationships, these endeavors will be more effective (Friere, 1970; McQuiston, Choi-Hevel, and Clawson, 2001; Wallerstein, 1992).

The Evolution of the SHERO's Program

The sexual health promotion program that we describe in this chapter was tailored to the needs of Latina adolescents through a series of empowerment and participatory evaluation activities. The evaluation work was conducted by a collaborative team of staff members from a community-based HIV/AID service organization (Project VIDA) and evaluators from a local university (DePaul University). Project VIDA entered this partnership in order to improve and expand its HIV prevention program for Latina adolescents that had existed for two years. The SHERO's (female version of "heroes") program was created in 1995 in response to increasing rates of unplanned pregnancy, HIV, and other sexually transmitted infections (STIs). The community recognized the need to offer sexual health promotion services to young Latina women. The program included two primary components: (1) community outreach aimed at providing sexual health information and supplies (e.g., condoms) to young women in their community and social settings, and (2) a group-based HIV prevention intervention focused on HIV/AIDS knowledge and risk reduction skills training. A young Mexican American woman served as the group facilitator, and community speakers from various agencies related to sexual and reproductive health presented the majority of the information to the participants.

In the first years of the collaboration, we did a process evaluation to improve our understanding of the sexual health needs of Latina adolescents in the community. We explored the sociocultural and contextual factors that impact these young women's sexual decision making and behavior. We then made programmatic changes and did an outcome evaluation to obtain formal data regarding the impact of the program on participants' knowledge, attitudes, and behaviors.

Theoretical Foundations

The program evaluation and development activities were based on three theoretical foundations: empowerment evaluation, participatory action research (PAR), and narrative ethnography. Empowerment evaluation and PAR are particularly effective when working with groups that have experienced oppression and marginalization. This is because they not only give community members an active voice in the evaluation and research process but also offer agencies new skills and resources that can enhance and improve their future programs (Suarez-Balcazar and Harper, 2003). In the current project, the DePaul evaluators became a resource for Project VIDA by sharing their evaluation skills and assisting the agency to develop their own systems of self-evaluation (Fetterman, 1996; Zimmerman, 2000). Project VIDA, on the other hand, provided knowledge and experience in working with community members, which was invaluable in ensuring that the needs of Latina adolescents were met.

Further, during the process evaluation more than 100 Mexican American female adolescents from the community served by Project VIDA participated in a range of formal evaluation and feedback activities including focus groups, individuals interviews, and satisfaction surveys. These young women also spoke with members of our collaborative team to enhance our understanding of their sexuality and their everyday lives. This interaction helped us develop methods and measures that would be most relevant for young women in their neighborhood.

We chose to incorporate a narrative ethnographic approach, since it serves to empower oppressed groups within society, such as Latina adolescents, and gives voice to the lived stories and narratives of these populations (Harper et al., 2004; Mankowski and Rappaport, 2000; Rappaport,

2000). Throughout the project, we worked collectively with Latina adolescents to reveal the narratives and stories that were present at multiple systemic levels, including the individual, agency, and neighborhood or community. The team used this information to modify the SHERO's program so that it would help young women recognize the range of community and cultural narratives that serve as barriers to sexual self-protection (e.g., gender-specific stereotypes and norms related to sexual activity) and assist them in creating new empowering narratives that promote personal strength and sexual health.

The "Modified" SHERO's Program

We modified several aspects of the SHERO's intervention based on the information gained from the formal process evaluation activities (e.g., the general theoretical orientation of the intervention, the format of the sessions, and the specific content of each of the sessions). In addition, information gained from interactions between members of the collaborative team and the participants was critical to incorporating the voices of these young women into the new program. Several youths shared their impressions regarding the positive and negative aspects of the sessions, speakers, and activities and offered advice about ways they could be improved. Young women whose friends did not attend all the sessions also shared reasons for their absence that included personal scheduling conflicts, family responsibilities, or disinterest in the program and/or activities.

The new content included a greater focus on the major issues that were impacting the sexual health of Latina adolescents in the community such as teen pregnancy, having sexual relationships with older men, and gang affiliation. We also created more time in the group for participants to talk about their understanding and awareness of their bodies, with a specific focus on sexual health awareness and promotion. Specific sessions were devoted to sexual and reproductive health, and all sessions emphasized positive and responsible sexuality for those who chose to be sexually active.

Structure and Content of the SHERO's Program

The modified SHERO's intervention is a nine-week group-based sexual health promotion program that provides Latina female adolescents between the ages of twelve and twenty-one with information, resources, and coping skills to help them manage environmental, interpersonal, and individual-level stressors that place them at risk for negative sexual health outcomes. Each of the weekly sessions includes activities and exercises that assist the participants in recognizing the range of community and cultural narratives that serve as barriers to health promotion and self-protection (e.g., gender-specific stereotypes and norms related to dating and sexual activity). The program also explores other sociocultural and environmental influences on sexual activity.

Culturally Specific Elements of the SHERO's Program

To promote empowerment and sexual health, some aspects of the SHERO's intervention were designed to challenge cultural norms and beliefs related to heterosexual interactions and sexuality. Thus, the intervention is aligned with the concept of "subverting culture" presented by Ortiz-Torres, Serrano-Garcia, and Torres-Burgos (2000). These authors assert that culture should not be used as a vehicle for the further oppression of women and state that HIV risk reduction interventions for Latina women must include a critical examination of the aspects of culture that both promote and impede prevention efforts. The SHERO's program challenges gender-based inequalities and double standards; it facilitates changes in social norms and beliefs that affect sexual risk behaviors, instead of idealizing existing oppressive cultural norms. Our belief is that a positive and honest account of sexuality will increase the likelihood that participants will make healthy choices. In the following sections we describe several central cultural components of the program that address the promotion of sexual health, with an emphasis on creating new healthy stories and narratives. Table 10.1 includes samples of program activities related to these components.

Sexual and Reproductive Health

Although the topic of menstruation is frequently discussed between Latina mothers and their adolescent daughters, sexual issues such as contraception, conception, and sexual/reproductive anatomy are often ignored (Koss and Vargas, 1999). Since Latina females often receive the cultural message that they are to be inexperienced in sexual matters and should

TABLE 10.1
The SHERO's Sexual Health Promotion Program

Cultural elements	Additional sample activities
Sexual/reproductive health	*Condom lineup:* Participants place cards with various steps to condom use in the most appropriate order and discuss the complexity of condom use.
Sexual pleasure	*Personal sexual risk assessment:* Participants explore the potential consequences of various sexual activities and then conduct an individualized sexual risk assessment.
	Responsibility for actions: Participants brainstorm ways to introduce condom use to sexual partners that would not be seen as "ruining the mood" (e.g., presenting condoms as a gift after a romantic dinner).
Role of religion and pregnancy	*Pregnancy reality:* Activity detailing the costs and benefits of teen pregnancy. Youth are given a set amount of money to plan for a new baby and discuss the financial, physical, emotional, and social realities of being a teen mother.
Sexual assertiveness and communication	*T.A.L.K.:* Participants are encouraged to apply communication and negotiation skills for protective sexual health behaviors related to (*T*iming, *A*ssertiveness, *L*ocation, *K*nowing what to say) through interactive role-plays and discussion.
Gang culture and affiliation	*Gang Rituals:* Interactive discussion about the impact of gang affiliation (e.g., gang rituals) on sexual health and well-being.

suppress desires to be sexual, discussions about the physical maturation of their bodies and the emergence of sexual feelings as a normal part of their development are either nonexistent or fairly limited (Holland et al., 1994). As strongly as Latino culture promotes young women to be virgins when they marry, such standards differ greatly from those ascribed to young men. Latino males are expected to engage in premarital sex, be more sexually experienced than their female partners, and have multiple sex partners (Marin, 1996).

Group discussions during the initial sessions of the SHERO's program revealed that several young women had family and friends who became pregnant during their teenage years. Although these interactions alerted the young women to the challenges associated with early parenthood, most shared that their family members never discussed these early pregnancies with them. In fact, these youth mentioned that strict parental rules about dating and relationships limited dialogue about sex and childbearing, with these topics being reserved for discussions about marriage and life after a college degree was earned.

Given the components of this traditional narrative, we integrated activities designed to increase knowledge of one's body in order to maintain sexual and reproductive health. This was a distinct departure from an intervention that focused strictly on disease prevention. Thus, we incorporated new messages that awareness about one's body and the changes related to physical maturation were not shameful but instead signaled the importance of caring about health. The new narrative also provided the language to communicate with health care professionals or community agencies about signs of infection or other medical concerns.

Sexual Pleasure

The theme of sexual pleasure is influenced by how cultures construct gender roles. *Marianismo* incorporates suffering as a part of the female identity and maintains that sex is solely a function of the sacrament of marriage—a source of pleasure for males. Women are expected to be forgiving of their male partner's sexual sins (e.g., promiscuity or unfaithfulness), subservient, and submissive (Koss and Vargas, 1999; Gomez and Marin, 1996). *Machismo,* on the other hand, dictates the expression of manhood via behaving strongly, demonstrating sexual prowess, and asserting authority over women (Marin, 1996).

These cultural factors are not only central to the meanings placed on womanhood and manhood but also define heterosexual relationships. We promoted a new narrative that acknowledged the limitations of the traditional gender roles and included an awareness of young women's healthy sexuality. Participants were also able to associate sex with the physical expression of love and pleasure, and realize that they could exercise a choice in its expression in order for sex to be a mutually positive experience.

Role of Religion and Pregnancy

Religious themes consistent with Catholicism, whose teachings affect the vast majority of participants in our program, also influence gender expectations regarding sexual decisions and behaviors. Stemming from the symbolism embodied by the Virgin of Guadalupe, females often receive mixed messages regarding sexual practices; motherhood is held at high esteem because it promotes new life, but chastity is regarded as honorable (Rodriguez, 1994). Thus, in many Latino communities, condom use is not advocated, since it prevents the possibility of bearing children and impacts the expectation for motherhood (Unger and Molina, 1999).

The new narrative emphasized the development of a social support network open to a diversity of views and also created space for girls to think critically about whether they have received mixed messages based in religious teachings. This new narrative reinforced the idea that knowledge about and use of condoms do not need to tarnish a young woman's reputation; it shows she cares about protecting her own health and the health of others. The program also increased the young women's awareness about the impact of their personal choices about sex and safer sex practices on their futures. The consideration of childbearing as a solution to problems at home or as an attempt to secure a long-term relationship with a boyfriend was discussed in light of the responsibilities of teenage motherhood and its impact on future goals (e.g., educational).

Sexual Assertiveness and Communication

Themes related to sexual silence influence a Latina woman's comfort discussing sexual issues with her male partner (Marin, Gomez, and Hearst, 1993). For instance, a Latina adolescent may be reluctant to initiate a discussion about safer sex because of possible rejection by her partner and/ or fear of negative perceptions about her character due to her knowledge about sex. Difficulty communicating with sexual partners may also be exacerbated in sexual relationships with older male partners. The imbalanced power differential in such relationships presents risks of sexual coercion, sexual exploitation, and risky sexual behaviors (Harper et al., 2002; Miller, Clark, and Moore, 1997).

In the revised intervention, we identified common communication challenges in sexual relationships and aimed to strengthen participants' problem-solving skills and use of assertive communication. During the initial cycles of the SHERO's intervention, participants were asked to share their personal perspectives about safer sex in different situations. Since many participants were not comfortable identifying difficulties in their own interactions with male partners and did not want to give the impression that they were either sexually *inexperienced* or sexually *experienced,* this activity was usually met with silence. Thus, we created photographs of Mexican American couples that were taken in the surrounding neighborhood and showed them as stimuli for stories and discussions regarding communication difficulties experienced by romantic couples. Participants then evaluated the role each partner played in a relationship and discussed difficulties that may arise when significant age differences exist between partners.

Another new narrative related to assertiveness evolved during the course of modifying a session on role models and self-esteem. During the initial activity, we asked participants to describe unique qualities about various goddesses based on stories and pictures that made them positive female role models. In conversations with the young women, they remarked that they were unable to relate to the stories of the goddesses because they either were mythical figures from cultures with which they were not familiar or were from time periods that were too distant to relate to.

As a result of this feedback, we modified the session to ask participants about their personal definitions of a goddess or a positive female role model. We then asked who in their lives fit the criteria they mentioned. Participants were also asked to identify which females they admired in the media and why. The young women realized that they could embody the admirable qualities of their identified role models (e.g., mothers, aunts, grandmothers) by making their needs known to others, especially in sexual situations (e.g., asking partners about their sexual histories). Youth also discussed ways that they can shift the balance of power in relationships by employing the strategies used by their role models. By discussing safer sex issues with their partners, they viewed themselves as committed and responsible for their own health, as well as the health of their partner.

Gang Culture and Affiliation

In many impoverished communities, gang affiliation offers an array of perceived benefits to young women, such as a sense of belonging, status, power, control, identity, guidance, excitement, and protection (Calabrese and Noboa, 1995; Joe and Chesney-Lind, 1995; Molidor, 1996). Gangs also bring increased risk for negative health outcomes, as gang involvement among female adolescents has been associated with increased rates of participation in multiple risk behaviors, including sexual risk behaviors (Harper and Robinson, 1999). These realities about gangs were closely tied to the environment within which many of the youth in the SHERO's program live. Gang lines clearly mark boundaries of the surrounding neighborhoods and represent limitations on young women's selection of potential sexual partners, and on their futures more generally. The old narratives involved a perceived elevated status associated with gang affiliation, either as a gang member or as a dating/sexual partner of a male gang member. Some young women felt that the only way they could gain respect and love was through dating a gang member. They often did not think about their own personal safety concerns or about the negative aspects of such affiliations.

New narratives incorporated knowledge about the risks to personal safety and sexual health associated with being a gang member, being in a romantic relationship with a male gang member, and the dangers of gang initiation rituals. We shared the HIV risks associated with gang fights where exposure to open wounds and blood was common. One particular story involved a ritual known as "pulling a train," whereby gang members stand in line to successively have sex with one female. As one male pledge moved up in the line, he learned that his younger sister was the female with whom everyone was having sex. By understanding the personal behavioral and emotional risks posed by different situations, participants were more likely to live up to their best intentions to behave safely and, more important, to enact safer behaviors.

Evaluating the Impact of the SHERO's Program

To test the effectiveness of the SHERO's program, we conducted an outcome evaluation using a quasi-experimental pretest-posttest control group research design. Since it would not be practical to randomize young women into different conditions, we chose to use a quasi-experimental design. Latina adolescents in the community where the SHERO's program was developed would receive the full nine-week SHERO's program, and young women in a neighboring community would receive a standard sexual risk reduction curriculum often used in school-based programs. The decision not to randomly assign participants to programs was also influenced by the young women who had participated in the process evaluation, as they raised concerns about splitting up young women who came to the program with their friends (this would likely occur with randomization). They were also instrumental in deciding to offer a minimal treatment comparison condition as opposed to a no-treatment control so that all adolescents would receive some type of service.

We recruited Mexican American female adolescents between the ages of twelve and twenty-one through street outreach, school and community agency outreach, and peer networks from two neighboring, sociodemographically similar communities. A total of 183 young women participated in the SHERO's program, and 199 participated in the minimal treatment comparison condition. The two neighborhoods combined make up the largest Mexican community in the midwestern United States and the largest urban Mexican community after East Los Angeles (Pugh, 1997). With regard to employment, community members are concentrated in lower-skilled occupations, with 47 percent holding jobs as operators, fabricators, and laborers and only 6.4 percent employed in managerial and professional positions (Casuso and Camacho, 1995). According to the Chicago Police Department's biennial report for 1999 and 2000, out of the total number of crimes committed in 2000 within the district that encompasses both neighborhoods, 67 percent were property crimes and 32 percent were violent crimes. Young women from these two communities do not interact often due to gang lines separating the communities.

Most of the youth in this evaluation were fifteen years old and had completed ninth grade at the time of their participation in the evaluation. Furthermore, more than 90 percent of the participants lived with their parents or a family member, currently attended school, and were Catholic. Most participants also indicated that they spoke English and Spanish. With regard to generational status and acculturation type, more than 65 percent considered themselves to be second-generation Mexican Americans who identified strongly with both Mexican and American cultures.

We collected information for the evaluation from participants at three time points: pretest, posttest, and two-month follow-up. The posttest occurred at the end of the nine-session program for the participants in the SHERO's condition and at the same time for the participants in the comparison condition. Our primary method of assessing the outcomes of the intervention was self-report questionnaires completed by the adolescents. We measured behavioral factors such as the number of vaginal sex partners, condom carrying, and intentions to abstain from having sex. In addition, we measured contextual/ecological factors, including attitudes toward condoms, peer norms, and beliefs about sexual assault. Finally, we measured AIDS knowledge and STI knowledge. All participants in this evaluation were compensated for their time.

We found significant results on a variety of contextual/ecological, knowledge, and behavioral outcome measures. Overall, there was a significant difference in AIDS knowledge scores across the three time points, which improved for participants in SHERO's but remained the same for those in the comparison group. With regard to STI knowledge, scores increased significantly over time for SHERO's participants compared with nonparticipants. The program also had a positive influence on attitudes toward condoms, particularly at posttest, when participants in the SHERO's program reported more positive attitudes than those in the comparison group. Peer norms about condoms and sexual relationships were also positively impacted, particularly at posttest, when participants in the intervention group reported that their peers had more positive attitudes about condoms than the peers of adolescents in the comparison group. Such findings among SHERO's participants may be impacted by their peers who attended program sessions. At posttest, most (64 percent) of the intervention group participants indicated that they always came to the intervention sessions with friends.

With regard to beliefs about sexual assault, we found that participants changed their perceptions of sexual interactions that involve forced sex/ sexual assault. The young women in SHERO's were significantly less likely than those in the comparison group to view forced sex as justified when a woman "leads a man on" or when she has engaged in "token refusal" of sexual intercourse (i.e., indicating "no" when meaning "yes"). These results are particularly noteworthy because they indicate that SHERO's influenced participants' views that forced sexual intercourse is never justified. Participants also believed that a woman should not feel obligated to satisfy a man in circumstances in which she is believed to have "led him on."

Among behavioral outcomes, we found that the SHERO's participants were more likely than those in the comparison group to express an intention to abstain from having sex at posttest. There was also a trend in the difference between the two groups at the two-month follow-up on the number of times they had vaginal sex during the past two months, with the comparison group reporting more sex partners than the SHERO's participants. SHERO's participants were also more likely to carry condoms at posttest.

Conclusion

By working together to reveal the various narratives and stories that were present in the individuals, agency, and community, we all came to develop respectful and mutually beneficial relationships and to create a culturally, developmentally, and linguistically appropriate SHERO's sexual health promotion program. The young women who were involved in this project learned how to protect themselves from unplanned pregnancy and infection with STIs, including HIV. They critically examined many culturally sensitive issues and have been empowered with new skills and viewpoints that will assist them in confronting multiple environmental and relational stressors. They also developed new social support networks with other young women with whom to share similar life experiences and narratives and to help reinforce the new skills and knowledge. Many of the Latina participants in the program expressed their excitement about being able to play an active part in the shaping of the sexual health promotion program. These young women have expressed an increased sense of empowerment and fulfillment, since they were able to be active participants in a social change effort in their own community.

REFERENCES

Anaya, Henry D., Cantwell, S., and Rotheram-Borus, M. 2003. Sexual risk behaviors among adolescents. In *Preventing youth problems,* ed. Anthony Biglan, Margaret C. Wang, and Herbert J. Walberg, 113–143. New York: Kluwer Academic/Plenum.

Baumeister, Lisa M., Flores, E., and Marin, B. 1995. Sex information given to Latina adolescents by parents. *Health Education Research* 10 (2): 233–239.

Beattie, Peter M. 2002. Beyond machismos: Recent examinations of masculinities in Latin America. *Men and Masculinities* 4 (3): 303–308.

Calabrese, Raymond L., and Julio Noboa. 1995. The choice for gang membership by Mexican-American adolescents. *High School Journal* 78 (4): 226–235.

Casuso, Jorge, and Eduardo Camacho. 1995. Latino Chicago. In *Ethnic Chicago: A multicultural portrait,* ed. Melvin G. Holli and Peter D. Jones, 346–377. Grand Rapids, MI: Eerdmans.

Fetterman, David M. 1996. Empowerment evaluation: An introduction to theory and practice. In *Empowerment evaluation: Knowledge and tools for self-assessment and accountability,* ed. David M. Fetterman, S. J. Kaftarian, and A. Wandersman, 3–48. Thousand Oaks, CA: Sage.

Friere, Paulo. 1970. *Pedagogy of the oppressed.* New York: Seabury Press.

Gomez, Cynthia A., and Barbara V. Marin. 1996. Gender, culture, and power: Barriers to HIV-prevention strategies for women. *Journal of Sex Research* 33:355–362.

Harper, Gary W., Doll, M., Bangi, A. K., and Contreras, R. 2002. Female adolescents and older male sex partners: HIV-associated risk. *Journal of Adolescent Health* 19:1–2.

Harper, Gary W., Lardon, C., Rappaport, J., Bangi, A. K., Contreras, R., and Pedraza, A. 2004. Community narratives: The use of narrative ethnography in participatory community research. In *Participatory community research: Theories and methods in action,* ed. Leonard A. Jason, C. Keys, Y. Suarez-Balcazar, R. R. Taylor, M. Davis, J. Durlak, and D. Isenberg, 199–217. Washington, DC: American Psychological Association.

Harper, Gary W., and Lavome Robinson. 1999. Pathways to risk among inner-city African-American adolescent females: The influence of gang affiliation. *American Journal of Community Psychology* 27 (3): 383–404.

Holland, Janet, Ramazanoglu, C., Sharpe, S., and Thomson, R. 1994. Achieving masculine sexuality: Young men's strategies for managing vulnerability. In *AIDS: Setting a feminist agenda* ed. Lesley Doyal, J. Naidoo, and T. Wilton, 122–148. London: Taylor and Francis.

Joe, Karen A., and Meda Chesney-Lind. 1995. Just every mother's angel: An analysis of gender and ethnic variations in young gang membership. *Gender and Society* 9 (4): 408–431.

Koss, Joan D. 1997. The Maria paradox: How Latinas can merge Old World traditions with New World self esteem. *Cultural Diversity and Mental Health* 3 (2): 156–157.

Koss, Joan D., and Luis A. Vargas. 1999. *Working with Latino youth: Culture, development, and context.* San Francisco: Jossey-Bass.

Mankowski, Eric S., and Julian Rappaport. 2000. Narrative concepts and analysis in spiritually-based communities. *Journal of Community Psychology* 28 (5): 479–493.

Marin, Barbara V. 1996. Cultural issues in HIV prevention for Latinos: Should we try to change gender roles? In *Understanding and preventing HIV risk behavior: Safer sex and drug use,* ed. Stuart Oskamp and Suzanne C. Thompson, 157–176. Thousand Oaks, CA: Sage.

Marin, B. V., C. Gomez, and N. Hearst. 1993. Multiple heterosexual partners and condom use among Hispanics and non-Hispanic whites. *Family Planning Perspectives* 25:170–174.

McQuiston, C., S. Choi-Hevel, and M. Clawson. 2001. Protegiendo nuestra comunidad: Empowerment participatory education for HIV prevention. *Journal of Transcultural Nursing* 12 (4): 275–283.

Miller, K. S., L. F. Clark, and J. S. Moore. 1997. Sexual initiation with older partners and subsequent HIV risk behavior among female adolescents. *Family Planning Perspectives* 29 (5): 212–214.

Molidor, Christian E. 1996. Female gang members: A profile of aggression and victimization. *Social Work* 41 (3): 251–257.

Ortiz-Torres, B., I. Serrano-Garcia, and N. Torres-Burgos. 2000. Subverting culture: Promoting HIV/AIDS prevention among Puerto Rican and Dominican women. *American Journal of Community Psychology* 28 (6): 859–881.

Pugh, Ralph. 1997. Pilsen/Little Village. *Chicago History: The Magazine of the Chicago Historical Society* 26 (1).

Rappaport, Julian. 2000. Community narratives: Tales of terror and joy. *American Journal of Community Psychology* 28 (2): 1–24.

Rew, L., K. Chambers, and S. Kulkarni. 2002. Planning a sexual health promotion intervention with homeless adolescents. *Nursing Research* 51 (3): 168–174.

Rodriguez, Jeanette. 1994. *Our Lady of Guadalupe: Faith and empowerment among Mexican-American women.* Austin: University of Texas Press.

Suarez-Balcazar, Yolanda, and Gary W. Harper. 2003. Community-based approaches to empowerment and participatory evaluation. *Journal of Prevention and Intervention in the Community* 26 (2): 1–4.

Torres, J. B., V. S. H. Solberg, and A. H. Carlstrom. 2002. The myth of sameness among Latino men and their machismo. *American Journal of Orthopsychiatry* 72 (2): 163–181.

Unger, Jennifer B., and Gregory B. Molina. 1999. The UCLA multidimensional condom attitudes scales: Validity in a sample of low-acculturated Hispanic women. *Hispanic Journal of Behavioral Sciences* 21 (2): 199–212.

Wallerstein, Nina. 1992. Powerlessness, empowerment, and health implications for health promotion programs. *Health Promotion* 6 (3): 197–205.

Zimmerman, Marc A. 2000. Empowerment theory: Psychological, organizational, and community levels of analysis. In *Handbook of community psychology,* ed. Julian Rappaport and Edward Seidman, 43–63. New York: Plenum Press.

Chapter 11

"Cien Porciento Puertorriqueña"
(Puerto Rican, 100 Percent)

Xaé Alicia Reyes

The title of this chapter comes from a popular song played at Puerto Rican festivals, where the catchy phrase gets people to sing along and affirm their Puerto Ricanness. What is it like to be a Puerto Rican female in the continental United States? We can answer this question by drawing on the responses of Puerto Rican girls. I approached this question by using literature by Puerto Rican writers raised in the United States as a catalyst to gauge high school students' sense of identity and their reflections on whether they could or could not relate to the themes within the works. My research team and I collected data through open-ended questionnaires, journal entries, and recorded class discussions and then analyzed them through reflective dialogues (Freire 1972) between me (a college professor) and a graduate student doing an independent study project. This approach created a multilayered dialogue where the research team exchanged data collection strategies, reflections, and analyses of responses.

The Researcher's Positionality

The *puertorriqueñas* in this study share my ethnic background, although they are more than a generation younger and their socialization process has been different. A common element in our lives is the notion of coming from a country that is considered neither state nor republic. Santa Ana (2004) describes the situation of Puerto Ricans as a people who suffered as a colony of two great empires, the Spanish and the American. The political uncertainty of the island has led to a series of tensions that influence the identity construction of Puerto Ricans as they relate to the dynamics of power brokering both here and on the island. In his wonderful anthology *Boricuas* (1995), Roberto Santiago includes René Marqués's essay "The Docile Puerto Rican." The essay presents commentary on relationships between North Americans and Puerto Ricans, with descriptions of a benevolent, condescending attitude toward Puerto Ricans and an attitude that resembles servility adopted by Puerto Ricans as a response to what Marqués calls a "colonial guilt complex" (p. 157). Relatedly, Antonia Darder (Darder 1991; Darder, Torres, and Gutiérrez 1997) has explored the dynamics of silencing and voicelessness among bicultural and bilingual students. Darder attributes the loss of self-validation among bicultural students to systematic, institutionalized practices that perpetuate hegemonic relationships that marginalize them. Student journals recount watershed moments in K–12 schooling experiences where the students recognize that they can identify ethnically only with custodians and cafeteria staff. The message they internalize is that this is what they can aspire to.

Latina Identity Study: Puerto Rican Girls

For our initial research we conducted a number of interviews with groups of young Latinas in two different urban settings. We asked a total of forty high school students to tell us about their identities and to describe the influential Latinas they were familiar with. In this first stage of the study, we included all girls who considered themselves Latina. Another consideration for inclusion was the girl's interest in being part of a peer group that met regularly and her willingness to dialogue about topics and complete a survey. Initially, some students hesitated to speak about their identities because they either were born in the continental United States or were unable to communicate in Spanish. They explained that their peers would single them out for these two reasons as not being "true" Puerto Ricans. From this large group of respondents we came to focus on a smaller group for the core of our research study. The group that eventually self-selected by choosing to participate in a high school reading club included only Puerto Rican girls. Their high school is located in an urban setting with an increasing number of Latinos and West Indian students. It is on the outskirts of a major city that, like many other U.S. cities, is expanding into the suburbs.

The reading group activities evolved into a more focused analysis starting by exposing the girls to ethnic literature by Puerto Rican writers in the United States and moving to reading group activities that allowed a more focused analysis. We were motivated in this approach by the fact that the girls in this study were all of Puerto Rican descent. We considered the use of this literature as a catalyst to generate dialogues (as in Freire) that might validate the students' voices and experiences. It was an important element in fostering discussion and reflection by the high school students that could enhance and perhaps pique their interest in writing.

Why U.S. Ethnic Literature as a Catalyst?

When I began studying the education of Latinos in the United States, I realized that most of the literature written in English that I had been exposed to, even in Puerto Rico, was from mainland U.S. writers' perspectives. Literature in Spanish was presented from the perspectives of Peninsular, Latin American, and Puerto Rican writers. I saw some glimpses of the effects of migration in the writings of Julia de Burgos, José Luis González, Pedro Juan Soto, and others now included in the canon of Puerto Rican literature, but the writings of Puerto Ricans and other Latinos who grew up and were educated in the United States, such as Nicholasa Mohr, Judith Ortiz Cofer, Jesús Colón, and others, were excluded from the literary canon in Puerto Rico. Their writings, too, resonated with many of my experiences, and so their exclusion in the curriculum left me with a vacuum. I felt that these writings would also resonate with the experiences of the girls in our study and that it was important to introduce the girls to these authors.

As the project evolved, the interest and commitment of the participants became more formalized, and they became "the Latina reading group." Invitations to participate from the girls at the mediation site to their friends yielded about twenty-four members. We defined the roles of the research team by designing a survey to glean demographic data and other aspects of students' backgrounds.

Our review of curricular materials at the school noted gaps that rendered the students in our population invisible. These gaps resulted from not including any literature or history related to Puerto Ricans and not touching on issues of immigration from the island. My interest was in the potential for empowerment and strengthening of the Latina girls' understandings of their identities through reading and reflection about Latino ethnic literature in the United States. These readings could provide personal narratives that voiced some of the girls' own feelings of exclusion in the curriculum and in the social environment of the school.

A number of the participants engaged in the reading club as a social outlet, a place where they could be with friends and talk about their ethnic and cultural experiences. The school provided a space, and the librarian and the school board funded the purchase of an anthology, *Latino Writers in the U.S.: A Literary Reader.*

The number of students in the group was affected by students being pulled out of the class for ESL instruction, as well as relocation of students, yielding a final, stable sample size of twelve participants. The full group fluctuated to a maximum of twenty at any given time.

We decided to focus on the richness of reading and writing. Students were allowed to select the readings. They then participated in discussions and explored the similarities in their experiences and those of the writers or their protagonists. Additionally, graduate students involved in the project communicated with me via e-mail, at office meetings, and by phone to discuss strategies and work plans for the group. We discussed particular readings and ways of gleaning information.

Early Stages of the Study: Perspectives on Culture and Identity

Initially, I examined the Latina girls' written reflections using responses to open-ended questions (LeCompte and Preissle 1993). One of the initial survey questions students responded to asked what they thought was a "Latina/o perspective" among writers. Most of their responses indicated that this was related to what the authors chose to write about. Hence, writing about what it means to be Latino and Latino experiences is what the girls understood as the "Latino perspective."

In their discussions, the girls examined the notion of culture. What did "culture" mean to them? This query resulted in some students stating, "Latino writers write like other writers, there is no difference between people." In other words, some students have internalized the "I don't see color/difference" as the accepted behavior in their setting. Others mentioned traditions such as the "*quinceañera* party" and holiday foods. In these cases, the understandings of culture are based on what the traditional curriculum promotes—celebration of foods and music once a year in a multicultural day—as the essence of cultural identity.

In the context of the greater school population, the events, curriculum, and "props" that could enhance Latino students' involvement are a peripheral concern rather than one central to the school environment. For example, at the school there are no images reflective of Latino cultures, no topics in the curriculum or courses about the ethnic groups' histories, no events such as ethnic celebrations, concerts and plays, and no signs in Spanish. This unintentional neglect borders on exclusion of this segment of the school population.

We adopted the use of autobiographies to identify topics that were relevant to the students' backgrounds and interests. In their essays, the students spoke of their identities, the language spoken at home, who lived in their homes, and their life goals. Many stated they were Puerto Ricans, spoke Spanglish, or code switched with friends and spoke Spanish at home. Most students lived in large, extended families; fewer lived with single parents. As stated earlier, this school is located in an increasingly urban area that was once a suburb to a major city. As is typical of ethnic communities, many of those who can afford upward mobility have relocated to the suburbs. Most students would be considered to be of low- to middle-class socioeconomic status. Most of the students stated that they wished to go to college and also to have families, yet in many cases these are the very students who are placed outside of the college-bound track in the school.

Literature, Identity, and Gender

One book that students eagerly selected was Esmeralda Santiago's book *When I Was Puerto Rican.* Students questioned the use of "was" in this title and interpreted it as indicating a reluctance to stay Puerto Rican. The issue of identifying as Puerto Rican in spite of living in the United States seemed to resonate strongly with the students, in contrast with the author's position of placing her Puerto Rican identity in the past. The protagonist's mother became a working woman and was criticized by neighbors in Puerto Rico based on a gender expectation of stay-at-home motherhood venerated on the island through the first half of the twentieth century. The arrival of factories through Operation Bootstrap and the deployment of men to the U.S. war efforts beginning with World War I and migrant work in the United States and Hawaii brought about the "working woman" phenomenon. Students shared that "everybody wants mothers to work in the U.S." and "everybody thinks that Hispanic mothers are lazy and take welfare, but it isn't true. My mother works and is working for our family."

Male dominance in Latino culture is also present in Santiago's book. The gendered roles of that era, in which the male was expected to be the sole breadwinner and the mother a homemaker, did not resonate with the students in this generation. They claimed that both parents were expected to work as soon as children reached school age.

The issue of being responsible for siblings as a "birthright" of the oldest child (only if female) was also discussed in Santiago's work. This brought about complaints from the students indicating that the females are still expected to do all the household chores from which the males are exempt from by virtue of being males. One student went as far as describing her younger brother as "baby king," and another said her siblings referred to her as "mamita." Thus many of the students could personally relate to the protagonist's caretaker role.

Body image was discussed by referring to a passage in Santiago's book in which the mother spoke of working in a brassiere factory making bras for "American" women that were too small to fit anyone she knows. Although different prototypes of female images were discussed, Jennifer Lopez was held by all the students as the epitome of Latina beauty. The issue of body shape was a dominant theme in the self-concept the young women constructed; it was grounded deeply in the media personalities of their day, in addition to the perception of what the girls felt was attractive to their male peers. These preferences were neither scrutinized nor resisted in the discussions but rather accepted as the ideal standards.

A poem called "The Sounds of Sixth Street" by Martita Morales in the *Boricua* anthology prompted further discussion. Morales's selection focuses on racial politics among Puerto Ricans as they internalize rejection in U.S. society. The students were asked to consider why the narrator in Morales's poem rebels, and they proceeded to tie the narrator's rebellion to the historical period in which the poem was written. What the students drew from Morales's poem was the possibility of self-expression to communicate concerns and denounce situations of inequity. Before reading this selection, they had considered this possibility only in hip-hop and rap lyrics—forms of expression that are seldom considered poetry or legitimate writing in traditional classrooms.

Discussions of these writings led to dialogue on media influence. Responding to reflective questioning, students stated "that Latina mothers are depicted in the media as single poor and welfare moms." In terms of professional images in the media, students said, "The Latina always works as a maid in the movies, like J Lo in *Maid in Manhattan,* so people think that the only thing we do is clean." This discussion lent validity to the narratives of Mary Romero's life experiences in the book *Maid in the U.S.A.* (1992), where she shared her experiences as a child of a domestic worker and was poignantly described as a "baby maid" while in a supermarket with her mother. Students also pointed out how Latino men are often shown on the news, alongside African American men, as criminals and troublemakers, both in news reports and in entertainment programs.

Teachers are also influenced by media stereotypes and continue to perpetuate them through their discourses related to expectations. Interviews of teachers regarding increasing numbers of Latino students at their school revealed negative stereotypes about Latinos, along with lower expectations about their academic potential (Reyes 2003). The students in our study were not immune to the effects of stereotype expectations on their self-concept. A more focused study would be needed to determine how the intersection between teachers and media influenced their episodes of disidentification. It might also explain their hesitation when it came to talking about self-reported identities.

What It Means to Be Puerto Rican: In School and in the United States

Using Judith Ortiz Cofer's poem "A Latin Deli: An Ars Poetica" as a catalyst, the girls discussed differences among Latinos. The girls pointed to differences in foods and musical genres and, on deeper levels, to perceptions about them held by their non–Puerto Rican peers. Some mentioned that Latinas from other ethnic groups criticized their Spanish and accused them of being more Americanized, implying that they were less strict in how they relate to male peers. One student stated, "This girl [from X ethnic group] said that the only reason boys were attracted to Puerto Rican girls is because they were easy. That made me so mad." Some made comments in which they positioned Puerto Ricans as socially and culturally inferior to other Latino ethnic groups. The points they made reflected the challenges of the social context within the school setting. Students felt that they were looked down upon by teachers who themselves bought into these hierarchies. They described Puerto Rican students as "loud," and they were also accused of "always being in big groups in the hallways." This perception was corroborated in data from teacher interviews in other students' projects.

Other elements of Cofer's story included descriptions of images of the Virgin Mary in the deli. Students described their perceptions of the use of religious icons as an element placing Catholicism as a central "uniting cultural factor." On the other hand, the different avocations of the Virgin Mary separated the Puerto Rican students from those of Mexican descent. For example, in businesses located in areas more heavily populated by one ethnic group, the distinctiveness of icons and images in the stores and restaurants, and even the availability of artifacts sold, were reflected. Thus we find a focus on Our Lady of Guadalupe among Mexicans, on La Caridad del Cobre among Mexicans, and on La Providencia among Puerto Ricans.

The girls described their reactions to Puerto Rican foods much like Ortiz Cofer did when she became excited while purchasing foods from the island. The students stated that certain foods reminded them of their experiences in Puerto Rico. Music also forged an emotional tie to the island. One student was quick to point out that, in spite of these statements, "Eating the food and speaking Spanish don't make you 'Spanish' [*sic:* 'Puerto Rican'] . . . it's having the blood." This demonstrates a perception that the external elements are less defining of identity vis-à-vis the genetic lineage or biological ancestry.

Aurora Levin Morales's "Puertoricanness" evoked a discussion of students' memories of their homeland and their visits to the island. Their comments regarding the freedom and sense of safety when on the island, as compared with the city they currently live in, reflect the areas they are from on the island. In most cases they are from island towns rather than cities, where urban living conditions, including issues of safety, are similar to the those in the United States. The proliferation of gated communities and reported crime statistics point to patterns similar to those in the United States.

The most poignant responses related to their dual identities as they identified with Morales's sense of being "trapped between two cultures." These insights show a sophistication for which students are seldom given credit: the ability to select linguistic and cultural codes as needed for acceptance and communication with different sets of peers. If these skills were valued and encouraged in schools, our Latinas would be more self-confident and empowered to succeed.

Many of the students in this study exhibited artifacts that promoted and asserted their Puerto Rican identity in items of clothing; one of the most prominent of these is the Puerto Rican flag. This usage is often controversial because on the island wearing the Puerto Rican flag or exhibiting it in your car, house, or office is viewed as a nationalist symbol associated with independence from the United States. However, when Puerto Ricans immigrate and are immersed in communities with other immigrants who display their national flags, they feel compelled to act in the same way.

In some cases these practices begin in middle school and high school, where identity formation becomes an important developmental transition. Cultural events in classrooms and other areas that are not inclusive of their backgrounds begin to alienate the students, who cling to artifacts that reinforce their ethnic identities.

Conclusion

In this study of Puerto Rican high school girls in the United States, we attempted to identify patterns that emerge when the social context of school and of the host community challenge girls' sense of self. This study provides an example of how the use of ethnic literature can fill gaps in the social studies and history curriculum, enhance the literary canons in English literature, and generate discussions that reveal patterns of identity and adjustment across cultures. An overarching goal of this work is to develop educators with the skills to empower bicultural students to develop voice and access better academic and social opportunities (Trueba 1989).

The characteristics of Puerto Rican migration are unique because they include elements of the lives of other Latino groups, but this combination makes us more complex (Torre, Rodríguez Vecchini, and Burgos 1994). Although we are immigrants, we are also American citizens. This facilitates circulatory migration between Puerto Rico and the United States and contributes to our seeing the departure for either place as a hopeful move, albeit a disruptive one. American citizenship makes our relationship similar to that of Chicanos because of the subordinate status both groups are relegated to. We find ethnic commonality with both indigenous and African descendants, although there is some denial of the presence of these elements among us. Our slightly more benevolent history of integration conditions us to expect more accepting social attitudes toward difference than those we actually confront.

The focus on females is pertinent, and as we corroborated in this study, there are still vestiges of *machismo* in the lives of the Puerto Rican girls expressed through the gendered roles related to mothering and home-making. The awareness that the girls have regarding the inequities in these role assignments will hopefully make a difference in their understandings of their own roles. Again, as mentioned earlier, these students' insights show a sophistication for which they are seldom given credit: the ability to choose linguistic and cultural codes according to the context and the group they needed to communicate with. Valuing and encouraging these skills in our schools and classrooms would empower and enhance the self-confidence of our Latinas in academic and social settings.

Exposure to writing as a vehicle for self-expression is another consequence of this work. In an exit survey, students were asked whether the reading group experience influenced their thinking. One student responded that reading this literature "makes me confident and pushes me to do better and influences me to achieve my goals." Another stated, "I taught myself to speak Spanish and act in many ways of the Puerto Rican culture. Every bit of me is natural, and I am indeed a Puerto Rican American."

In the case of the Puerto Rican girls in this sample, comparing their experiences to those shared by the authors they studied seems to have given them opportunities to reflect on what was missing in their own lives and their academic settings. Their responses to the literature provide a basis for a critical analysis of their situations and potential. This study may inspire further use of Freirian dialogue and transformative reflection in classroom discussions. As students develop voice, we may find more avenues to strengthen their academic engagement and enhance their potential for success.

Acknowledgments

I am deeply indebted to Heather Rae Wohlgemuth for her willingness to engage in inquiry and reflection as we gleaned data for this exploration of Puerto Rican identity through responses to ethnic literature.

REFERENCES

Darder, Antonia. 1991. *Culture and power in the classroom: A critical foundation for bicultural education.* Westport, CT: Bergin and Garvey.

Darder, Antonia, Rodolfo Torres, and Henry Gutierrez, eds. 1997. *Latinos and education: A critical reader.* New York: Routledge.

Freire, Paulo. 1972. *Pedagogía del oprimido.* Mexico City: Siglo Veintiuno editores.

Latino writers in the U.S.: A literary reader. 2001. Evanston, IL: McDougal Littell/Houghton-Mifflin. Nextext publishing.

LeCompte, Margaret, and Judith Preissle. 1993. *Ethnography and qualitative design in educational research.* 2nd ed. San Diego, CA: Academic Press.

Matos, Luis Pales. 2000. *Poesía selecta/selected poems.* Translated by Julio Marzán. Houston, TX: Arte Público Press.

Reyes, Xaé Alicia. 1994. The social context of Puerto Rican public high school and the retention of return migrant students. Ph.D. diss., University of Colorado–Boulder.

———. 2000. Return migrant students: Yankee go home? In Sonia Nieto (ed.), *Education of Puerto Ricans in U.S. Schools,* 39–67. Mahwah, NJ: Erlbaum.

———. 2003. Teachers' (re)constructions of knowledge: The other side of fieldwork. *Journal of Latinos and Education* 2 (1): 31–37.

Romero, Mary, 1992. *Maid in the U.S.A.* New York: Routledge, Chapman, and Hall.

Santa Ana, Otto, ed. 2004. *Tongue tied: The lives of multilingual children in public education.* Lanham, MD: Rowman and Littlefield.

Santiago, Roberto, ed. 1995. *Boricuas: Influential Puerto Rican writings—An anthology.* New York: Ballantine.

Torre, Carlos A., Hugo Rodríguez Vecchini, and William Burgos, William, eds. 1994. *The commuter nation: Perspectives on Puerto Rican migration.* Rio Piedras: Editorial Universidad de Puerto Rico.

Trueba, Henry. 1989. *Raising silent voices: Educating linguistic minorities for the 21st Century.* New York: Harper and Row.

Wohlgemuth, H. R. 2004. The effects of multicultural literature on Latina high school students. Master's thesis, University of Connecticut.

Chapter 12

Getting Connected

The Expanding Use of Technology among Latina Girls

Robert W. Fairlie and Rebecca A. London

Young people across the United States are embracing technology in its various forms—such as cell phones, text messaging, Web site access, digital photography, and digital music. These technology "hooks" underpin a society that has been quick to embrace new technologies and use them in creative ways. Yet not all young people are making use of these innovations, and many do not have access to personal computers. The term "digital divide" is frequently used to describe the gap between those who do and those who do not have access to technology, and the resulting gap in opportunity and influence.

The United States as a whole, and Latinos in particular, experienced rapid growth in the use of computers and the Internet over the past several years (U.S. Department of Commerce 2002). In 1997, 38 percent of Latinos used computers, and 11 percent used the Internet. By 2001, 50 percent of Latinos were using computers and 32 percent were using the Internet. More recent data indicate that Internet use for English-speaking Latinos was as high as 60 percent in 2004 (Pew Internet and American Life Project 2005). Children are more likely than adults to use computers and the Internet. The U.S. Department of Commerce (2002) reported that rates of Internet use increased tremendously for youth under age of eighteen.[1]

The expanding use of computers and the Internet has important economic consequences for Latinos. Information technology skills are becoming increasingly important in the labor market, and the Internet is "expected to become a primary medium for communications, commerce, education, and entertainment in the 21st century" (U.S. General Accounting Office 2001: 3). Indeed, among Internet users, 61 percent of Latinos look for employment online (Pew Internet and American Life Project 2005).

In this context, the use of technology among Latina girls is of primary importance. Although school-age girls have begun to close the gender gap in science and math coursework, they continue to lag behind boys in technology-related coursework, particularly at the advanced level (American Association of University Women Educational Foundation 1998). Latina girls will need to use computers in order to compete academically. Access to computers and the Internet at home positively affects school attendance, high school graduation, and other educational outcomes (Attewell and Battle 1999; Schmitt and Wadsworth 2004; Fairlie 2005; Beltran, Das, and Fairlie 2005). One might expect that education and economic status are interlinked so that poorer children do not have the same access to computers as youth from economically stable families. Research indicates that even after taking into account differences in family income, computers in the home play an important role in improving educational outcomes.

As has been mentioned, home computer access is related to educational achievement and economic status. Youth from economically disadvantaged communities are more likely to have access to computers at school than at home. It has also been suggested that disparities exist across and within school districts in the pace and quality of technology adoption. Poorer communities, including those with higher concentrations of minorities, lag behind in terms of computer technology and access (Tomás Rivera Policy Institute 2002). When the computer-to-student ratio is low, students spend less time on the computer and may be limited to use during certain classes or for certain projects. Community technology centers (CTCs) or other community-based organizations also provide access. Recent research has shown that minority youth who participate in these types of programs gain tremendous knowledge related to technology (London et al. 2005). Technology can empower youth by giving them the opportunity to share their personal experiences or messages with others, use this self-expression to promote public awareness, and give them the skills and confidence to pursue a broad range of educational and career paths.

Because computer and Internet access is not equally available to people of all socioeconomic backgrounds in the United States, many public and private programs have been created in recent years to improve access to technology. For example, in the federal government alone, the

Departments of Agriculture, Commerce, Education, Health and Human Services, Housing and Urban Development, Justice, and Labor all have programs designed to bridge the digital divide. One of the largest programs, known as the E-rate program, provides discounts to schools and libraries for the costs of telecommunications services and equipment, with the level of discount depending on economic need and rural location (Puma, Chaplin, and Pape 2000).

The Present Study

To show how computer access and use have changed among Latina girls over time, we have documented trends in home computer and Internet access and use, as well as variations across Latina subgroups, age, and income level. We also examine the factors that predict home and Internet access. Our data are from the Computer and Internet Use Supplements to the 1998 to 2003 Current Population Surveys (CPS), conducted by the U.S. Bureau of the Census and the Bureau of Labor Statistics. The data are representative of the entire U.S. population and include interviews with approximately 50,000 households, including approximately 4,500 Latino households. The CPS contains a wealth of information on computer and Internet use by families and individuals not found in other government data sources. We also discuss three innovative and important programs designed to increase Latina girls' participation in the fields of science, mathematics, engineering, and technology.

Computer and Internet Access at Home and in Other Locations

There has been a dramatic rise in home computer access among all Latinos, and for Latina girls in particular, between 1998 and 2003 (see Figure 12.1).[2] For example, in 1998, 27 percent of Latinos (adults and children) had a computer at home. By 2003, 49 percent had a computer, an increase of 81 percent. Latina girls saw an even larger increase, from 28 percent with a computer at home in 1998 to 58 percent in 2003; the rate for Latina girls more than doubled in just six years.

Yet not all families with home computers have access to the Internet. Internet service, particularly broadband or other high-speed access, can be

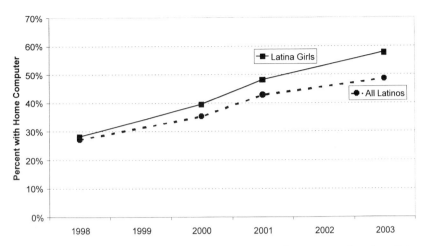

Figure 12.1. Changes in Home Computer Access for All Latinos and Latina Girls, 1998–2003

expensive for some families. In particular, although 58 percent of Latina girls had home computers in 2003, only 44 percent had home Internet access. In general, Latina girls are more likely than other Latino subgroups to have a home computer and Internet access. In fact, the home Internet access rate for girls more than quadrupled during this six-year period (as shown in Figure 12.2). In comparison, the Internet access rate for all Latinos increased threefold. In both cases, this is tremendous growth over the period.

All Latino subgroups increased their access to computers at home, but disparities among these groups exist, as is shown in Figure 12.3. In 2003, unspecified Latina groups (a designation that includes Cubans) had the highest combined rate of home computer ownership, followed by Puerto Ricans, Central and South Americans, and then Mexicans.[3]

Among subgroups, we find a similar pattern in Internet access at home. As shown in Figure 12.3, Mexican girls were the least likely to have Internet access at home (38 percent), and other Latinas were the most likely (67 percent). The rate of increase in Internet access among these groups is comparable.

The speed of Internet access varies depending on whether one uses broadband or other high-speed technology, or dial-up access. In 2003,

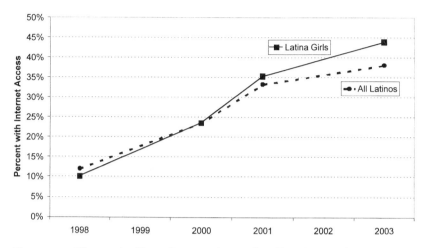

Figure 12.2. Changes in Home Internet Access for All Latinos and Latina Girls, 1998–2003

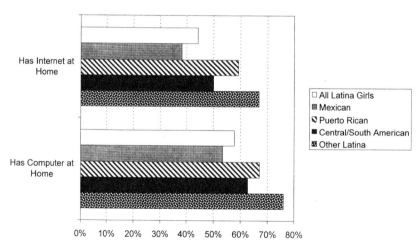

Figure 12.3. 2003 Home Computer and Internet Access by Subgroup, Latina Girls Ages 5–17

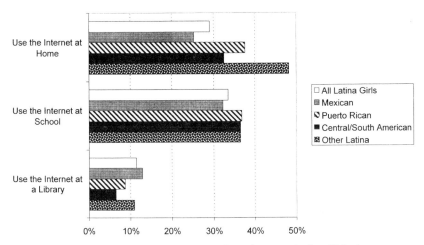

Figure 12.4. 2003 Locations of Internet Use by Subgroup, Latina Girls Ages 5–17

high-speed access among Latina girls and Latinos in general trailed behind dial-up access. For instance, in 2003, 15 percent of Latina girls had high-speed Internet access at home, whereas 29 percent had dial-up access. Because speed of Internet connection is critical in navigating the Internet, and because broadband markets are expanding, we anticipate that the percentage with high-speed access will continue to grow.

Locations of Internet Use

Thus far, we have described access to computers and the Internet at home. We anticipate, however, that young people will access technology elsewhere as well, particularly in school. Figure 12.4 shows where Latina girls used the Internet in 2003 in total and by subgroup. Home and school were the two primary places that Latina girls used the Internet, with school use slightly more prevalent than home use (33 percent compared with 29 percent). About 11 percent of Latina girls used the Internet at libraries; Mexican girls were more likely to use the Internet at libraries than other subgroups, which may be due in part to their having fewer computers and less Internet access at home.

It is important to note that only one-third of Latina girls reportedly accessed the Internet at school. To date, 92 percent of all instructional classrooms in U.S. public schools have computers with Internet access, with an average of 3.5 computers per classroom (U.S. Department of Education 2004). This discrepancy may reflect the fact that it is the parent who reports on use of technology in the CPS, and parents may understate the amount and locations of Internet use outside of the home for their child(ren).

Differences in Access to Home Computers

As we have seen, not all Latina girls have equal access to home computers and the Internet. Table 12.1 shows that in addition to ethnicity, other characteristics are associated with access. For instance, older girls (aged fourteen to seventeen) were more likely to have computers at home than younger girls (aged five to nine): approximately 64 percent compared with 51 percent. These older teens were also more likely to have Internet access at home.

Family income was also related to access. Latina girls from families with higher incomes were more likely to have a computer at home than those from lower-income families. About three-quarters of girls with family incomes of $50,000 or greater had a computer at home, compared with 40 percent of girls whose family incomes were below $20,000. An even greater disparity exists in Internet access. Just under one-quarter of Latina girls from very low-income (under $20,000 per year) families had Internet access at home, compared with about 71 percent of those in families with annual incomes over $50,000.

Finally, immigrant status and language use are associated with computer and Internet access. U.S.-born Latina girls were much more likely to have a home computer and Internet access than immigrant Latina girls. Girls living in families in which the adults speak Spanish at home were also at a disadvantage in terms of computer and Internet access. When some English was spoken, about 64 percent of the girls had a computer at home, and they were more than twice as likely to have Internet access.

Language may be an important factor related to computer and Internet use for a number of reasons. As it turns out, the Internet is less global than it is sometimes portrayed; the overwhelming majority of sites are in English. Spooner and Rainie (2001) report estimates from VilaWeb.com indi-

TABLE 12.1
Home Computer and Internet Access for Latina Girls Current Population Survey, 2003

	Access to home computer	Access to Internet at home	Sample size
Age-group			
Ages 5–9	50.9%	38.9%	760
Ages 10–13	59.9%	46.3%	537
Ages 14–17	64.2%	48.0%	537
Family income			
$0–20,000	40.4%	24.2%	452
$20,000–30,000	52.2%	38.1%	329
$30,000–50,000	65.9%	46.8%	422
$50,000 or more	75.4%	70.7%	361
Immigrant status			
Immigrant	44.8%	28.8%	310
Native-born	60.2%	46.9%	1,524
Language spoken at home by parents			
Spanish only	39.1%	23.6%	485
Not Spanish only	64.3%	51.2%	1,349

NOTE: All estimates are calculated using sample weights provided by the CPS.

cating that 68 percent of Web pages are in English, whereas only 3 percent are in Spanish. The Organization for Economic Cooperation and Development (2001) also reports that 94 percent of links to secure servers are in English. Although computer software is available in languages other than English, it is not clear how widely it is used. Perhaps because of this, Latinos living in households where Spanish is the only language spoken were less than half as likely to use the Internet as other Latinos (U.S. Department of Commerce 2002). Although these results do not control for differences in income or education, they are suggestive of the importance of language and content.

The findings reported here indicate that there are important differences across subgroup, age, immigrant status, language spoken at home, and family income in Latina girls' access to technology. These factors tend to be related. For instance, we saw that both family income and immigrant status are important characteristics related to access to technology. However, it is well documented that many immigrants to the United States have lower income levels than others living in the United States, and it is therefore difficult to know if it is immigration status per se that is driving the results, or other factors related to economics. To tease apart the independent effect of each of these factors, we conducted a multivariate statistical analysis to identify which factors influence home computer and Internet access. We describe the findings in the next section.

Determinants of Home Computer and Internet Access

What factors influence having a computer in the home and access to the Internet? Clearly not all families want a computer or Internet access, and this preference may depend on exposure to and the perceived usefulness of these technologies. Preferences may also be related to the child's age, where the family lives, and the adults' use of computers at work. Parent education and income are also likely to be important determinants of who purchases a computer and connects to the Internet.

In Table 12.2 we provide a summary of the factors that influence home computer and Internet access. In the first column are the effects of each factor on the probability of Latina girls having a home computer.[4] For instance, the number listed in the first column next to "Immigrant" indicates that being an immigrant reduces the likelihood of having a computer at home by 5 percentage points. On average, about 44 percent of Latina girls have a home computer (see the last row of the table). Thus the model predicts that when other factors such as family income and parent education are controlled for, 39 percent of immigrants will have home computers. Many of the factors, including immigration status, have a significant influence on home computer and Internet access for Latina girls.

TABLE 12.2
Logit Regressions for Home Computer and Internet Access
Current Population Survey, 1998–2003

	Effect of characteristic on probability of home computer access (Percentage points)	Statistically significant	Effect of characteristic on probability of home Internet access (Percentage points)	Statistically significant
Age	1.1	**	0.9	**
Ethnicity				
Mexican (reference category)				
Puerto Rican	12.5	**	9.6	**
Cuban	−4.3		−5.8	
Central or South American	9.4	**	3.7	*
Other Latino	6.7	**	4.6	*
Immigrant	−5.0	**	−3.7	*
Only Spanish spoken at home	−8.9	**	−7.6	**

TABLE 12.2 *(continued)*

	Effect of characteristic on probability of home computer access (Percentage points)	Statistically significant	Effect of characteristic on probability of home Internet access (Percentage points)	Statistically significant
Number of children in household	0.0		−1.2	**
Family income				
Less than $10,000 (reference category)				
$10,000–$15,000	4.8	*	3.7	
$15,000–$20,000	3.9		5.6	*
$20,000–$25,000	8.1	**	9.5	**
$25,000–$30,000	11.7	**	12.9	**
$30,000–$35,000	11.1	**	11.3	**
$35,000–$40,000	12.8	**	12.7	**
$40,000–$50,000	16.0	**	18.1	**
$50,000–$60,000	21.4	**	21.9	**
$60,000–$75,000	25.2	**	24.9	**
More than $75,000	22.3	**	24.1	**
Family owns home	7.9	**	4.7	**
Parent education				
Mother: high school dropout (reference category)				
Mother: high school graduate	6.3	**	5.2	**
Mother: some college	13.8	**	10.7	**
Mother: college graduate	15.4	**	11.9	**
Father: high school dropout (reference category)				
Father: high school graduate	7.0	**	7.9	**
Father: some college	13.3	**	10.7	**
Father: college graduate	16.6	**	16.3	**
Parent Internet use at work				
Mother uses Internet at work	6.4	**	3.0	
Father uses Internet at work	13.4	**	12.9	**
Region of the country				
South (reference category)				
North	1.3		2.8	
Midwest	−0.4		−3.9	*
West	4.7	**	−1.0	
Urbanicity				
Central city (reference category)				
Suburban	0.8		0.1	
Rural	−3.8	*	−3.5	*
Year				
1998 (reference category)				
2000	10.0	**	15.2	**
2001	15.8	**	24.4	**
2003	23.8	**	30.2	**
Rate of home access	44.1%		29.0%	
Sample size	6,212		6,212	

NOTE: All estimates are calculated using sample weights provided by the CPS. Regressions are estimated using logistic models.

* $p < .05$; ** $p < .01$.

Subgroup is also an important predictor of technology access at home, even after controlling for immigrant status, language spoken at home, and income. Puerto Rican girls, for instance, were 12 percentage points more likely to own computers than Mexican girls (which is the reference category) and 10 percentage points more likely to have access to the Internet at home. Central and South American girls, as well as other Latinas, were similarly more likely than Mexicans to have access to computers and the Internet at home. These results mirror those reported in Figure 12.2 and provide even stronger evidence because they control for other intervening factors, such as income.

Other cultural factors also influence technology access for Latina girls. Both immigrant status and language spoken at home independently affect the probability of computer ownership and Internet access. Foreign-born girls and girls who live in households in which only Spanish is spoken among the adults were much less likely to have home computers and Internet. These effects are independent of each other, indicating that immigrant acculturation apart from English-language acquisition influences access to technology for Latina girls.

Overall, language is an important determinant of computer ownership and Internet use even after controlling for education, family income, and immigrant status. Spanish-speaking Latinas have much lower rates of computer ownership and home Internet use than those who speak a language besides Spanish. This may be partly due to the fact that most software and Internet sites are in English, making computers less useful or more difficult to use for Spanish-only Latinas (Spooner and Rainie 2001; Organization for Economic Cooperation and Development 2001). Foreign-born Latinas come from countries with substantially lower rates of computer ownership and Internet use than in the United States, thus limiting their potential exposure to computers.

Family size also plays a role. Although the number of children in the household does not affect home computer ownership, the probability of Internet service decreases with the number of children in the household. This may be due to the increased costs associated with raising more children. In addition, the likelihood of having a home computer or Internet service increases by nearly 1 percentage point as Latina girls become one year older.

The importance of income in determining who has home access to technology is evident from the results reported in Table 12.2. The higher the family income, the more likely Latina girls are to have computer and

Internet access. Although some poor Latino families may view computers as a worthwhile investment, they may not be able to finance the purchase of one. Similarly, monthly Internet charges may deter some low-income families from signing up for service. Our estimates indicate that Latina girls with annual family incomes of $50,000 or more were more than 20 percentage points more likely to have a computer and home access to the Internet than were girls living in families with less than $10,000 of family income.

Another factor that affects the ability of Latino families to purchase computers is whether they own a house. Home ownership is an important component of a family's wealth and can be used to finance computer purchases such as with a home equity line. Latina girls living in households where the parents own the home were 8 percentage points more likely to have a home computer and 5 percentage points more likely to have home Internet access than those living in households that rent.

As expected, parent education is an important determinant of owning a home computer. With each increasing level of education for the mother and father, there is a substantially larger probability of owning a home computer. Latina girls who have two college-educated parents were more than 30 percentage points more likely to have a home computer and Internet access than were girls whose parents did not graduate from high school, even after controlling for the higher income that is associated with more education. The strong relationship between education and home computer ownership may reflect the effect of wealth or long-term income on purchasing computers, but it may also reflect preferences for computers based on exposure or perceived usefulness.

Another factor that influences exposure to computers is whether the mother or father uses the Internet at work. Latina girls whose parents use the Internet at work were substantially more likely to have a computer and Internet at home. These parents may have a computer at home because they are more familiar with how to use it or need it to work at home.

Geographic differences were also important in determining computer ownership and Internet access among Latina girls. We found that Latina girls residing in the western United States were 5 percentage points more likely to have a home computer than those living in the South. Computer ownership was also higher in the West than in any other region of the country even after controlling for family characteristics and whether the girl lives in a rural or urban area. Latinas living in rural areas were 4 percentage points less likely than Latinas living in central cities to own computers and to have Internet access at home. Latino families residing in the West and in central cities may be more exposed to technology and benefit more from using it.

In sum, the proportion of Latina girls with home computers rose by 24 percentage points from 1998 to 2003, and the proportion with home access to the Internet rose by 20 percentage points. Our analyses show that home computer ownership and Internet access are not due to only one factor, such as higher family income or education. Instead, they are a function of multiple characteristics of the child, the family, and where they live.

Characteristics of the child that increase the likelihood of computer and Internet access at home are being an older child and having been born in the United States. Families that have more access speak a language other than Spanish, have a higher income, own their home, and have highly educated parents who use the Internet at work. Families with more access also live in central cities or suburbs. Within this group of Latina girls, Cubans have the most and Mexicans the least access.

Overall, we find that access to home computers and the Internet access is expanding rapidly for Latina girls, despite high levels of poverty and language barriers. Next we present three examples of community-based efforts that have contributed to girls' increased access to and use of technology.

Programs to Increase Latina Girls' Participation in Technology

Across the United States, communities are mobilizing to bridge the digital divide and increase Latinos' access to information technology. We will describe three different approaches currently being used to increase girls' participation in technology and other nontraditional fields.

The MAXIMA project, which was launched in 2000 by faculty members at New Mexico State University, aims to encourage the participation of young women and minorities in the fields of science, technology, engineering, and math. The project builds teachers' capacity to create more positive attitudes toward technology and increase girls' academic achievement in nontraditional fields.

The MAXIMA project initially included twenty-four teachers and thirty-nine Latina girls. This was a longitudinal project that followed these girls from fourth to sixth grade. Teachers attended a series of summer institutes aimed at expanding their content knowledge in science, mathematics, and technology, providing an instructional framework for a multicultural setting, and integrating technology into their professional development and their classrooms. Summer activities were supplemented with monthly teacher meetings, access to robotics equipment or other classroom supplies, and a personal laptop for each teacher.

The original thirty-nine Latina students in MAXIMA visited the university campus for one day to participate in the Southern New Mexico Science, Engineering, Mathematics, and Aerospace Academy, the Engineering Lego Lab, chemistry demonstrations, and other activities on campus that involve mathematics and science.

Results from the evaluation of MAXIMA indicate that when their teachers learn about appropriate pedagogy that maximizes student learning, Latina girls have flourished and report that both math and science are subjects that they enjoy. The program shows the importance of offering professional development for teachers to understand the needs and interests of Latina students to encourage them to consider a math, science, or engineering career in their postsecondary education.

In another program, Latina girls in North Central Washington have a unique opportunity to learn about computer technology and improve their mathematics and science skills by participating in the Breaking Boundaries Summer Day Camp. Located in Okanogan County, Washington, Breaking Boundaries is a free eight-week summer camp offered exclusively to Latina girls. The main purpose is to provide girls from disadvantaged backgrounds with the opportunity to make more informed decisions about their futures, and in particular to orient these girls toward delaying childbearing, completing high school, and pursuing a higher education.

Breaking Boundaries began in 2003 and started by recruiting twenty-five seventh- and eighth-grade girls to spend their summer learning about science and technology and participating in more traditional summer camp activities such as swimming, boating, and backpacking. The girls attend the camp each summer for up to three years and learn progressively more challenging and interesting technology applications each year (e.g., from basic keyboarding in 2003 to digital photography and video in 2005). The camp also includes nutrition education, which is important because these girls are in one of the highest risk groups for juvenile diabetes. Breaking Boundaries will begin another three-year cycle with new seventh and eighth graders in the summer of 2006.

In addition to summertime activities, girls receive mentoring and tutoring throughout the school year. These activities are designed to reinforce skills learned in the summer and to help the girls progress through high school and into a career in a field related to science, mathematics, or technology.

Sister to Sister/Hermana a Hermana (STS/HAH) is an arts and leadership organization that works with girls and young women of color aged nine to eighteen living in the Ward 1 community of Washington, D.C. It offers workshops and group activities in neighborhood centers and schools to promote healthy communication, creative self-expression, community building, and life skills development.

The Girls Multimedia Workshop, a youth-led project of STS/HAH, provides technology instruction, mentoring, and academic support with the aim of creating safe, structured environments, positive learning experiences, and greater opportunities for girls and young women. Workshops led by young women expose girls to the visual arts, performing arts, and digital media. Participants are trained to use digital media equipment such as digital video and photography cameras, iMacs, and more. The STS/HAH participants for 2005 are developing a new documentary called *The Ripple Effect: Our Stories,* which includes the voices and stories of girls and young women in their community.

STS/HAH is expanding the life choices for Latina girls and young women in Washington, D.C. Participants are Latina (both born in the United States and immigrant), African American, and Asian. Services offered by STS/HAH are bilingual, cross-cultural, and inclusive. STS/HAH encourages girls and young women to see the best within themselves and within one another, and to identify across racial and cultural boundaries.

These programs, and many others around the country, are working to assist Latina girls to move into educational and career paths that contain few Latinas. The programs bridge issues of economic disadvantage and language barriers to provide unique opportunities and supports. These programs recognize that special efforts are necessary to move girls into math, science, engineering, and other technology-related fields. Even among girls who choose more traditional careers, computer and Internet skills are critical for them to be competitive in education and a variety of labor markets.

Summary

There have been large increases in Latina girls' home access to computers and the Internet between 1998 and 2003. In particular, the rate of home computer access among Latina girls aged five to seventeen increased from 28 percent to 58 percent over the six-year period, an increase of 107 percent. Internet connections at home more than quadrupled, increasing from 10 percent in 1998 to 44 percent in 2003. These girls appear to be adapting to technology even more quickly than Latinos of all other ages.

NOTES

We would like to thank Susan Brown of the MAXIMA project, Stefanie Cruz of Sister to Sister/Hermana a Hermana, and Donna Evans of Breaking Boundaries for sharing their work with us. Oded Gurantz provided excellent research assistance. We gratefully acknowledge funds from the William T. Grant Foundation and the Community Technology Foundation of California that were provided in support of this research.

1. The report does not present statistics by both age and ethnic background.

2. The CPS did not collect computer and Internet use data in 1999 and 2002.

3. Although the CPS data separately identify Cubans, we group them with other unidentified Latino groups because there are so few Cuban girls in our sample.

4. We include data from 1998 to 2003 to increase sample sizes and precision in the regression. All regressions are run using logistic models and are adjusted with weights provided by the CPS.

REFERENCES

American Association of University Women Educational Foundation. 1998. *Gender Gaps: Where Schools Still Fail Our Children.* Washington, DC: AAUWEF.

Attewell, Paul, and Juan Battle. 1999. Home Computers and School Performance. *Information Society* 15: 1–10.

Beltran, Daniel O., Kuntal K. Das, and Robert W. Fairlie. 2005. Do Home Computers Improve Educational Outcomes? Evidence from Matched Current Population Surveys and the National Longitudinal Survey of Youth 1997. Department of Economics University of California, Santa Cruz, unpublished manuscript.

Fairlie, Robert W. 2005. The Effects of Home Computers on School Enrollment. *Economics of Education Review* 24:533–542.

London, Rebecca A., Manuel Pastor Jr., Rachel Rosner, Lisa Servon, and Antwuan Wallace. 2005. The Role of Community Technology Centers in Youth Skill-Building and Empowerment. Center for Justice, Tolerance, and Community, University of California, Santa Cruz, unpublished manuscript.

Organization for Economic Cooperation and Development. 2001. *Understanding the Digital Divide.* Paris: OECD Publications.

Pew Internet and American Life Project. 2005. *A Decade of Adoption: How the Internet Has Woven Itself into American Life.* Washington, DC: Pew Research Center.

Puma, Michael J., Duncan D. Chaplin, and Andreas D. Pape. 2000. *E-Rate and the Digital Divide: A Preliminary Analysis from the Integrated Studies of Educational Technology.* Prepared for the U.S. Department of Education by the Urban Institute.

Schmitt, John, and Jonathan Wadsworth. 2004. Is There an Impact of Household Computer Ownership on Children's Educational Attainment in Britain? Centre for Economic Performance Discussion Paper No. 625.

Spooner, Tom, and Lee Rainie. 2001. *Hispanics and the Internet.* Pew Internet and American Life Project. Washington, DC: Pew Research Center.

Tomás Rivera Policy Institute. 2002. *Latinos and Information Technology: The Promise and the Challenge.* Prepared for the IBM Hispanic Digital Divide Task Force.

U.S. Department of Commerce. 2002. *A Nation Online: How Americans Are Expanding Their Use of the Internet.* Washington, DC: U.S. Government Printing Office.

U.S. Department of Education. 2004. *Internet Access in U.S. Public Schools and Classrooms: 1994–2002.* National Center for Education Statistics 2004–011. Washington, DC: U.S. Government Printing Office.

U.S. General Accounting Office. 2001. *Telecommunications: Characteristics and Choices of Internet Users.* Washington, DC: U.S. Government Printing Office.

Part 4

Developing Initiative

Chapter 13

La Felicidad

Predictors of Life Satisfaction and Well-Being among Latina Girls

Charu Thakral and Elizabeth Vera

> I worry about the girls I see sitting in my classroom who don't seem interested in anything. What excites these girls? What do they care about? I am afraid if these girls can't find a focus soon, they will get sidetracked by a boy, end up pregnant, no diploma, no job, and no hope.
> —Seventh-grade teacher at an urban public school, sharing her perception of her Latina students

It is easy to be pessimistic about the plight of urban Latina girls. Teenage pregnancy and school dropout are among the ever-present stereotypes that professionals working with Latinas confront. The field of psychology has done little to challenge such stereotypes. One of the long-standing criticisms of psychology has been that it focuses largely on weaknesses and deficits. Furthermore, attempting to "fix" problems, instead of promoting healthy development, has been the focus of most mental health professionals. This bias toward the negative is vividly exemplified within the literature investigating girls of color.

Due to the overemphasis on the problems that Latinas encounter during adolescence, far less is known about the successes, aspirations, and psychological wellness of these girls. As a result, professionals who work with Latinas have an unbalanced understanding of the mental health and strengths of these girls.

It is noteworthy that within the past several years, researchers who study adolescents have begun to shift their focus away from predicting specific problem behaviors and toward identifying competencies and resources that both foster healthy outcomes and prevent a host of mental health problems (Larson 2000). This shift reflects an acknowledgment that even when youth do not exhibit concrete problems (e.g., pregnancy, substance abuse), they may not necessarily grow up to become happy, adjusted, productive adults (Catalano et al. 1999; Larson 2000).

Proponents of this perspective that focuses on strengths and assets, called "positive psychology" (Seligman and Csikszentmihalyi 2000), highlight the need for mental health practitioners to focus on strengthening existing skills and increasing the competencies of their clients. Consistent with the study of positive psychology and mental health promotion is a large field of research known as "subjective well-being" or "life satisfaction." Understanding what constitutes well-being and the routes to achieving happiness offers opportunities for enhancing clients' quality of life.

Subjective well-being, also referred to as "subjective happiness," refers to the self-evaluation of life satisfaction (Robbins and Kliewer 2000). Research in the subjective well-being field attempts to uncover the reasons that individuals are satisfied with their lives (Diener 2000). In concert with this effort, we sought to provide a better understanding of the factors that enable urban Latina adolescents to flourish and achieve life satisfaction. This is an important issue because many mental health practitioners, based on the existing negative literature on this population, might not expect these girls to be satisfied with their lives.

Diener et al.'s (1999) model of subjective well-being consists of both cognitive and affective components. Cognitive evaluations of subjective well-being are assessed through one's global judgment of life satisfaction. Affective reactions (i.e., predominant moods and emotions) are assessed by evaluations of one's degree of experiencing pleasant and unpleasant emotions. Thus, subjective well-being is defined by three interrelated factors: global life satisfaction, positive affect, and negative affect (Lightsey 1996; Robbins and Kliewer 2000). "Global life satisfaction" is defined as a positive evaluation on one's life as a whole. "Positive affect" and "negative affect" refer to the frequency of positive and negative emotions, respectively. While this model has been supported by past studies, its usefulness for understanding the well-being of Latina adolescents has not been tested.

Research in the field has explored a number of factors involved in the prediction of subjective well-being. Subjective well-being is related to many aspects of personality such as self-esteem, optimism, self-efficacy, hardiness, and agreeableness (Diener 1996; Diener et al. 1999; Lightsey 1996; Lucas, Diener, and Suh 1996), as well as demographic factors such as income level, education, and marital status (Oishi et al. 1999). Research has found that levels of well-being do not vary by gender, race, or social class. However, the criteria on which life satisfaction is judged may vary among groups.

Up to this point, the majority of subjective well-being research reviewed has focused on individual (as opposed to interpersonal) factors that relate to life satisfaction. However, external resources such as perceived social support have also been shown to have a critical role in the psychological adjustment and well-being of adolescents in the general population (Stice, Ragan, Randall 2004; Scholte, Lieshout, and von Aken 2001; Lewinsohn et al. 1994).

It may be particularly important to examine the role of perceived social support from family and peers in predicting well-being in Latina adolescents because the majority of Latin American cultures have a strong identification with and attachment to both nuclear and extended family (i.e., familism as a core value; McNeill et al. 2002). Because family functions as a natural support system throughout the lifetime in Latino cultures, examining the importance of support in regard to life satisfaction among these girls is critical.

In an attempt to investigate the extent to which Diener et al.'s (1999) model of subjective well-being may be applicable to an urban, Latina adolescent population, we designed the current study. Identifying the factors related to happiness and life satisfaction of Latina adolescents has important implications for practitioners who work with this population. Such data will be useful in the design of culturally tailored prevention programs aimed at enhancing life satisfaction and promoting mental health in Latina youth.

Purpose

We sought to identify factors that most significantly predicted life satisfaction and well-being in a sample of urban Latina adolescents living in a large midwestern city. Based on previous research, we selected a number of factors for examination as potential predictors of life satisfaction: achievement motivation, positive and negative affect, optimism, hope, self-esteem, and social support.

Participants

The study included forty-nine urban Latina adolescent girls. Ninety percent of our participants were Mexican American, with the remaining 10 percent being Puerto Rican or Central American. The study participants were enrolled in a public urban school in a large midwestern city and ranged in age from 12 to 15 years (average = 13.26). The average academic grade per student through self-report was a C.

According to the data available from state records, the sample reflects the demographic profile of the school as a whole. The ethnic breakdown of the school is 68.4 percent Hispanic, 10.5 percent black, 9.7 percent white, 11.3 percent Asian American, and less than 1 percent Native American. Eighty-seven percent of the students enrolled in the school are categorized as low income (i.e., students came from families whose incomes qualified for free breakfast and lunch programs in school, suggesting family incomes are below the national poverty level).

In terms of immigration status, the majority (75 percent) of students in the school are second generation (born in the United States); the remaining 25 percent were born in other countries and came to the United States as small children. We did not specifically ask the girls in our sample to report their generational status. In the school as a whole, 39.5 percent of the students are eligible for transitional bilingual programs based on their English-language proficiency. While this is not an indication of immigration status per se, it suggests that many of the students are bilingual English and Spanish speakers. Academically, students in the school overall performed significantly lower than the state average in terms of standardized test scores (Illinois State Report Card 2003).

We recruited participants in combination with a school-based outreach program aimed at enhancing decision-making skills, career aspirations, and identity exploration. All students in the seventh and eighth grades were eligible for participation in the outreach program. Students involved with the program who chose to and obtained parental permission completed the research survey.

Instruments

The questionnaire included demographic questions and seven measures.

Students were asked to designate their sex (boy or girl), age, nationality/race/ethnicity, and an estimate of their typical grades in school. The nationality/race/ethnicity question was left open-ended so that the students could use their own words to describe their heritage. Only students whose response was coded Hispanic/Latino were included in this study. For their grades, students were asked whether they would describe themselves as someone who gets mostly As, Bs, Cs, or Ds and Fs. Each of the seven measures, listed here, was found to have adequate statistical reliability and validity in the current study:

1. The Achievement Motivation–Denver Youth Survey (Huizinga 1989) consists of thirteen items that measure motivation to achieve future outcomes associated with school, job, family, and community.
2. The Positive and Negative Affect Schedule(PANAS; Watson, Clark, and Tellegen 1988) consists of twenty items that assess emotions. For example, participants are asked how frequently they feel excited, happy, frustrated, and angry. The PANAS consists of two scales (ten items each) measuring positive and negative affect.
3. The Children's Hope Scale is a six-item scale developed by Snyder et al. (1997) to examine one's perceived ability to obtain future goals (e.g., believing that one knows how to get what one wants in life).
4. The Life Orientation Test (Scheier and Carver 1985) consists of eight items that measure optimism, or one's expectations about the potential to experience positive things in life (e.g., looking on the bright side of things, expecting good things to come out of bad situations).
5. The Hare Area-Specific Self-Esteem Scale contains ten items that measure girls' perceptions of their worth and importance among their peers, in the home environment, and in the school environment.
6. The Vaux Social Support Record consists of nine items that measure satisfaction with perceived emotional advice, guidance, and social support from family, friends, and school personnel.
7. The Satisfaction with Life Scale (SWLS; Diener et al. 1985) is a five-item measure of satisfaction with the quality of one's life that includes items such as "Overall, my life is satisfying."

Results

Table 13.1 lists the average scores and variability within the sample on each of the variables. On average, as a group, the participants were moderately satisfied with life, felt supported, hopeful, and optimistic, and experienced similar levels of both positive and negative emotions. They also reported moderate levels of self-esteem. There was large variation in the life satisfaction measure, which may suggest that participants were more likely to respond in extreme ways to the questions on the scale (e.g., being very satisfied or very dissatisfied).

We examined relationships between the different variables by computing correlations (see Table 13.2). We found that life satisfaction, our index of subjective well-being, was significantly related to all variables except achievement motivation. In other words, there were moderately strong, positive relationships between life satisfaction and all the predictor variables except for negative affect, which is significant in a negative direction. Perceived social support was related to all variables except achievement motivation.

Even though achievement motivation did not significantly relate to life satisfaction, the girls' goals included some achievement in academics and career. The three most frequently endorsed goals were to have a happy family, have a good-paying job, and get a college education. The least frequently endorsed goals included being popular, having a lot of money, and helping out around the house. Table 13.3 provides a list of the average results for the sample.

To predict life satisfaction, we ran a stepwise multiple regression statistical analysis. We found that both negative affect and positive affect were the best predictors of life satisfaction. The statistical details are shown in Table 13.4. These analyses suggest that urban Latina girls who had lower levels of unpleasant emotions and higher levels of positive emotions also demonstrated higher levels of life satisfaction.

Discussion

Subjective well-being research focuses on the factors that contribute to high perceived "quality of life." This study reveals that some urban Latinas are optimistic and hopeful, have positive self-esteem, and feel supported. The findings highlight the psychological strengths of these adolescent

TABLE 13.1
Means and Standard Deviations for Predictor Variables (N = 49)

Variable	M	SD	Range
Life satisfaction	21.71	7.95	5–34
Achievement motivation	53.73	4.73	36–63
Hope	22.55	5.86	10–35
Optimism	21.75	3.43	11–29
Positive affect	32.36	5.95	20–46
Negative affect	27.46	5.18	16–41
Self-esteem	29.29	4.86	18–38
Social support	11.38	3.52	2–18

TABLE 13.2
Intercorrelations of Predictor Variables

Variable	1	2	3	4	5	6	7	8
1. Life satisfaction	—							
2. Achievement motivation	.113	—						
3. Hope	.595**	.156	—					
4. Optimism	.634**	.230	.509**	—				
5. Positive affect	.690**	.165	.714**	.677**	—			
6. Negative affect	−.648**	−.121	−.225	−.385*	−.339*	—		
7. Self-esteem	.637**	.150	.677**	.615**	.702**	−.416**	—	
8. Social support	.593**	.102	.637**	.482**	.499**	−.403**	.651**	—

* $p < .05$; ** $p < .01$.

TABLE 13.3
Means and Standard Deviations for Areas of Achievement Motivation (N = 49)

Achievement Motivation	M	SD
Having a happy family	4.63	.612
Having a good-paying job	4.60	.559
Having a college education	4.59	.618
Helping out around the house	3.92	.820
Having a lot of money	3.87	.998
Being popular	2.42	1.16

TABLE 13.4
Summary of Regression Analysis of Variables Predicting Life Satisfaction

Variable	B	SE ß	Beta
Constant	16.64	11.39	
Achievement motivation	−.0032	.164	−.020
Hope	.194	.240	.150
Optimism	.417	.323	.197
Positive affect	.322	.225	.257*
Negative affect	−.619	.163	−.434*
Self-esteem	−.088	.266	−.057
Social support	.230	.309	.107

* $p < .05$.

girls, helping to create a sorely needed balance to the common negative images of this group.

This study shows the factors that relate to life satisfaction, or subjective well-being, in a sample of urban Latina adolescents. Life satisfaction was most strongly related to both positive and negative emotional states.

These empirical findings not only have implications for theory development and future research; they also have practical utility for mental health practitioners and other professionals who work directly with urban Latina adolescents. More specifically, this information can contribute to both the design and the implementation of intervention and prevention programs targeted at mental health promotion for this population in school or community settings.

The important role of negative affect in predicting life satisfaction indicates the need for programs to incorporate the teaching of strategies for coping with stress and difficult emotions (e.g., anger, disappointment, frustration) in addition to teaching help-seeking behaviors to adolescent girls. A family-based or peer-based approach that increases the availability of social support for precisely these purposes may be warranted.

The importance of programs that build social support for adolescent girls is echoed in previous research that has examined the utility of enhancing social support for adolescents experiencing symptoms of psychological disorders (Stice, Ragan, and Randall 2004). The current data would suggest that such support is important for girls as a healthy component of living, even though it was not related to their achievement motivation.

In addition to the implications for practitioners, our findings also have implications for future research on subjective well-being in urban adolescent populations and Latina adolescents in particular. This study is one of a few that aim to extend the field's knowledge of subjective well-being in urban adolescent girls.

Limitations

As is the case with many studies that examine psychological phenomena in historically underrepresented groups, this study has a number of methodological considerations that limit our ability to generalize the findings to all Latinas. First, our sample size was large enough for the analyses conducted, but it was too small to examine the variables simultaneously, as is possible in high-level statistical procedures like structural equation modeling. Second, the participants were geographically very homogeneous: the girls all lived in the same neighborhood and attended the same school. Therefore, it is hard to know to what extent the findings would be confirmed with urban Latina girls outside this community. Third, it would be interesting to examine the impact of generational status or family structure on life satisfaction of the sample participants. A lack of sufficient range of age at immigration to the United States prevented the analysis of such effects. Fourth, as is the case with all self-report data, it is difficult to know whether our survey methodology accurately measures the hope, optimism, achievement motivation, self-esteem, and social support of the study participants or whether social desirability played a role in their responses. Even with these imperfections, the data were useful in the preliminary examination of subjective well-being in a population of youth often neglected in the research.

Conclusion

The overall results of this study suggest that within this sample of poor, urban Latina girls, future aspirations were positive, and psychological well-being was related to both inner resources and the quality of interpersonal relationships. These findings contribute to a more balanced portrayal of psychological functioning of urban Latina youth and challenge existing negative stereotypes.

REFERENCES

Baumeister, Roy, Campbell, Jennifer D., Krueger, Joachim, and Vohs, Kathleen D. 2003. Does high self-esteem cause better performance, interpersonal success, happiness, or healthier lifestyles? *Psychological Science in the Public Interest* 4: 1–44.

Ben-Zur, Hasida. 2003. Happy adolescents: The link between subjective well-being, internal resources, and parental factors. *Journal of Youth and Adolescence* 32:67–79.

Caldwell, Roslyn, Silverman, Jenna, Lefforge, Noel, and Silver, N. Clayton. 2004. Adjudicated Mexican American adolescents: The effects of familial emotional support on self-esteem, emotional well-being, and delinquency. *American Journal of Family Therapy* 32:55–69.

Carvajal, Scott C., Garner, Randall L., and Evans, Richard I. 1998. Dispositional optimism as a protective factor in resisting HIV exposure in sexually active inner-city minority adolescents. *Journal of Applied Social Psychology* 28 (23): 2196–2211.

Catalano, Richard F., Burgland, M. Lisa, Ryan, Jeanne A., Lonczak, Heather C., and Hawkins, David. 1999. Positive youth development in the United States: Research findings on evaluations of positive youth development programs. Washington, DC: Department of Health and Human Services, National Institute for Child Health and Human Development.

Cheng, Helen, and Furnham, Adrian. 2003. Attributional style and self-esteem as predictors of psychological well being. *Counseling Psychology Quarterly* 16:121–130.

Coley, Rebekah L., Kuta, Ann M., and Chase-Lansdale, P. Lindsay. 2000. An insider view: Knowledge and opinions of welfare from African American girls in poverty. *Journal of Social Issues* 56 (4): 707–726.

Diener, Ed. 1996. Traits can be powerful, but are not enough: Lessons from subjective well-being. *Journal of Research in Personality* 30 (3): 389–399.

———. 2000. Subjective well-being: The science of happiness and a proposal for a national index. *American Psychologist* 55 (1): 34–43.

Diener, Ed, and Diener, Marissa. 1995. Cross-cultural correlates of life satisfaction and self-esteem. *Journal of Personality and Social Psychology* 68 (4): 653–663.

Diener, Ed, Emmons, Robert, Larsen, Randy, and Griffin, Sharon. 1985. The Satisfaction with Life Scale. *Journal of Personality Assessment* 49:71–75.

Diener, Ed, and Fujita, Frank. 1995. Resources, personal strivings, and subjective well-being: A nomothetic and idiographic approach. *Journal of Personality and Social Psychology* 68 (5): 926–935.

Diener, Ed, Suh, Eunkook M., Lucas, Richard E., and Smith, H. L. 1999. Subjective well-being: Three decades of progress. *Psychological Bulletin* 125:276–302.

Garbarino, James. 2001. An ecological perspective on the effects of violence on children. *Journal of Community Psychology* 29:361–378.

Harvard Civil Rights Project. 2004. *Losing our future: How minority youth are being left behind by the graduation rate crisis.* Cambridge, MA: Civil Rights Project at Harvard University.

Huebner, E. Scott. 1991. Correlates of life satisfaction in children. *School Psychology Quarterly* 6 (2): 103–111.

Huizinga, D. 1989. Denver youth survey youth interview schedule. Institute of Behavioural Science, Boulder, Colorado.

Illinois State Report Card. 2003. http://webprod1.isbe.net/ereportcard/publicsite/getSearchCriteria.aspx.

Larson, Reed W. 2000. Toward a psychology of positive youth development. *American Psychologist* 55:170–183.

Leadbeater, Bonnie J. R., Way, Niobe, and Raden, Anthony. 1996. Why not marry your baby's father? Answers from African American and Hispanic adolescent mothers. In Bonnie J. R. Leadbeater and Niobe Way (eds.), *Urban girls: Resisting stereotypes, creating identities* (pp. 193–209). New York: NYU Press.

Lewinsohn, Peter M., Roberts, R. E., Seeley, J., Rohde, P., Gotlib, I. H., and Hops, H. 1994. Adolescent Psychopathology: II. Psychosocial Risk Factors for Depression. *Journal of Abnormal Psychology* 103 (2): 302–315.

Lightsey, Owen Richard. 1996. The role of psychological resources in well-being: A reply. *Counseling Psychologist* 25 (4): 699–705.

Lucas, Richard E., Diener, Ed, and Suh, Eunkook. 1996. Discriminant validity of well-being measures. *Journal of Personality and Social Psychology* 71 (3): 616–628.

Magaletta, Phillip R., and Oliver, J. M. 1999. The hope construct, will, and ways: Their relations with self-efficacy, optimism, and general well-being. *Journal of Clinical Psychology* 55 (5): 539–551.

Marsella, Anthony J. 1998. Urbanization, mental health, and social deviancy: A review of issues and research. *American Psychologist* 53:624–634.

Masten, Ann S. 2001. Ordinary magic: Resilience processes in development. *American Psychologist* 56(3): 227–238.

McCullough, Gable, Huebner, E. Scott, and Laughlin, James E. 2000. Life events, self-concept, and adolescents' positive subjective well-being. *Psychology in the Schools* 37 (3): 281–290.

McNeill, Brian W., Prieto, Loreto, Niemann, Yolanda Flores, Pizarro, Marc, Vera, Elizabeth M., and Gomez, Sylvia. 2001. Current directions in Chicana/o psychology. *Counseling Psychologist* 29:5–17.

Niemann, Yolanda. 2001. Stereotypes about Chicanas and Chicanos: Implications for counseling. *Counseling Psychologist* 29:55–90.

Oishi, Shigehiro, Diener, Ed, Lucas, Richard E., and Suh, Eunkook M. 1999. Cross-cultural variations in predictors of life satisfaction: Perspectives from needs and values. *Personality and Social Psychology Bulletin* 25:980–990.

Peterson, Christopher. 2000. The future of optimism. *American Psychologist* 55 (1): 44–55.

Robbins, Steven, and Kliewer, Wendy. 2000. Advances in theory and research on subjective well-being. In S. D. Brown and R. Lent (eds.), *Handbook of counseling psychology* (pp. 310–345). New York: Wiley.

Rodriguez, Norma, Mira, Consuelo B., Myers, Hector F., Morris, Julie K., and Cardoza, Desdemona. 2003. Family or friends: Who plays a greater supportive role for Latino college students? *Cultural Diversity and Ethnic Minority Psychology* 9 (3): 236–250.

Salguero, Carlos, and McCusker, Wendy. 1996. Symptom expression in inner-city Latinas: Psychopathology or help seeking? In Bonnie J. R. Leadbeater and Niobe Way (eds.), *Urban girls: Resisting stereotypes, creating identities* (pp. 328–336). New York: NYU Press.

Scheier, Michael, and Carver, Charles S. 1985. Optimism, coping, and health:

Assessment and implications of generalized outcome expectancies. *Health Psychology* 4:219–247.

Scholte, Ron H., van Lieshout, Cornelis, and van Aken, Marcel. 2001. Perceived relational support in adolescence: Dimensions, configurations, and adolescent adjustment. *Journal of Research on Adolescence* 11 (1): 71–94.

Seligman, Martin E. P., and Csikszentmihalyi, Mihaly. 2000. Positive psychology: An introduction. *American Psychologist* 55 (1): 5–14.

Shorey, Hal, Snyder, C. R., Yang, Xiangdong, and Lewin, Michael R. 2003. The role of hope as a mediator in recollected parenting, adult attachment, and mental health. *Journal of Social and Clinical Psychology* 22 (6): 685–715.

Snyder, C. R. 1995. Conceptualizing, measuring, and nurturing hope. *Journal of Counseling and Development* 73:355–360.

Snyder, C. R., Hoza, Betsy, Pelham, William, and Rapoff, Michael. 1997. The development and validation of the Children's Hope Scale. *Journal of Pediatric Psychology* 22:399–421.

Stice, Eric, Ragan, Jennifer, and Randall, Patrick. 2004. Prospective Relations between Social Support and Depression: Differential Direction of Effects for Parent and Peer Support? *Journal of Abnormal Psychology* 113 (1): 155–159.

Suh, Eunkook, Diener, Ed, Oishi, Shigehiro, and Triandis, Harry. 1998. The shifting basis of life satisfaction judgments across cultures: Emotions versus norms. *Journal of Personality and Social Psychology* 74 (2): 482–493.

Watson, David, Clark, Leanna, and Tellegen, A. 1988. Development and validation of brief measures of positive and negative affect: The PANAS scales. *Journal of Personality and Social Psychology* 54 (6): 1063–1070.

Way, N., and Robinson, Melissa G. 2003. A longitudinal study of the effects of family, friends, and school experiences on the psychological adjustment of ethnic minority, low-SES adolescents. *Journal of Adolescent Research* 18 (4): 324–346.

Chapter 14

La Salud

Latina Adolescents Constructing Identities, Negotiating Health Decisions

Yvette Flores

> I call myself Mexican. What influenced me to say I'm
> Mexican is the fact that people, I guess, fear them. I guess
> I thought that by having that title, maybe people would
> just leave me alone to live my life. My mom never really
> said, "You're Mexican." She just wanted me to be *myself.*
>
> —Ana, age fifteen

Ana is tall, with dark hair and almond-shaped brown eyes. She attends an urban high school where students of Mexican origin have a high dropout rate. She has agreed to participate in a focus group to discuss young Latinas' thoughts, hopes, and aspirations.[1] She is outspoken and has strong opinions. Her parents are immigrants; they work long hours and lack the time to guide her regarding school. They tell her she should avoid dangers and bad influences, but they are unable to offer her a road map to negotiate her bicultural context at school, in the community, or at home. In spite of this, Ana is doing well in school. She hopes to graduate and go to college.

This chapter reports on the findings of focus groups held with Latina ninth graders in three cities of Northern California in the late 1990s. The project was guided by three questions: (1) What do Latina adolescents consider to be risk factors for them? (2) How do Latina adolescents make decisions to avoid risky behaviors? And (3) what role does ethnic identity play in the life of early adolescents? Ultimately, the study aimed to identify the factors that promote resilience and help young women like Ana succeed despite poverty, discrimination, and limited social and environmental resources.

Perspectives on Risk and Resilience

A recent policy report by the National Coalition of Hispanic Health and Human Service Organizations (COSSMHO) concluded that Latina adolescents were a population at extreme risk, given their high rates of "new morbidities," including school dropout, pregnancy, substance abuse, suicidality, and use of weapons (COSSMHO 1999). Three of the four more serious threats to girls' health and education—pregnancy, depression, and substance abuse—are more prevalent among Latinas than among African American or Asian American girls (Centers for Disease Control 1998). Moreover, these trends seem to be worsening over time, particularly as a result of increased acculturation and loss of cultural practices. These researchers conclude that a loss of protective cultural factors and family support compromise the health and well-being of Latina adolescents (COSSMHO 1999; Flores in press-a).

Although the risk factors Latina adolescents face are well documented, less is known about the protective factors that allow young Latinas like Ana to thrive. Latinas born and raised in the United States require bicultural competence, the ability to negotiate both the culture of the family and that of the larger social context, in order to succeed academically and socially (Falicov 1999; Vargas-Reighley 2004). Bernal and Knight (1993) argue that this process can be facilitated by a young person's sense of belonging to an ethnic group (ethnic self-identification), particularly in the face of ethnic or racial discrimination. Specifically, girls who feel a connection to the ethnic origin of their families *and* who know about and participate in ethnic rituals and traditions have better mental health and academic achievement. Few studies have asked Latina adolescents themselves what they perceive to be risks and what they consider to be protective factors, or what influences affect their health decisions. This is the central focus of this chapter.

Methodology

Female adolescents were recruited to participate in focus groups to discuss ethnic identity and health concerns. We examined several domains: the adolescents' ethnic identification; the factors that influenced that identification; perceived risks; sources of support; normative pressures to engage in early sexuality, smoking, drinking, and use of drugs; aspirations; and how the adolescents negotiated health decisions.

Procedures

Students were recruited from three schools, one urban high school, one suburban high school, and one semirural middle school with high Latino enrollment. One undergraduate research assistant of the same gender and ethnicity as the participants facilitated each focus group. An additional research assistant served as recorder and made process notations and observations. The focus groups' discussions were audiotaped and transcribed. One junior high group was conducted in Spanish. The remaining groups were conducted in English, although the participants often used Spanish.

Content analysis of the transcription was carried out to identify and elucidate themes (Creswell 1997). The principal investigator and a research assistant not familiar with the project analyzed each transcript independently of the other. Only themes with a 95 percent concordance rate between raters are reported in this chapter.

Participants

Five female focus groups were conducted, with a total of sixty students participating. The adolescents ranged in age from fourteen to fifteen years and included two groups of ninth graders in a predominantly Chicano junior high school ($N = 30$), two groups of high school freshmen in an urban, ethnically diverse high school ($N = 20$), and one group of freshmen in a suburban, predominantly European American high school ($N = 10$).

Results

Ethnic Self-Identification

The majority of the students were of Mexican descent and second generation; half of the sample reported their parents were born outside of the

United States. Most immigrant parents had been born in Mexico; a few were born in Central America or the Caribbean. Three students reported being racially mixed. One had a European American parent, one had an African American parent, and one had a Filipino parent.

Nearly all the junior and senior high school students identified as Mexican, regardless of place of birth. Students in the predominantly European American school chose a variety of labels. One chose the label "Chicana," one used "Puerto Rican," and one called herself a "Flipsican" (to reflect her Filipino-Mexican ethnicity). Another student stated she was black and Mexican, and one stated, "I say I'm Mexican and Spanish." At the more ethnically diverse high school, several students who had a Central American and a Mexican parent chose the label "Mexican," stating that it was easier: "A lot of people don't know where my mom's country is, so I just say Mexican."

Factors That Influenced Ethnic Identification

Most students did not recall why or when they had started labeling themselves with their chosen descriptor. Very few students had discussed their ethnicity with their parents or other family members. Several students began identifying as Mexican as a result of interactions with their peers. For example, one student in the predominantly European American high school discussed the first time she called herself Mexican: "I would have to say I was twelve in the seventh grade. I really started to identify myself as Mexican. That was after the fact that a group of Mexican girls started calling me a wannabe white girl. I found that really offensive. That was basically when I started identifying myself as that, Mexican."

A junior high school student stated: "Chicana—because someone told me that, from all, that everything put together (Spanish, indigenous, etc.), mixing, everybody came up with Chicano." Another high school student stated that she began to use the label "Chicana" after her brother came home from college and told her that is what she was.

While the students described the majority of their parents as desiring their daughters to be Mexican, few parents actively discussed this or taught their daughters Mexican cultural rituals or practices. Few students were aware of how their parents labeled themselves. When a discussion of ethnic labeling occurred, it was mostly among siblings.

Ethnicity of Peers

Most of the students in the junior high school described their friends as predominantly Mexican. This is not surprising, since 80 percent of the student body is of Mexican origin, and most students socialized primarily within their own ethnic group. In the urban, ethnically diverse high school, students had primarily Mexican or other Latina friends but indicated having friendships with European American girls as well. A few girls labeled these friends "whitesicans"—white people who think they are Mexican.

Students in the predominantly European American high school indicated they had friends from various ethnic groups. In this sample of predominantly Mexican-identified adolescents, ethnic self-identification appears to be influenced less by family than by context. While most of the parents were immigrants, few of them actively encouraged, taught, or promoted a Mexican ethnic identification among their daughters. Those girls who attend schools where there are large numbers of Mexican students appeared more comfortable with the label, and they socialized with and dated primarily other Mexican youth.

Perceived Risks

When the girls were asked to indicate what they perceived to be the major challenges or problems facing Latinas, teen pregnancy emerged as the primary issue across all three schools. In the junior high school, three girls knew of Latina girls who had babies and were not attending school. Twelve of the junior high school girls mentioned they had older teenage cousins who had been pregnant while in high school. Half of the sample ($N = 30$) identified cigarette smoking, and forty girls noted alcohol as serious threats to their health.

Normative Pressures to Engage in Early Sexuality

None of the junior high school students disclosed engaging in sexual behavior, and only five of the high school girls acknowledged having had sex. The sexually active girls included two fourteen-year-olds and three fifteen-year-olds. Moreover, all the girls indicated that they felt a lot of pressure from males to engage in sex. A junior high school student stated,

"I don't want to ruin my reputation; guys want to get with you and then they talk and no one respects you." The high school students also described experiencing a great deal of pressure from male peers to date and have sex.

Most of the Mexican-origin girls were not allowed to date. Consequently, many of the girls had secret boyfriends and saw them without parental knowledge. The girls who were sexually active disclosed that they had not had casual sex, only sex with their boyfriends. Most of the girls dated males over sixteen years of age with whom sex "just happened." None of the five girls who were sexually active reported condom use. While all the girls had received sex education and had information about sexually transmitted infections (STIs) and the risk of HIV, they did not feel they could negotiate condom use with their boyfriends. One stated, "Guys just pressure you too much; you don't have time to plan." Another said, "We were both virgins, and we plan to marry after high school, or if I get pregnant, so we don't really worry about it. We want to have a big family." Another stated, "If we suggest condoms, they are going to think we are doing it with others."

Negotiating Sex

Most of the girls were abstinent. They indicated several reasons to avoid sex, including fear of parental disapproval, not wanting to get pregnant, not having a boyfriend, protecting their reputation, and wanting to graduate from high school.

None of the girls had discussed sex openly with their parents. However, most of the girls expressed a desire to have greater communication with their parents, particularly their mother, regarding sexuality. In general, while the girls perceived the lack of information regarding sexuality and the limited communication with their parents on the subject as threats to making wise decisions, their awareness of their parents' views and values served a protective function, helping girls choose not to have sex.

Normative Pressures to Smoke, Drink, and Use Drugs

The girls reported moderate drug use, mostly at home and with romantic partners. More than half the sample ($N = 36$) said they had tried alcohol at least once. Three of the high school girls smoked cigarettes on occasion, and all denied any drug use other than marijuana. None of the girls reported frequent use of alcohol; however, all the sexually active girls reported drinking on "their dates." One girl indicated that her boyfriend smoked weed, but she was afraid to try it. Another stated, "Weed is all around; you just have to be strong and say no, that's stupid, I am not going to do that."

Of the three girls who admitted smoking marijuana, two had smoked with older siblings. They often smoked at home after school and laughed that their parents had no idea they had the drug in the house: "They probably would think it was oregano or something, they [parents] are so innocent. Mexican parents really don't know what is going on these days." All three girls who smoked marijuana drew a clear distinction between alcohol, marijuana, and other drugs, which they saw as more serious and which they would not even try.

The girls who smoked cigarettes and drank alcohol stated that they had encountered a great deal of peer pressure. In fact, most of the girls saw peer pressure to drink as part and parcel of going to school. In addition, the girls recognized that they are often bombarded with media messages that glorify alcohol use and smoking. One said, "It's everywhere, magazines, billboards, music, TV . . . you just have to make a choice and decide what you want to do."

Negotiating Use of Licit and Illicit Drugs

The girls who had not tried alcohol, cigarettes, or any drug stated that they had made the choice based on concerns about their parents. One girl stated, "As it is I am not allowed to go anywhere; if I got caught doing any of that, I would be grounded for life." Another stated, "My parents don't tell me not to smoke or drink, but they do say that we are not 'that kind of people.' . . . What they mean is that only *cholos* and *cholas* get high." Several girls resonated with this statement, echoing their experiences with parents who did not directly tell them how to act but gave them examples of family members or neighbors who were not acting appropriately.

However, most of the girls complained about hypocritical parental attitudes. One stated, "My parents both smoke and drink but then tell us how bad this stuff is for us. What are we supposed to think?" Despite their dissatisfaction with the degree of communication with their parents, all the girls expressed great empathy for the level of stress, workload, and problems their parents experienced. "You know, they do the best they can, they have so many responsibilities; life here [in the United States] is hard."

Sources of Support

Most girls identified few sources of support. They felt they could not talk to their parents about sex and the pressures they experienced at school related to alcohol or other drug use, or experiences of perceived discrimination. Most girls in both high schools and the junior high felt that school administrators did not understand them. Furthermore, many girls sensed a pervasive context of prejudice where they were stereotyped, devalued, and misunderstood because they were culturally different or spoke with an accent. In the urban high school, most of the girls named a school counselor as the sole source of support in their lives.

A few girls considered girlfriends the main source of support. However, several girls noted that they could not always trust other girls, particularly when it comes to guys. Few girls felt their parents understood their social and academic situation well enough to provide support. The pervasive feeling among the girls was of not being understood.

Future Aspirations

The girls were asked what they foresaw doing in five and ten years. The junior and senior high school students indicated they would have graduated from high school and hoped to have a good job that paid well. These girls had no specific career plan in mind. Within ten years all the girls expected to be married, with children, and working. Two of the girls stated they would like to attend college, but none had any specific plans.

Differences between Junior and Senior High School Girls

All the girls were ninth graders. However, half of the participants attended the junior high, and the others went to two senior high schools. The girls in junior high school were less likely to drink, smoke, or engage in sexual behavior than their high school peers. High school girls reported more peer pressure to drink, smoke, and have sex.

Ethnic identification was influenced primarily by the school setting. Those attending predominantly Mexican schools and who had mostly Mexican friends chose that label for themselves. Girls who had a non-Mexican parent were more likely to choose the label "Latina."

In Their Own Voice: Making Good Health Decisions

The girls were asked what would help them make good health decisions and what they could tell parents and educators regarding their needs and desires. The girls felt they had little power to negotiate condom use or to say no to sex. They expressed a desire that boys not pressure them to have sex or drink. As one said, "Tell the guys not to hassle us about, you know, doing it."

Girls also desired greater communication with their parents on matters of health; this was particularly true among the girls who had immigrant parents. One stated, "Our parents need to take the initiative and talk to us . . . let us know they can handle talking about sex and stuff." Another said, "They are so old-fashioned, you know. They don't know what is going on, and we need them to tell us what they want us to do and support us a little more, you know."

Girls talked about their need to be treated fairly at school and to be regarded as individuals, not as stereotyped members of an ethnic group. As one said, "It is so hard, you know. You walk around school, and either you are invisible and no one cares about you, or they come at you with attitude like they are thinking, oh, she's just another Mexican, no good, up to no good, gonna amount to nothing." Another girl echoed this feeling: "We just want to live our life, you know, go to school, learn, figure out what we are going to do when we are older . . . we need respect, that's it."

Lessons Learned

The high-risk behaviors affecting young Latinas were not prevalent in this sample of junior and senior high school girls, despite the fact that the girls received minimal direct support or guidance from their families regarding health decisions. The majority of the young women identified as Mexican or Latina and appeared to have internalized key cultural values, despite the absence of direct cultural instruction from their parents. As others (e.g., Bernal and Knight, 1993) have found, ethnic identification, even when unexamined, may serve a protective function for these young women. Perhaps identification with their ethnic group provides a sense of belonging that increases these girls' self-esteem and prevents risky behaviors.

While the parents did not actively guide their daughters' behavioral

choices, the parents' cultural values may have fulfilled a protective function for the young women. Participants considered the impact of their behavior on their parents and often used parental values as a reason to avoid
situations of risk. They also credited parental strictness as a deterrent to
getting into trouble. While the girls did not articulate an adherence to traditional Latino values, their actions reflected respect for their parents, an
understanding of the stresses parents faced, and behaviors in accordance
with implicit parental rules. While ethnic identification per se appeared
not to influence how these young women negotiated health decisions,
those who attended predominantly Mexican schools had peers who also
had internalized similar values in the home. For students in more culturally homogeneous schools, it may have been easier to adhere to parental
rules and values given the similar cultural background of their friends.

The young women acknowledged facing strong pressure from boys
to have sex and drink alcohol. Despite the fact that they could not seek
support from their parents to refuse these advances, most girls found the
strength to avoid such situations. These young women often expressed
cultural values as sources of strength: not wanting to have a bad reputation, not disappointing their parents, and fear of even greater parental
restriction of their freedom.

The girls understood and experienced the influence of peers and the
need to fit in while being an individual. Most of the junior high school
students were concerned that the transition to high school would bring
more pressure to engage in high-risk behaviors. None of the girls felt they
could protect themselves indefinitely without support from parents and
less pressure from males.

Few of the girls had a life plan; they mirrored the societal expectation
that women will marry and have children and work to help support the
family. The few girls who expressed a desire to attend college were students in the suburban high school and had more exposure to college and
career planning.

In sum, the findings of this study indicate that despite significant peer
pressure, these young women demonstrated great agency to avoid engaging in high-risk behaviors in a context of minimal perceived support.
They had to rely on their own internalized cultural values, sense of family
obligation, and individual strength, but they could not articulate specific
strategies to withstand the pressure from peers to have sex, drink, and
smoke.

The cultural divide between immigrant parents and U.S.-born or U.S.-raised children may have led to a sense of isolation for the girls. Likewise, economic conditions may have limited the availability of time parents had available to support, guide, and communicate actively with their daughters. Furthermore, the young women did not perceive the schools as sites of support, since previous experience indicated that their cultural uniqueness would be problematized and devalued.

Policy Implications

The findings presented in this chapter have important policy implications. First, it is clear that Latina adolescents want and need greater parental involvement in their life. Existing studies document the importance of parental support and increased communication with their children during the adolescent period; thus action research programs focusing on Latino parent-adolescent communication and youth empowerment are necessary to support young Latinas' journey into adulthood. Likewise, primary prevention programs must be developed to bridge the cultural differences between immigrant Latino families and their offspring. Immigrant parents in particular need to increase their understanding of the social context of their daughters to promote greater support of their daughters' health decisions. The young women participants in this study utilized their cultural knowledge and internalized cultural values as a tool to avoid high-risk behaviors. This cultural knowledge can be expanded and supported and can serve as a vehicle to foster greater parent-child communication.

The second implication is that although the young women exhibited agency in making health decisions, they need a wider repertoire of negotiation skills. The girls expressed a desire for the boys to decrease their pressure, which suggests a limited sense of power to negotiate with their male peers. Therefore, it is crucial to offer young women the skills to communicate directly and actively with males and develop a greater sense of agency regarding their health decisions.

Primary prevention programs need to be designed that foster behavioral self-efficacy within a culturally congruent and respectful context.[2] These programs ought to include information on how to negotiate safe sex with a partner. Young men also need programs that increase their awareness of and respect for the experiences of young Latinas.

Third, the participants in this study expressed a sense of isolation. They mentioned few mentors, such as older sisters or other advocates. Although they expressed future academic and career aspirations, they lacked sufficient knowledge or planning to attain them. This shows the need for professional Latinas to engage more actively with young women who lack extrafamilial sources of support. The future of young Latinas largely rests on those of us who have had the privilege to hear their needs and wants expressed in their own voice.

NOTES

1. The term "Latina" is used to be inclusive of the young women who were biracial and of mixed Mexican and other Latino backgrounds. The majority of the participants, however, chose to call themselves Mexican or Mexican American.

2. A model program of this type is Nahui Ollin Teotl—The Essence of the Four Movements, a Group Mentoring Program for Latinas and Young Women of Color in Middle and High School offered by the National Latina Health Organization in Oakland, California. The after-school program offers talking circles on sexism, racism, body image, and spirituality. The program is designed to promote skills to make healthy life decisions, increase girls' awareness *and* understanding of issues that affect them as young women of color, and to create a safe environment where girls can explore positive life choices. See http://www.latinahealth.org/programs.html.

REFERENCES

Bernal, Martha E., and George P. Knight, eds. 1993. *Ethnic Identity: Formation and Transmission among Hispanics and Other Minorities.* Albany: State University of New York Press.

Center for Disease Control. 1998. Youth Risk Surveillance-United States, 1997. *MMWR* 47:50.

COSSMHO. 1999. *The State of Hispanic Girls.* Washington, DC: COSSMHO Press.

Creswell, John. 1997. *Qualitative Inquiry and Research Design: Choosing among Five Traditions.* Thousand Oaks, CA: Sage.

Falicov, Celia. 1999. *Latino Families in Therapy: A Guide to Multicultural Practice.* New York: Guilford Press.

Flores, Yvette. In press-a. Latino Children and Adolescents. In *The Oxford Encyclopedia of Latinos and Latinas in the United States,* ed. Deena J. Gonzalez and Suzanne Oboler. Oxford: Oxford University Press.

————. In press-b. Latino Parenting. In *The Oxford Encyclopedia of Latinos and Latinas in the United States,* ed. Deena J. Gonzalez and Suzanne Oboler. Oxford: Oxford University Press.

Guendelman, Sylvia, J. B. Gould, M. Hudes, and B. Eskenazi. 1990. Generational Differences in Prenatal Health among the Mexican American Population: Findings from HHANES 1982–84. *American Journal of Public Health* 80 (suppl.): 61–65.

Vargas-Reighley, Rosalva. 2004. *Bi-cultural Competence and Academic Resilience among Immigrants.* Levittown, PA: LFB Scholarly Publishing.

Zambrana, Ruth, ed. 1995. *Understanding Latino Families: Scholarship, Policy and Practice.* Thousand Oaks, CA: Sage.

Chapter 15

Latina Adolescent Motherhood
A Turning Point?

Stephen T. Russell and Faye C. H. Lee

Teenage motherhood is often regarded as a significant mistake, and much has been written about the risk factors for pregnancy and early motherhood among Latina adolescents. This focus on the problem of teenage pregnancy has limited attention to the sources of strength and success in the lives of Latina adolescent mothers. How does motherhood affect the other critical relationships in the lives of young Latinas: their relationships with parents and partners? How does it affect their educational aspirations, commitment, and success? How can we build from the strengths of young mothers to plan program strategies for pregnant and parenting Latina teens? In this chapter we focus on twenty-seven Latina adolescent mothers, their sources of strength, and their ideas about programs for pregnant and parenting teens like themselves.

Latina youth have among the highest pregnancy rates in the United States. The national Latino teen birthrate is twice that of non-Latino whites (Driscoll et al., 2001), and in California Latino adolescents are more than three times more likely to become parents than are whites (U.S. Department of Health and Human Services, 2001). Thus, in spite of the recent well-publicized declines in the overall teen pregnancy rate in the United States, current data highlight the social problem of Latina teen pregnancy. For Latina teens in the United States, the personal challenges of teen pregnancy and parenthood are often compounded by economic (poverty) and cultural factors (language, immigrant status, and traditional Latino cultural values and norms). At the same time, becoming a teen mother does not automatically lead to exclusively negative outcomes. Some Latina teen mothers describe renewed hope and aspirations for the future both for themselves and for their children. In this chapter, they tell of their hopes and dreams and the strengthening of relationships with family and partners as results of early motherhood.

Strengths among Latina Teen Mothers: A Life Course View

A person's life trajectory, or pathway through life, involves an interweaving of individual agency within the constraints and opportunities of the social context (Elder and Russell, 2000; Koss-Chioino and Vargas, 1999). Two important elements of life course trajectories are relevant: transitions and turning points. *Transitions* are life events that require reorganization of the daily functions of life (Graber and Brooks-Gunn, 1996). *Turning points* are a unique form of life transition. They are moments or events in the life course that cause lasting changes in trajectories of development, or at least some significant reorientation of life's priorities. Turning points can create opportunities, or they may reinforce existing constraints and further confine an individual's life path (Rönkä, Oravala, and Pulkkinen, 2002). Becoming a mother during the teenage years often marks a turning point because it fundamentally alters the course of life, either for better or for worse.

Three mechanisms are helpful for understanding turning points and their influences on life trajectories (Elder and Russell, 2000). The concept of *interdependent lives* acknowledges the multiple sources of influence that social relationships have in the lives of youth during times of life change. For the Latina teen mother these would include her partner, family, and friends, as they are crucial relationships with important cultural value for many Latinas (Clayson et al., 2003; Oropesa, 1996). *Situational imperatives* are characteristics of the new life situation that fundamentally shape one's responses to a life turning point (Elder and Russell, 2000). The situational imperatives of teen motherhood may be dramatic, including the sudden responsibilities and burdens of parenthood (often single parenthood), along with the prospect of fundamental changes in the teen mother's social support and relationships. Finally, the *accentuation principle* holds that a person's adaptation to a life turning point is based on an interaction between the requirements of the new situation and an individual's life history (Elder and Russell, 2000). Teen pregnancy may accentuate maladaptive behaviors that led to premature parenthood in the first place (Rönkä et al., 2002), or it may reorient a young mother toward greater responsibility and planfulness for the sake of her child (SmithBattle and Leonard, 1998). The accentuation principle suggests that the strengths that exist in a teen mother's life—whether her aspirations, sources of support, or cultural values—may be uniquely activated at this turning point.

While the research literature is dominated by discussions of the harmful consequences of teen pregnancy and parenthood, there are small bodies of work that recast these issues. Much of this work has identified teen motherhood as a possible adaptive response to life in poverty (Geronimus, 1991, 1992). Subcultures defined by poverty may support and reinforce teen pregnancy and early motherhood because these may be the only adult roles available to teens who have limited access to the life options that are valued in the dominant culture (SmithBattle, 2000).

Thus, some research suggests the possibility that the transition to motherhood can be a positive turning point for some young women. Our chapter focuses on strengths in the lives of Latina teen mothers, but we in no way intend to minimize the personal challenges faced by teen parents and their children (Moore et al. 1993; Ahn 1994; Robert and Bong 1999). Given these challenges, there is a clear need for teen pregnancy prevention and intervention efforts, and there is strong evidence that such programs can make a positive difference in the lives of young mothers and their families (Camarena, Minor, Melmer, and Ferrie, 1998). There is a pressing need for teen pregnancy prevention and intervention approaches that are grounded in the unique needs and experiences—and strengths—of Latino young people (Russell, Lee, and Latino/a Teen Pregnancy Prevention Workgroup, 2004).

A Study of Latina Teen Mothers in California

This chapter draws from a qualitative study of parenting Latina teens' perspectives of adolescent pregnancy prevention programs (Driscoll et al., 2003). We interviewed twenty-seven Latina teen mothers aged fifteen to nineteen (average age seventeen), each with one child (ages 1 to 36 months; 9.8 months average age). Half were immigrants, and half were born in the United States. All lived in California, half in the highly urbanized San Francisco Bay area, and half in the more rural south-central valley. While the challenges of life as an adolescent mother were central to our discussions with these young women, in this chapter we focus our attention on their stories about aspirations and sources of strength. Many told of positive changes in their aspirations and their key sources of social, emotional, and instrumental (tangible help such as child care, financial assistance, or transportation) support.

The Latina teen mothers in our study were contacted through pregnancy prevention programs. They were interviewed individually and face-to-face by youthful interviewers who were trained by the research team. Interviews were conducted in either English or Spanish (nine, or 33 percent in Spanish), depending on the respondent's preference, and were held at locations that were most convenient for the teen mom. The interviewers followed a protocol that consisted primarily of open-ended questions designed to elicit and probe respondents' candid and detailed views of the recommended practices for teen pregnancy prevention programs, as well as to uncover unexpected issues. Before asking questions about the pregnancy prevention program in which they were participating, we asked about how pregnancy and motherhood had changed key dimensions of their lives, including their school and work life, and relationships with their partners (the father of their babies) and parents.[1]

We used two approaches to analyze our interview data. First, the authors reread transcripts to identify key quotes or passages that described sources of strength for Latina adolescent mothers. We wished to allow these young mothers to speak for themselves about strengths in their lives. Second, we categorized their responses to provide basic descriptive information and to analyze the data. We conducted chi-square tests of possible group differences based on respondents' location (Bay Area or Central Valley) or country of birth, and conducted analysis of variance based on respondents' age and the age (in months) of their children. These quantitative results are integrated into our discussion of the interview questions and are reported in endnotes.

Higher Educational Aspirations and Performance

Adolescent mothers said motherhood increased their aspirations for the future and believed education was needed for a better future. Half (thirteen) gave specific examples of how motherhood improved their educational aspirations and performance. As one young mother said, "I just don't want to live the life I'm living right now. I want to go higher because I know I can. I got a whole life ahead of me." Several teens described specific visions for the future. For example: "I plan on getting my high school diploma and my GED in December. And then I want to go to a community college around here, but eventually, like in ten years from now, I want to have maybe my master's degree, at least my bachelor's degree in paralegal."

Teen mothers also spoke of the importance of education in their roles as mothers:

> If you don't finish high school, what's going to happen when your kids want you to help them with their homework and you don't know because you never finished [high school]? It's about being helpful with your kids, and you know to help them have a good education, and you'd be able to say, "Well I finished high school, and I was pregnant with you." Having them feel good about you being [their] parent and you being able to teach them. I think it's always important to finish school.

Most of the teen moms discussed their future education in generalities and did not seem to have clear educational goals. But even when they did not know much about post–high school education, they recognized the potential value of education and expressed interest in continuing their schooling. This young mother is an example: "For me I put more importance on school to get further ahead. Before I didn't have anybody, so it didn't matter to me, and school was last for me, but now it's first." Becoming a mother altered her educational aspirations, although she had little understanding of higher education. She continued: "So what kind of colleges are out there? Because I don't even know myself. I don't even know what college I want to go to yet. I want to go, but I don't even know what, how it works. [I don't know the] difference between degrees."

Like most parents, many of the teen mothers in our study were motivated by their desire to care for and support their children and by their desire for positive outcomes for their children. For example, an eighteen-year-old mother who was interviewed shortly before the beginning of her senior year at an adult-education school described how she had dropped out of school in the seventh grade and was living with her future in-laws on about $500 per month from "welfare." This is how her son motivated her: "Just knowing that my son's there, and every time I look at my son, [I think], I have to get a job, I have to get everything together, because I don't want him to be like me. I don't want him to be struggling all the time for money, struggling for transportation, for everything."

Many teen moms became more committed to education and said they studied harder. An eighteen-year-old described her experience: "Well, I wasn't really going to school before I had got pregnant. When I was about four months pregnant, I went back to school, and I wanted to get an education because I always seen myself as graduating." Another teen mother described her grades: "I brought them up more. Instead of talking in school, I did my work, concentrated more about what the teacher was saying and everything because I want to get out of there. I want to get a good job."

For these Latina teens, becoming a mother made them more aware of the responsibilities of supporting themselves and their babies. Most of the interviewees linked education with improved career options and economic well-being and success: "Without an education you haven't anything, you have nothing, no house, no car, nothing." Many described education as an investment in the future.

Hope for the future, higher educational aspirations, and improved attitude toward and performance in school appeared to be among the most significant positive outcomes of becoming a mother for the teens in our study. We also found that the Latina teen mothers who reported improvements in their schooling were significantly more likely to say that their parents should be included in pregnancy prevention programs.[2] This speaks to the notion of interdependent lives and the role that key supportive relationships, particularly with immediate and extended family, may play for Latina teen mothers. We turn our attention to this topic in the following sections.

Improved Relationships with the Baby's Father

Eight of the teen mothers (approximately one-third) reported that their relationships with the fathers of their babies had improved since they had become parents. They described increased closeness, instrumental support such as help with caring for children and providing transportation or money from their partners, and a conscious change of their interactions for the sake of their child. In terms of closeness, when asked about her relationship with the baby's father one mother said, "Actually it's gotten better because we've been talking lately, getting along." Another said, "He likes her. He adores her. Every time he's at home, he's playing with her, even though he's tired he's playing with her." One teen mother pointed out that the relationship initially worsened but had improved over time: "At first it made us separate, but now we're closer together because we realize the responsibility. So actually it brought us together." Another mother talked about the help her partner provides: "After she was born, things were better, and he's been more helpful, he changes her diapers, he plays with her, he'll watch her, if he doesn't go to work and I have to go to school, he'll watch her. So actually it united us more." Two of the teen mothers talked about improvements in their relationships with their partners because of the need to set an example for their child. In explaining the ways that the relationship improved one mother said, "Now that we have the baby we try not to argue, not to fight, not to do anything because of the baby, because they learn everything. And we don't want for her to get married at a young age or something like that."

All but two of the teen mothers thought that involving the fathers of babies was an important strategy for programs that serve pregnant and parenting teens. Most of the responses were simply that programs should include both parents because raising a child should be the responsibility of both mothers and fathers.

One said that fathers should be involved so that they can better understand the young mothers' experience. She commented:

> [Yes,] so that they can see what mothers have to go through. So they can also share the moment, good or bad, share it with the mothers. And they also need help . . . maybe like also doing some groups for fathers, later in the day when they're home. Maybe men and women both going so they can talk to them so they can also know. Because sometimes, men don't always talk realistically. . . . They don't know what women have to do.

Although only one-third of participants reported improved relationships with their child's father, most agreed that programs have the potential to improve those relationships.

Positive Relationships with Parents

Parents are an important lifelong source of social support and may play a particularly important role in the lives of pregnant and parenting teens. In our study, ten Latina teen mothers reported improved relationships with their mothers, and seven reported improved relationships with their fathers. Increased closeness was a common theme: "Well, you know, after I had the baby, I think I'm closer to my parents, because I'm always going to their house."

Mothers were prominent among positive supporting relationships for these Latina teen mothers, particularly for those living in the Central Valley. We found that Latina teen mothers living in the Central Valley were significantly more likely than those living in the Bay Area to report that their relationships with their mothers had gotten better since they had their babies.[3] Only two of the eleven Bay Area teen mothers reported better maternal relationships, while nine out of sixteen Central Valley teen mothers reported better relationships with their own mothers. The reason for this difference may be that Latinas living in the Central Valley have a more family-based local culture. Another possible explanation is that the stresses of living in urban areas further alienate urban Latina teen mothers from their families. In describing their relationships with mothers, the young women mentioned emotional closeness and instrumental, daily support as common themes.

When asked if her relationship with her mother had gotten better or worse, one young mother said, "I would say better. Because she's really always there for me, and we became a lot closer, and she's so close to my daughter, so it's like bonded us more." One mother explained that the relationship had improved because motherhood has given her a better understanding of her own mother: "I guess I understand what she's going through." On the other hand, one teen mother said that the relationship had gotten better because she and her mother had changed from adversaries to friends: "It's gotten better. Because before, I used to yell a lot at my mother. I even wanted to hit her, and not now. So now we're like two friends."

The daily, instrumental support that mothers provide to teen mothers was another common theme that seemed to underlie the closeness that had developed in improved relationships: "I think my mom and I are even closer together. Because I would always leave. I wasn't home. And my mom helps me some. Like right now, she helps me." One teen mother described the improved relationship with her mother as linked to the help her mother provides, but also to the better relationship between her mother and her partner: "It got me together with my mom. She takes care of the baby when I don't have a chance to, and me and her can talk more freely. She also gave my husband an opportunity to know her better." Finally, one teen mother said the following about her relationship with her mother:

[It has gotten] better I think. . . . she helps me. When I take a shower, she gets her or sometimes if we're going somewhere like a family reunion, I'm in a hurry, and she gives her a bath, and then she changes her. . . . When I go to the WIC, when I have my appointments, she takes care of her sometimes when she can.

In this example, the teen mother describes some fundamental ways in which her relationship with her mother had changed, but she views that change as generally positive because the everyday assistance that her mother provides in raising her child has brought them closer together.

Only seven of the teen mothers reported better relationships with their fathers after their child was born; none of the Spanish-speaking teen mothers reported improved relationships with their fathers. However, it is not surprising that those who reported better relationships were significantly more likely to also report better relationships with their mothers.[4] While closeness was the theme that characterized improved relationships with mothers, improved communication seemed to be an important theme with fathers. One teen mother said, "He's kind of an introverted person, but ever since the baby's came along, he's opened up more, so our relationship's even better." Another said "It got better . . . because before we used to like argue a lot, and now we don't argue because she's there." This teen mother expressed a sentiment similar to others who talked about the baby's father—that the conscious effort not to argue in front of the baby has improved the relationship.

Several of the Latina teen mothers who reported improved relationships with their own fathers talked about the advice that their fathers gave them about raising their children. When asked whether her relationship with her father had gotten better or worse, one teen mother said, "I think better. Well, he tells me to take care of her well and to teach her good things." Our quantitative analyses revealed that teen mothers who reported improved relationships with their fathers had significantly older babies.[5] If giving advice is an important aspect of the Latina father-daughter relationship, Latina fathers may have more advice as the child gets older, and so the father-daughter relationship may also be strengthened.

We found that Latina teen mothers whose relationships with their fathers improved were also significantly more likely to report improvements in their schooling (whether in attendance, grades, or motivations and aspirations).[6] In describing their relationships with their fathers, none of the Latina teen mothers talked specifically about education. However, it may be that those whose fathers both are present and offer support are at an advantage either in terms of the structural aspects of their lives (financial support and child care) that allow them to pursue education or in terms of having their fathers' encouragement and support for educational goals and aspirations.

Finally, two-thirds (seventeen) of the Latina teen mothers in our study described the potential benefits of including their parents in pregnancy prevention and teen parenting programs. Older teen mothers were significantly more likely to say that it is desirable to include parents in programs for pregnant and parenting teens.[7] Most of those in favor of including parents talked about the important role of the extended family in a baby's life. One teen mother put it this way:

> I think it should because, that way, it makes your family stronger. . . . maybe they should have a class in the morning or at night, and all the family members could come, and they could sit down and make a family goal sheet for a week or a month [and schedule] maybe this day that person can help out with the baby with this.

This Latina mother believed that family involvement in the program could strengthen the family system and offer the potential for instrumental support for her and her child.

Conclusions: Strengths among Latina Teen Mothers

Our study reveals important strengths in the lives of Latina teen mothers. In summary, some of these mothers had a renewed commitment to education, experienced improved relationships with their babies' fathers, and were closer to their own parents. These strengths appear to be interdependent, suggesting a strengthening of family ties at this important life turning point. Young women who reported improved relationships with their own fathers were likely to report better relationships with their mothers as well, and those who reported sources of relational strength were more likely to report renewed commitment to education. What we cannot know is whether the instances of strength that we found are examples of true turning points in these young women's lives, or of accentuation of preexisting strengths in their relationships and aspirations. Clearly motherhood was an important transition for all the women we interviewed; the degree to which it will fundamentally reshape their life paths remains in question and may not be apparent (to a researcher or to them) until many years from now.

In assessing the implications of this study, we note that our sample was limited to Mexican American teen mothers in two areas of California. It is also limited to teen mothers who were participating in community-based programs; these young women may be more motivated and may have more resources and support than teen mothers who do not participate in such programs. It is also important to acknowledge our own values and perspectives: while we believe that teen pregnancy and parenthood do not automatically lead to negative outcomes, we do believe that early parenthood limits life options for young parents and their children.

In closing, we ask how adolescent parenting programs can build from the strengths that young Latina women bring with them. What program innovations might help foster some of the strengths that were revealed in our discussions with these young mothers? We know from prior research that the family is very important within traditional Latino culture (Clayson et al., 2003; Oropesa, 1996). Many of the young women in our study talk about how their families support them in their new role as mothers. This underscores the notion of interdependent lives and the importance of family as the central and obvious source of strength when young women are faced with the situational imperatives of early motherhood. Regarding educational goals and aspirations, many of the Latina teen mothers we interviewed expressed ideas that were consistent with advice given in teen pregnancy prevention programs and by others with U.S. values. That is, many of them talked about the importance of getting a good education to improve conditions for themselves and their children. This indicates teen mothers may be in the midst of a life transition that could, in fact, become a turning point. As many already do, prevention programs should take advantage of this teachable moment and provide the information the girls need to further their education, while building from strong family ties when they are present in the lives of young mothers.

Denner and Guzmán introduced the current book with a focus on the links between research on Latina girls and the many programs and policies that directly affect these girls' lives. In fact, our study was guided by an emphasis on understanding effective program practices from Latina teen mothers' perspectives. Programs for pregnant and parenting teens may work to influence a teen's life trajectory by trying to enhance a young mother's capacity; however, these programs generally do not focus on the fundamental limitations and constraints of their social contexts. As Erickson (1998) points out, larger socioeconomic and cultural considerations are fundamental to both the causes and consequences of early motherhood. These young mothers do not, however, speak of the social constraints that operate in their lives. Instead, their suggestions for effective programs (e.g., to include male partners and family members) are framed in ways that emphasize the benefits to the individual mother and child. We continue to wonder: Is it possible for programs that work with pregnant and parenting teens to intentionally focus on social and economic justice issues that underlie teen pregnancy and parenting? In what ways can young mothers become engaged to work not only for a better life for themselves and their children but also for better opportunities for all young women?

NOTES

The Latina/o Teen Pregnancy Prevention Workgroup of the Division of Agriculture and Natural Resources (ANR) of the University of California includes Michael S. Brockman (University of Arizona), Anne K. Driscoll (UC Davis), Peggy Gregory (UCCE Kings County), Marilyn Johns (UCCE San Mateo County), Darlene Liesch (UCCE Kern County), Fe Moncloa (UCCE Santa Clara County), and Carla Sousa (UCCE Tulare County).

The research described in this chapter was made possible in part by funding from a UC MEXUS grant (principal investigator Anne K. Driscoll), as well as through University of California ANR workgroup funding. We thank the participants in our study. We also thank Karen McCluskey, Leticia Carrillo, Denise Alvarado, and Ashley Waddington for their contributions to the research team.

1. All interviews were taped and transcribed. After transcription, Spanish interviews were translated into English, after which an independent bilingual reader read both transcripts (English and Spanish version) to assure accuracy.

2. Two-by-two chi-square analyses: $\chi^2(1) = 3.16, p = .08$.

3. Two-by-two chi-square analyses: $\chi^2(1) = 3.90, p = .05$.

4. Two-by-two chi-square analyses for Spanish-speaking and improved paternal relationship: $\chi^2(1) = 3.85, p = .05$; for improved paternal and maternal relationships: $\chi^2 (1) = 3.96, p = .05$.

5. The average age (in months) of the babies of teen mothers who reported improved relationships with their own fathers was 16.14, compared with an average age of 7.38 months for babies whose mothers reported no change in or worsening relationships with their fathers: $F(1) = 6.18; p = .02$.

6. Two-by-two chi-square analyses: $\chi^2 (1) = 6.43, p = .01$.

7. The average age of those who thought that including parents in programming was a good idea was 17.23, compared with an average age of 16.38 among teen mothers who thought that the inclusion of their parents would not be a good program strategy: $F(1) = 3.44$; $p = .08$.

REFERENCES

Ahn, Namkee. 1994. Teenage childbearing and high school completion: Accounting for individual heterogeneity. *Family Planning Perspectives* 26 (1): 17–21.

Camarena, Phame M., Kris Minor, Theresa Melmer, and Cheryl Ferrie. 1998. The nature and support of adolescent mothers' life aspirations. *Family Relations* 47:129–137.

Clayson, Zoe Cardoza, Xochitl Castenada, Emma Sanchez, and Claire Brindis. 2003. Intersections of culture, health, and systems in California Latino communities. In *Sexual and reproductive health promotion in Latino populations: Parteras, promotoras y poetas: Case studies across the Americas,* edited by M. I. Torres and G. P. Cernada, 293–306. Amityville, NY: Baywood.

Driscoll, Anne K., M. Antonia Biggs, Claire D. Brindis, and Ekua Yankah. 2001. Adolescent Latino reproductive health: A review of the literature. *Hispanic Journal of Behavioral Sciences* 23 (3): 255–326.

Driscoll, Anne K., Michael S. Brockman, Peggy Gregory, Melina M. Bersamin, Marilyn Johns, Faye C. H. Lee, Darlene Liesch, Fe Moncloa, Carla Sousa, Stephen T. Russell, and Denise Alvarado. 2003. In their own words: Pregnancy prevention needs of Latino teen mothers. *California Journal of Health Promotion* 1:118–129.

Elder, Glen H., Jr., and Stephen T. Russell. 2000. Surmounting life's disadvantage. In *Negotiating adolescence in times of social change,* edited by L. J. Crockett and R. K. Silbereisen, 17–35. New York: Cambridge University Press.

Erickson, Patricia I. 1998. *Latina adolescent childbearing in East Los Angeles.* Austin: University of Texas Press.

Geronimus, Arline T. 1991. Teenage childbearing and social and reproductive disadvantage: The evolution of complex questions and the demise of simple answers. *Family Relations* 40:463–471.

———. 1992. Teenage childbearing and social disadvantage: Unprotected discourse. *Family Relations* 41:244–248.

Graber, Julia A., and Jeanne Brooks-Gunn. 1996. Transitions and turning points: Navigating the passage from childhood through adolescence. *Developmental Psychology* 32 (4): 768–776.

Koss-Chioino, Joan D., and Luis A. Vargas. 1999. *Working with Latino youth (culture, development, and context).* San Francisco: Jossey-Bass.

Lee, Bong Joo, and Robert M. Goerge. 1999. Poverty, early childbearing, and child maltreatment: A multinomial analysis. *Children and Youth Services Review* 21 (9/10): 755–780.

Moore, Kristin Anderson, David E. Myers, Donna Ruane Morrison, Christine Winquist Nord, Brett Brown, and Barry Edmonston. 1993. Age at first childbirth and later poverty. *Journal of Research on Adolescence* 3 (4): 393–422.

Oropesa, Ralph S. 1996. Normative beliefs about marriage and cohabitation: A comparison of non-Latino whites, Mexican Americans, and Puerto Ricans. *Journal of Marriage and the Family* 58:49–62.

Pérez, Sonia M., and Luis A. Duany. 1992. *Reducing Hispanic Teenage Pregnancy and Family Poverty: A Replication Guide.* Washington, DC: National Council of La Raza.

Robert, G. M., and L. J. Bong. 1999. Poverty, early childbearing, and child maltreatment: A multinomial analysis. *Children and Youth Services Review* 21 (9/10): 755–780.

Rönkä, Anna, Sanna Oravala, and Lea Pulkkinen. 2002. "I met this wife of mine and things got onto a better track": Turning points in risk development. *Journal of Adolescence* 25 (1): 47–63.

Russell, Stephen T., Faye C. H. Lee, and Latino Teen Pregnancy Prevention Workgroup. 2004. Practitioners' perspectives on effective practices for Hispanic teen pregnancy prevention. *Perspectives on Sexual and Reproductive Health* 36 (4): 142–149.

SmithBattle, Lee. 2000. The vulnerabilities of teenage mothers: Challenging prevailing assumptions. *Advances in Nursing Science* 23 (1): 29–30.

SmithBattle, Lee, and Victoria Wynn Leonard. 1998. Adolescent mothers four years later: Narratives of the self and visions of the future. *Advances in Nursing Science* 20 (3): 36–46.

U.S. Department of Health and Human Services. 2001. 1999 natality data set [CD-ROM]. CD-ROM Series, 21(12).

Chapter 16

Conclusion
Latina Girls, Social Science, and Transformation

Bianca L. Guzmán and Jill Denner

As Fine and associates (2000) have stated, our obligation as socially conscious researchers is to "come clean at the hyphen, meaning that we interrogate in our writings who we are as we co-produce the narratives we presume to collect, and we anticipate how the public and policy makers will receive, distort, and misread our data" (108). To this end, this conclusion begins with a reflection on how this book has transformed our own research, giving the reader a clear picture of why we chose to include only research that specifically focuses on the positive functioning of Latina girls. We then review the main points of each chapter and the implications of the collective findings for social science research.

Bianca's Story

As I sit in my small home office to write this conclusion, I think about the two years that Jill and I have spent editing this book. It has been a journey of self-discovery for me. I say this because during my graduate studies, I would tell others that I wanted to focus my research on Latina girls. My advisers and classmates did not know exactly how to react to this comment. I think the difficulty in responding to my research goals was a function of how psychology and the larger scientific community minimize the value of research on normal development in ethnic minority groups. The basic social science research then and now reflects a model of pathology for human nature, which is especially true for individuals of color, and primarily stems from the medical model of health delivery.

The medical model suggests that human development is problematic and that science is the way we create solutions to physiological and behavioral pathology (Engel, 1977). This focus on identifying and fixing pathology is especially true when we examine the research on people of color from economically disadvantaged and immigrant communities. Based on this model, it is no wonder that much of the social science research and especially the psychological research is heavily focused on identifying deficiencies, abnormal behavior, and the amelioration of that behavior. Others have called this model the cultural deficit model (Jones and Thorne, 1987).

When I began my research career with Latina girls, I also used this deficit model. I was enrolled in a graduate community psychology program whose main tenet was to give voice to underrepresented groups and social issues. This is significant because even though faculty members were conducting fieldwork in local communities and examining issues of juvenile justice, sexual violence, and oppression, the theories they used and taught in the classroom were still primarily based on a cultural deficit model. There were a few models of empowerment (Rappaport, 1987) and resiliency (Garmezy, 1993), but these models were used as a tool to exercise critical thinking about the general social science research. When I conducted literature searches, I found that most research on Latina girls focused on school dropouts, teenage pregnancy, gang involvement, early childhood parenting, depression, and suicide. As a young social scientist, I assumed that conducting research based on a cultural deficit model was the appropriate approach for the work I wanted to conduct; although I knew about some empowerment theory, I did not have any evidence or previous research that actually used this model to conduct research with people of color.

My dissertation, which focused on teenage pregnancy and the educational aspirations of teenage mothers of color, is testament to my orientation during those days. I used a stress and coping model (Selye, 1978), which suggests that the greater the stress and the lower level of coping that someone has, the more pathology he or she will experience. As the conclusion in my dissertation states, I found pathology in that teenage mothers of color with high levels of stress also had lower levels of coping, and therefore they did not finish their high school education.

I realize now that my research contributed to a cultural deficit model without my having any intentions of furthering the stereotypical views of teenage mothers of color. From this I learned that researchers who conduct research on a marginalized group must take full responsibility for what we publish and what we do not.

As I look over my dissertation today, I realize that my thinking and scholarship around human behavior and especially around Latina girls have shifted to a model of positivism, empowerment, and resiliency. This has been a long process that began with my reading of many feminist essays (hooks, 1984, 2000; Reinharz, 1992; Trujillo, 1998). When I first read *Feminist Theory from Margin to Center* by bell hooks (1984), I knew that I had found a feminist theory that fit my own experience as a woman scholar of color. Through hooks's incisive and clear analysis of how women of color have experienced marginalization even in the feminist movement, I knew that my experiences as a Latina scholar conducting work with Latina and African American women was indeed a struggle for the legitimization of a field of study. This legitimization has become solidified for me through the conceptualization of this book.

The editing of this book has offered me the opportunity to understand that both social scientists of color and social scientists who conduct research on marginalized groups must find a safe space in which to present their work to ensure that the value of the work is understood and acknowledged. I firmly believe that this book has allowed the contributing authors a safe space in which to present their findings and to discuss the implications of their work.

Another component of feminist research theory that shifted the way in which I conduct my research and that we have used in this book is the concept of reflexivity (Campbell and Wasco, 2000; Cosgrove and McHugh, 2000; Hill et al., 2000). "Reflexivity" is defined as an awareness of the impact that the researcher has on the research process as a function of being part of the environment. As Fine and colleagues (2000) state, the social sciences have historically viewed and currently view the self of the social science observer (researcher) as a potential contaminant, something to be separated out, neutralized, minimized, standardized, and controlled. Furthermore, as Ruth Behar suggests, "We ask for revelations from others, but reveal little or nothing of ourselves; we make others vulnerable, but we ourselves remain invulnerable" (cited in Fine et al., 2000, 109). I am continually drawn to the work of feminist researchers because they clearly acknowledge the ways in which the research process influences the outcomes we report.

I realize that my transformation as a socially conscious scholar and scientist has come full circle with the editing of this book. Through the editorial process I have learned of the ways that Latina girls are resilient, how their ecological environments are dynamic, and the ways that they empower themselves and the individuals in their social networks. Through the process of reading the chapters of the book and interacting with the authors who contributed to it, I also learned that we have all been taught in the same cultural deficit model. Finally, writing from another perspective, as the authors in this book have done, even if we believe that perspective to be more in line with our own research values, is very difficult because we have never had a context in which to ground our writing.

Jill's Story

At the American Psychological Association (APA) conference in 1999, Jennifer Hammer, an editor at New York University Press, asked me if I would like to elaborate on the findings from my postdoctoral research to write a book on Latina girls. My initial reaction was surprise. I thought there must be a book of research on Latina girls in press somewhere in the United States. It would surely be published any day.

The following year at the same conference, Jennifer asked me again if I was interested. As I pondered the question, I realized that in fact there was no existing book that brought together research on Latina girls, and that one was sorely needed. Despite my enthusiasm for the book, I felt that the research would be better represented by a Latina woman, rather than by me, a white woman.

Three years passed, and still no book on Latina girls appeared. I thought about my two female mentors, Catherine Cooper and LaRue Allen, both of whom have studied Latino/a culture, and neither of whom are Latina. Their work had certainly made a contribution. Then, after talking with Latina students who urged me to make the research more widely available, I decided I would do it if I found a coeditor who could bring to the book her experience of growing up Latina in the United States. I met Bianca at the APA conference in 2002, at a dinner for women in community psychology. She shared my priority for linking research and practice, and seemed to understand that I felt a sense of personal responsibility to do this book. From our first meeting and up until now, she has asked me direct questions that help me to articulate my motivation for doing this book, and how I have changed as a result.

My initial plan for the book was to use it as an opportunity to bridge research and practice. To this end, I planned to include commentaries by practitioners on each chapter. I believed that this would force authors to go beyond knowledge generation to conduct research that would be useful for those who care about Latina girls. The commentaries were intended to provide the reader with clear examples of how the research could be applied to their interactions with Latina girls. But these commentaries proved challenging. First, we found few practitioners who wanted to take the time to read and write about research. Second, our timeline required us to commission chapters on data that were already collected, and as Bianca has described previously, most social science research builds from deficit models that value knowledge generation over utility. While the commentaries did not make it into the book, I hope that the readers of this volume participate in that very important next step of using the findings presented here to support Latina girls as they make positive choices for themselves and their communities.

Transformation and This Book

Many of the chapters present rich qualitative data in which the voices of Latina girls speak. The girls so eloquently speak of their struggles to find an identity that serves them and the communities in which they live. Their voices teach us that Latina girls are no different from any other human being in that they are actively interacting with their environment to create meaning in their lives. Most important, this book invites the reader to think about Latina girls as individuals who are happy and well adjusted. Having said this, the chapters in the book do not negate the fact that Latina girls in the United States live on the margins and that there is much work to be done on a social, political, and community level to ensure social justice for these young women.

We believe that one of the biggest contributions that this book offers students of social science, social scientists, educators, and mental health professionals is a way to think about the positive aspects of human behavior. Although the book is specifically about the lives of Latina girls, we believe that the concepts and theoretical grounding of the work presented here are applicable for many cultural groups. That is to say that the contributors to this book join many others who are challenging social science to shift the field from examining only pathology to acknowledging the positive role of resiliency and empowerment in human behavior (e.g., Seligman, 2004; Seligman and Csikszentmihalyi, 2000).

To this end, we know that several of the authors who wrote chapters in this book experienced a shift in the way they conceptualized their own work. Some authors told us that they could not conceptualize their work around resiliency and empowerment. As editors, we listened and continued to edit. As is apparent in the pages of this book, these authors were able to transform their own research agendas to interpret their data with resiliency and empowerment as a theoretical base. This theoretical shift in thinking is one that would benefit social science as a whole. We are pleased to say that this book is a step in the redirection of theorizing in the social science arena.

In the introduction to this book, we posed the question of how Latina girls are different from any other girls in the United States. Bianca asked this question of her six- and ten-year-old daughters and they replied that they are different because of their personality and how they react to other people. They also said that they are special just like everyone else.

Bianca's first reaction to this answer was to categorize it in terms of child development—they must be answering this way because of their level of cognitive maturity. As she thought more and more about their answer, it became apparent that they have tremendous insight into human behavior. These two young Latina girls understood that human beings are social animals by nature and that we all want to be considered special. Latina girls want to be just like everyone else, and the chapters in this book are a tribute to the special positive outcomes that Latina girls experience in the areas of negotiating family relationships, overcoming institutional barriers, accessing institutional support, and developing initiative.

Negotiating Family Relationships

In the collection of chapters on family, our main goal was to allow the reader a window into how Latina girls actively negotiate role expectations and relationships in their home environment. The studies were done independently with different populations across the United States, but the underlying theme of all these chapters is that Latina girls are challenging gender roles and transforming relationships. These chapters reveal how this negotiation is not a unidirectional process. That is, these young girls are influenced by their home environments, and they also influence their home environment in such a way that they are creating new cultural practices.

Jennifer Ayala's chapter on mother-daughter voices shows that while mothers are teaching their young daughters culturally specific expectations about sexual behavior, they are also learning from their daughters about how to liberate themselves from traditional Latino gender roles. In this chapter, we see how mothers and daughters describe loving bonds even within contested spaces of gender/culture negotiations. Daughters deeply respected the strengths of their mothers even as they critiqued some of their practices. Mothers in turn acknowledged the strength in their daughters, as they listened to or observed their daughters teaching them how to negotiate their own sexuality.

Angela Gallegos-Castillo describes the ways that Latina girls voice and contest their discontent around male privilege. The words of the young women in this chapter show how male privilege and entitlement harm not just young women but the whole family unit. These young women challenge their familial arrangements in order to decrease their burden of the household work and to teach their fathers and brothers that they, too, need personal time to pursue their own interests and personal goals. These acts of resistance and the creation of safe spaces show the reader how these young women are actively creating their own female consciousness and identity.

The chapters by Guzmán et al. and Romo et al. both argue that parents impart their morals and values around safe-sex behavior and education. Guzmán and associates illustrate that parents actively engage in sex-related conversations with their daughters even when parents feel uncomfortable doing so. This information clearly contradicts much of the literature that suggests Latino parents do not talk to their adolescent daughters about sex because of their conservative cultural and religious beliefs. On the contrary, the authors suggest that when Latina girls live in a two-parent household, whether or not the parents have conservative religious beliefs, they are more likely to have numerous conversations about sex and sexually. They also find that the risk of early sexual activity is reduced when both their mothers and fathers are in the household.

Romo and associates make the point that mothers are highly engaged in communicating with their daughters around issues of educational success. These authors illustrate that Latina mothers do not discourage their daughters from pursuing educational goals and that Latina girls are not at risk for early childbearing. Thus, a close parent-adolescent relationship enhances resiliency among Latina girls, protecting their well-being in multiple domains.

Overcoming Institutional Barriers

In this part our goal was to provide a deeper understanding of how the ecological environments in which Latina girls live impact the way they negotiate their social networks, career goals, and aspirations. Melissa Hyams discusses how gender and sexual identity formation intersect with school-based institutional rules and regulations. Hyams urges us to look critically at how the educational system is implicated in shaping the world of Latina girls. This research shows the ways in which young Latinas' abilities and knowledge about themselves as gendered and sexualized beings impact their educational experience.

Nancy Lopez's research focuses on how young Dominican American women resist and actively engage in reducing gender marginalization at school. Lopez describes the origin of a feminist consciousness for Dominican girls as a direct by-product of the behavior they have seen exhibited by their mothers. Lopez points out that in the Dominican Republic and in the commonwealth of Puerto Rico, women have served as vice presidents and as governors. Thus, a feminist perspective is not necessarily developed as a process of assimilation but may be a characteristic of women in the Caribbean that is passed down through the generations. She describes the complexity of gender roles as they intersect with U.S. culture in an inner-city high school.

The chapters by Wendy Rivera and Ronald Gallimore and by Deborah Marlino and Fiona Wilson discuss the career expectations and goals of Latina girls. Rivera and Gallimore find that many Latina girls aspire to attain careers that require higher education. They describe differences in academic achievement and support among those on different academic paths after high school. Many resources are available for these young women, including parents, peers, and school personnel. However, although many Latina girls have high career expectations and are earning good grades in school, they lack knowledge about the steps they need to take to attain certain careers. The authors recommend that school personnel should play an even bigger role in the career paths of Latina girls by linking them to role models and providing information to their families about the education and training required for various careers.

Deborah Marlino and Fiona Wilson provide detailed information about what types of careers Latina girls want to pursue. Most girls in their study listed professional careers, with the most popular choices including medicine, education, law, and government. Although the girls in this study lived in economically disadvantaged neighborhoods where college education is the exception, these authors found that Latina girls are determined to be different—to get a good education and to find financially rewarding professional careers. They want to use their success to give back to their families and make their communities stronger.

Accessing Institutional Support

The chapters in this part show the ways that ethnicity and ethnic identity intersect with institutional opportunities. The Latina young women described in these chapters seek educational and health promotion programs that allow them to explore who they are in relation to their own culture and the mainstream culture in which they live. Each chapter shows some innovative strategy for engaging girls in a way that values their cultural heritage and helps them question negative expectations about their abilities and life choices.

Xaé Alicia Reyes described how reading ethnic Puerto Rican literature is a way to prompt young Puerto Rican women to reflect on their ethnic background. In her reading group, the process of reading and writing became a vehicle for self-expression. As one student wrote, "[Reading and writing] makes me confident and pushes me to do better and influences me to achieve my goals." Another student stated, "I taught myself to speak Spanish and act in many ways of the Puerto Rican culture. Every bit of me is natural, and I am indeed a Puerto Rican American." The words of these young women clearly suggest that reading and discussing literature can teach girls about their culture and make them proud of who they are.

Gary Harper and associates invite us to think about how the constructs of *marianismo* and *machismo* (female and male gender roles) and *familismo* can advance health promotion for Latina girls. This is in contrast to the common use of these culturally bound constructs to explain negative health behaviors. These authors reconceptualized the constructs to provide a new way to create a culturally, developmentally, and linguistically appropriate sexual health promotion program. The participants in the program learned how to protect themselves from unplanned pregnancy and sexually transmitted infections. The young women learned to critically examine how culturally based gender roles affect their behaviors. Questioning those roles empowered them, providing them with new skills and viewpoints that will assist them in confronting multiple environmental and relational stressors.

Finally, Robert Fairlie and Rebecca London describe girls' access to the information technology skills that are becoming increasingly important in the labor market. At least half of all Latina girls living in the United States have access to a computer with Internet service either in the home or in a school/community setting. Overall, these authors find that ownership of home computers and Internet access are expanding rapidly for Latina girls, despite high levels of poverty, language barriers, and underfunded schools. They highlight three programs that meet the developmental and cultural needs of Latina girls.

Developing Initiative

The goal of the last part of the book was to show the different ways that Latina girls are negotiating risk and opportunity in their environments. The research by Charu Thakral and Elizabeth Vera challenges popular images of Latina girls by showing that many have happy and fulfilled lives. The authors state that although the young Latina girls who participated in their research came from poor neighborhoods, most still had positive views of their future. The authors also found that these young women had high levels of psychological well-being, which are related to both inner resources and the quality of interpersonal relationships. These findings contribute to a more balanced portrayal of psychological functioning of urban Latina youth and challenge existing negative stereotypes.

Yvette Flores discusses how Latina girls construct positive self-identities and negotiate health decisions. Flores makes the point that in order for Latina girls to succeed in the United States, they need bicultural competence—the ability to negotiate both the culture of the family and the larger social context—in order to succeed academically and socially. Flores argues that this process can be facilitated by a young person's sense of belonging to an ethnic group (ethnic self-identification), particularly in the face of ethnic or racial discrimination. Specifically, girls who feel a connection to the ethnic origin of their families *and* who know about and participate in ethnic rituals and traditions have better mental health and academic achievement.

Stephen Russell and Faye Lee's chapter demonstrates that Latina girls who become parents in their teens can still lead positive and productive lives. The girls in their study are seeking to improve the quality of their life, as well as that of their children. The adolescent mothers in this study describe how motherhood increased their aspirations for the future and their belief that education is needed for a better future. As one young mother said, "I just don't want to live the life I'm living right now. I want to go higher because I know I can. I got a whole life ahead of me." Some of the adolescent mothers noted improved relationships with parents and with their child's father. Finally, the authors challenge us to create programs for adolescent mothers that engage young mothers to work not only for a better life for themselves and their children but also for better opportunities for all young Latina women.

Final Thoughts

The chapters in this book show how Latina girls are both different from and similar to girls from other cultural backgrounds. Latina adolescent girls face some of the same challenges as other ethnic girls, but they also face other unique challenges. Our intention for this book was to point out that although Latina girls may face many challenges related to oppression, race/ethnicity, gender stereotyping, and educational opportunities, most are leading happy and productive lives. We invite the reader to think reflexively about how to make meaning of the chapters. Think about what surprised you, and what failed to surprise you. We consider your act of reading this book and what you do next as the most important step in the transformation of both theory and practice.

REFERENCES

Campbell, Rebecca, and Wasco, Sharon. 2000. Feminist approaches to social science: Epistemological and methodological tenets. *American Journal of Community Psychology* 28 (6): 773–791.

Cosgrove, Lisa, and McHugh, Maureen. 2000. Speaking for ourselves: Feminist methods and community psychology. *American Journal of Community Psychology* 28 (6): 815–838.

Engel, George L. 1977. The need for a new medical model: A challenge for biomedicine. *Science* 196:129–136.

Fine, Michelle, Weis, Lois, Weseen Susan, and Wong, Loonmum. 2000. For whom?

Qualitative research, representations, and social responsibilities. In Norman K. Denzin and Yvonna S. Lincoln, Yvonna (eds.), *Handbook of qualitative research* (2nd ed., pp. 107–132). Thousand Oaks, CA: Sage.

Garmezy, Norman Z. 1993. Vulnerability and resilience. In D. C. Funder, R. D. Parke, C. Tomlinson-Keasey, and K. Widaman (eds.), *Studying lives through time* (pp. 377–397). Washington, DC: American Psychological Association.

Hill, Jean, Bond, Meg, Mulvey, Anne, and Terenzio, Marion. 2000. Methodological issues and challenges for a feminist community psychology: An introduction to the special issue. *American Journal of Community Psychology* 28 (6): 759–772.

hooks, bell. 1984. *Feminist theory from margin to center.* Cambridge, MA: South End Press.

———. 2000. *Feminism is for everybody.* Boston: South End Press.

Jones, Enrico E., and Thorne, Avril. 1987. Rediscovery of the subject: Intercultural approaches to clinical assessment. *Journal of Consulting and Clinical Psychology* 55:488–495.

Rappaport, Julian. 1987. Terms of empowerment/exemplars of prevention: Toward a theory of community psychology. *American Journal of Community Psychology* 15:121–148.

Reinharz, Shulamit. 1992. *Feminist methods in social research.* New York: Oxford University Press.

Seligman, Martin E. P. 2004. Can happiness be taught? *Daedalus* 132(2): 80–87.

Seligman, Martin E. P., and Csikszentmihalyi, Mihaly. 2000. Positive psychology: An introduction. *American Psychologist* 55:5–14.

Selye, Hans. 1978. *The stress of life.* Columbus, OH: McGraw Hill.

Trujillo, Carla. 1998. *Living Chicana theory.* Berkeley, CA: Third Women Press.

About the Contributors

Elise Arruda is a doctoral student in applied developmental psychology at Claremont Graduate University. She is currently doing research and evaluation at CHOICES (a nonprofit organization serving Latina women) and the Los Angeles Unified School District. Her career goals include continued research on adolescent development and dissemination of research through policy and evaluation.

Jennifer Ayala is currently Assistant Professor of Education at Saint Peter's College in New Jersey. She recently received her Ph.D. in social/personality psychology from the CUNY Graduate Center in New York City. A second-generation Latina with both Caribeña and South American ancestry, she is interested in issues of education (both formal and alternative spaces for education), health, and social justice for Latina/o communities and communities of color in general.

Audrey K. Bangi is currently a co-coordinator of a multisite HIV prevention project for urban youth. She has been involved in various HIV and violence prevention community-based research projects and mental health service provision with ethnic minority youth. Her interest in working with Latina adolescents stems from strong desires to engage in positive social change efforts affecting women's health and to provide more culturally appropriate programs to address their needs and realities.

Jill Denner is a Senior Research Associate at Education, Training, Research (ETR) Associates, a nonprofit agency focused on health education and promotion. Her work focuses on how research and youth programs can work together to promote the positive development of adolescent girls, the role of youth in systems change, and innovative community-based strategies to prevent sexual risk behaviors.

Mimi Doll has been working in the Latino/a community over the past seven years serving as an HIV prevention program evaluator, developer of health intervention curricula, and therapist. Working with Latina adolescents has served as a perfect intersection of several causes that are near and dear to her heart: promoting young women's health, well-being, and empowerment, as well as working for social justice (e.g., addressing health and economic disparities).

Robert W. Fairlie is an Associate Professor of economics and Director of the Master's Program in Applied Economics and Finance at the University of California, Santa Cruz. He was a Visiting Fellow at Yale University and is a research affiliate of the National Poverty Center at the University of Michigan and the Institute for the Study of Labor (IZA). His research interests include ethnic and racial patterns of self-employment, entrepreneurship, access to technology and the "digital divide," the effects of immigration on U.S. labor markets, racial patterns in unemployment and job displacement, welfare reform, education, and health insurance.

Aida L. Feria is the cofounder of CHOICES (a nonprofit organization serving Latina women) and is currently the Executive Director. Ms. Feria is an influential leader in the field of health promotion both locally and nationally. She has received numerous awards from local and national organizations for her service to the Latina community. In addition, she has served as a consultant to legislators, school districts, and city programs and has been featured in English- and Spanish-language print and broadcast media. Ms. Feria is also the proud parent of two young adult Latina women.

Yvette Flores is a licensed clinical psychologist and professor of Chicana/o studies at University of California–Davis. Her research examines the influence of gender, class, and migration on the physical and emotional health of U.S. Latina/os and Mexicans on both sides of the border.

Angela Gallegos-Castillo, Ph.D., is a Senior Research Associate at the National Council on Crime and Delinquency, an applied research center that explores alternatives to incarceration. Her research focuses on Latina/o youth health, violence prevention, and life experiences both inside and outside the criminal justice system, with a special interest in girls and young women.

Ronald Gallimore is Distinguished Professor Emeritus, Department of Psychiatry and BioBehavioral Sciences at the Graduate School of Education and Information Sciences, University of California–Los Angeles, as well as Chief Scientist at LessonLab Research Institute. He investigates the impact of differential cultural experiences on school adaptation and academic achievement. He also conducts longitudinal intervention projects to improve teaching in communities serving large numbers of Latino youth.

Bianca L. Guzmán is a community psychologist who conducts research on Latina health issues. Dr. Guzmán is the cofounder of CHOICES a nonprofit organization created eighteen years ago to serve Latina women in the San Gabriel Valley in Los Angeles. Dr. Guzmán is currently the director of research and evaluation of CHOICES; she also teaches at California State University, Los Angeles. She is the proud mother of two young Latina girls.

Gary W. Harper is a Professor in the Department of Psychology at DePaul University. He has been working in the field of HIV prevention with adolescents for twenty years, and his research and community work are focused on developing and evaluating culturally and developmentally appropriate sexual health interventions for various groups of ethnic minority youth. His interest in working with Latina adolescents stems from his desire to collaborate with Latino-focused community agencies so they can use evaluation and research strategies to give voice to groups of young people who experience oppression and marginalization in our society.

Melissa Hyams is a Visiting Assistant Professor in geography and women's studies at Northern Illinois University. Her work examines informal and institutional regulatory processes and practices constituting spaces and identities among young Latina Americans.

Claudia Kouyoumdjian is working toward her Ph.D. in the Child and Adolescent Development Emphasis in the School of Education at the University of California–Santa Barbara. Her research interests focus on parent-adolescent socialization on sexuality and education aspirations, particularly in relation to Latina girls.

Faye C. H. Lee is the 4-H Youth Development Advisor for the University of California, Cooperative Extension, in San Francisco County. She extends research-based information and conducts applied research to address community issues, particularly related to low-income, ethnic minority children, youth, and their families.

Rebecca A. London is an Associate Research Professor in the Center for Justice, Tolerance, and Community at the University of California, Santa Cruz, and a Research Affiliate at the National Poverty Center. Dr. London's research focuses on low-income families and youth in a public policy framework. Her recent research concentrates on the ways that community technology centers serve young people and how technology acquisition promotes other positive outcomes for high school students. Dr. London holds a Ph.D. in human development and social policy and an M.A. in economics, both from Northwestern University.

Nancy Lopez is an assistant professor of sociology at the University of New Mexico in Albuquerque. Lopez's book *Hopeful Girls, Troubled Boys: Race and Gender Disparity in Urban Education* (New York: Routledge, 2003) examines the race-gender gap in education among Dominicans, West Indians, and Haitians in New York City. She has also coedited a book entitled *Creating Alternative Discourses in Latino Education* (New York: Peter Lang, 2004) with Raul Ybarra. Her current research examines race and ethnic identity among Latino youth in New Mexico.

Deborah Marlino is a Professor of management at the Simmons School of Management in Boston. Her research interests include marketing strategy and consumer psychology. Current research, undertaken with Fiona Wilson, examines the career interests and motivations of young women of diverse backgrounds.

Erum Nadeem earned her Ph.D. in clinical psychology from the University of California, Los Angeles. Her research interests include Latino parenting and adolescent health, peer relations in urban schools, and community-based program development.

Ana Pedraza is a Health Educator/Prevention Counselor who specializes in addressing the multiple sexual health needs of Latina adolescents, including the provision of prevention services related to HIV, STIs, and pregnancy. Ana was a participant in the SHERO's program more than eight years ago and then became the Project Coordinator. Under her direction, the program more than doubled in size and expanded to provide sexual health services to Latina adolescents in multiple venues, including schools, community agencies, and health clinics.

Xaé Alicia Reyes was appointed Associate Professor at the University of Connecticut–Storrs in 1999. Her joint assignments are with the Neag

School of Education and the Puerto Rican and Latino Studies Institute. She received her Ph.D. from the University of Colorado in Boulder. Her recent publications include "Transnational Nomad in Academia: A Puerto Rican Perspective," in M. V. Alfred and R. Swaminathan (eds.), *Immigrant Women in the Academy: Negotiating Borders, Crossing Boundaries in Higher Education* (Hauppauge, NY: Nova Science Publishers, 2004); and "Teachers' (Re)constructions of Knowledge: The Other Side of Fieldwork," *Journal of Latinos and Education* 2, no. 1 (2003): 31–37.

Wendy Rivera is a doctoral student in the School of Education at the University of California–Los Angeles. Her research interests include the contributing factors and various pathways to the positive academic and career outcomes of immigrant youth.

Laura F. Romo is an Assistant Professor in the Child and Adolescent Development Emphasis in the School of Education at the University of California–Santa Barbara. Her research has focused on identifying culturally and developmentally appropriate ways to enhance Latino mother-adolescent communication about self-protective practices related to sexual behavior.

Stephen T. Russell is Associate Professor of Family Studies and Human Development in the John and Doris Norton School of Family and Consumer Sciences, University of Arizona. His research focuses on adolescent ethnic and sexual identities, sexuality development, and sexual health. He conducts research on adolescent pregnancy and parenting, and on the health and development of sexual minority youth.

Bernadette Sanchez is an Assistant Professor in the Department of Psychology at DePaul University. She conducts research on the mentoring relationships and academic achievement of urban Latino adolescents. She is interested in Latino adolescents because of her own experiences growing up as a Latina in the United States. She hopes to be a positive role model to other young Latina women.

Marian Sigman is a Professor in the Department of Psychology at the University of California–Los Angeles. She was the principal investigator of a large NIH-funded study that examined mother-adolescent communication about dating, sexuality, and AIDS among Latino dyads. Over the past decade, she has coauthored numerous publications related to these topics in top-tier journals.

Charu Thakral is currently working on her Ph.D. in counseling psychology at Loyola University of Chicago. She is presently completing her doctoral-level internship at Children's Memorial Hospital in Chicago. Her research interests include areas of study ranging from well-being to stress, coping, and resilience in ethnic minority children and adolescents. Her graduate work with mentors has fostered a commitment to the promotion of positive mental health in minority children.

Elizabeth Vera is a Professor of Counseling Psychology in the School of Education at Loyola University Chicago. Her research focuses on prevention and well-being in urban adolescents and their families, with an emphasis on Latino families. Dr. Vera teaches classes in prevention and outreach, family therapy, adolescence, and human development. She graduated with her Ph.D. from Ohio State University in 1993 and is the recipient of the 2002 Early Career Scientist-Practitioner Award from Division 17 of the American Psychological Association.

Previously an executive in private, public, and nonprofit organizations for fifteen years, *Fiona Wilson* is now an Instructor at Simmons School of Management, where she teaches marketing, strategy, and entrepreneurship. Her research focuses on women/girls and entrepreneurship.

Index